At the Creation of a
New Germany

At the Creation of a New Germany

From Adenauer to Brandt

An Ambassador's Account

George McGhee

Foreword by John J. McCloy

Yale University Press
New Haven and London

Designed by Sally Harris.
Set in Melior type by Rainsford Type,
Danbury, Connecticut, and printed in the
United States of America by Vail-Ballou
Press, Binghamton, New York.

Library of Congress Cataloging-in-
Publication Data

McGhee, George Crews, 1912–
    At the creation of a new Germany:
from Adenauer to Brandt : an ambassador's
account / George McGhee;
foreword by John J. McCloy.
        p.   cm.
    Bibliography: p.
    Includes index.
    ISBN 0–300–04250–7 (alk. paper)
    1. McGhee, George Crews, 1912–   .
2. Germany (West)—Politics and government.   3. Adenauer, Konrad, 1876–1967.
4. Brandt, Willy, 1913–   . 5. Germany
(West)—Relations—United States.
6. United States—Relations—Germany
(West).   7. Diplomats—United States—Biography.   8. Diplomats—Germany (West)—
Biography.   I. Title.
DD259.4.M36   1989
303.4'8243'073—dc19   88–10829
                                        CIP

The paper in this book meets the guidelines
for permanence and durability of the Committee on Production Guidelines for Book
Longevity of the Council on Library
Resources.

10   9   8   7   6   5   4   3   2   1

*To my dear wife, Cecilia,
who shared these experiences
faithfully and well*

Contents

Foreword

The most important reason for the peace and stability in Europe since 1945 has been the enduring alliance between the United States and Western Europe. Within the North Atlantic Treaty Organization no country is more important to the United States than the Federal Republic of Germany. The Federal Republic maintains the largest army and is the most important economic power in Western Europe. As a divided country in the heart of Europe, the security and stability of Germany is of the utmost concern to the United States. For these reasons the American ambassador to the Federal Republic must be a wise and perceptive leader who possesses the experience, judgment, and understanding necessary to represent the United States in this vital relationship. George McGhee, who served as ambassador to the Federal Republic from 1963 to 1968, was just such a distinguished appointment.

George McGhee had already had a noteworthy career in both the public and private sectors before he went to Germany. A geologist by training and a Rhodes scholar in the 1930s, McGhee later established his own oil producing firm before the Second World War. After a distinguished and decorated wartime record, he joined the Department of State in 1946 as a special assistant to William Clayton, the under secretary for economic affairs. McGhee later coordinated the Greek-Turkish Aid program, an effort that helped these two countries preserve their independence. From 1949 to 1953, first as assistant secretary of State for Near Eastern, South Asian, and African affairs, and then as ambassador to Turkey, he opened the first American contacts with many of the new nations of the developing world. (These efforts are described in McGhee's first book, *Envoy to the Middle World*.) Returning to the private sector, he was the director of a number of corporations, including several major multinationals. To all of these positions George McGhee brought an ebullience of spirit, an understanding of political and legislative process, and a practical sense for good management. In 1961 President John F. Kennedy appointed McGhee under secretary of political affairs, the post from which he advanced again to an ambassadorship, this time to the Federal Republic, in May 1963.

My own experiences with the new Germany gave me sympathy and understanding for the complexities and problems Ambassador McGhee would confront. When President Truman appointed me high commissioner to the Federal Republic of Germany in May 1949, our goal was to transform Germany from an occupied enemy into a trusted and reliable partner. Opposing our efforts was the Soviet Union, which sought to pressure and entice the Germans into looking for their future to the East. In spite of Soviet threats and blandishments, the United States was successful in bringing Germany into the Western community of nations. Chancellor Konrad Adenauer's government restored the hopes that the Weimar Republic had disappointed and laid the foundations of a stable liberal democracy. With U.S. assistance and encouragement, Adenauer also worked to bring about a lasting rapprochement with France. Along with such great French statesmen as Jean Monnet and Robert Schuman, the chancellor enthusiastically cooperated in the creation of the European Coal and Steel Community, and later the Common Market. Under the leadership of Economic Minister Ludwig Erhard, Germany used billions of dollars in Marshall Plan assistance to rebuild a thriving market economy, Europe's strongest and most productive. To secure Germany's defense and yet avoid the dangers of militarism, Germany's new armed forces were integrated into NATO. Under Adenauer's courageous leadership, Germany also began to make amends for Nazi crimes, providing restitution both to Jewish survivors and to the state of Israel. The success of American policy in the Federal Republic remains one of the great achievements in international diplomacy.

No situation, however, no matter how stable, lasts forever. When George McGhee arrived in Bonn in May 1963, he found Germany on the brink of numerous changes. The extreme tensions of the Cold War, created by the building of the Berlin Wall and the Cuban Missile crisis, were beginning to fade. The possibilities for negotiation with the Soviet Union, over such matters as a nuclear test ban and the nonproliferation of nuclear weapons, were improving. The Germans would need to adjust to the improving climate of East-West relations, an adjustment that would lead ultimately to a new policy toward Eastern Europe: Ostpolitik. The Federal Republic, with its increasing economic strength, would also have to shoulder more burdens and responsibilities within the Western alliance.

George McGhee provided patient and experienced leadership. As ambassador he cultivated friendships with German political, social, and economic leaders of all stripes, explaining American policy and listening to their concerns. In the politically charged atmosphere of the time, he made hundreds of speeches, fulfilling the demanding public role that is required of an American ambassador. Although I had known Ambassador McGhee earlier, we became closely associated while working on the "offset" payments question, the readjustment of the financial burdens of America's military role in the Federal Republic. George McGhee's counsel served me well on this difficult issue, and I am certain that his advice commanded respect and attention from the State Department. McGhee also enjoyed a good relationship with Presidents Kennedy and Johnson; neither always followed McGhee's advice, however, and sometimes that was costly to American interests. Yet McGhee's achievement was to maintain American prestige in Germany during a time of great change and turmoil.

George McGhee's reflections on this experience deserve careful study by historians and should be of interest to the general reader. Here are important lessons for policymakers as well, reminders of the necessity of careful negotiations, consultation, and planning with our most important ally. While many issues have changed, the necessity of a strong American-German partnership remains. For this relationship to grow and develop, the United States must demonstrate the flexibility and wisdom to adjust to new challenges while maintaining an eye on the enduring common interests of the two countries. To meet these challenges we will need more leaders of the character, wisdom, and judgment of George McGhee.

John J. McCloy

Preface

I have called this book *At the Creation of a New Germany* because I believe it best describes the critical period from the retirement of Konrad Adenauer in 1963 through the chancellorship of Ludwig Erhard and the Grand Coalition in 1966 under Kurt Kiesinger, which led to the first Social Democratic party (SPD) government in 1969 under Willy Brandt. Hans Gatzke, writing in *Germany and the United States*, notes: "If the keynote of the Adenauer era was stability, the next few years were characterized by movement and change" (1980, 207). I have written about this change.

Erhard succeeded Adenauer, continuing and accentuating close cooperation with the United States while distancing himself from France in reaction to Adenauer's largely personal policy of rapprochement with de Gaulle. With the developing mood of détente, in which the United States took the lead, and our increasing entanglement in Vietnam, Germans became restive under the restrictions of American tutelage. In general we welcomed this shift as producing a healthier, more normal relationship between the two countries. As ambassador I did not discourage it—both privately and in my public speeches I nudged the Germans in this direction.

In the elections of 1965 Adenauer relented in his implacable hostility to Ludwig Erhard, strengthening Erhard as the candidate for chancellor of the Christian Democratic Union (CDU), and the CDU won by a greater margin than under "dem Alten." With this election Erhard reached the height of his power. He established good relations with President Johnson and tried to fulfill German offset obligations to compensate for the foreign exchange costs of U.S. troops in Germany, but this was not rewarded by Johnson. Until Johnson himself called it off in 1964, Erhard had attempted to deliver German participation in the MLF, or multilateral force. Supported by Johnson, Erhard made a contribution to détente with his "peace note" to the East in 1966. But Erhard soon was buffeted by the German Gaullists and under attack because of a minor recession, and the weakened Free Democratic party (FDP) withdrew its support. With Erhard under great pressure, the CDU forced his resignation in 1966.

Kurt-Georg Kiesinger, minister president of Baden-Württemberg, succeeded Erhard in November 1966 in the Grand Coalition with the SPD under Willy Brandt, who became foreign minister. This sequence of events resulted in Kiesinger's turn toward France and a mild cooling of relations with the United States. Amid student riots and disagreements with the United States over the nuclear nonproliferation treaty, Brandt made a beginning in Ostpolitik with the Soviets and Eastern bloc countries. When Willy Brandt succeeded as the first SPD chancellor the following year, a complete cycle had been made. The transition to a new Germany had taken place.

Germany in the mid-1960s was a very different Germany from the one I first visited in 1930 at age eighteen. A friend and I got jobs as deck boys on a cotton boat sailing from Corpus Christi to Bremen. My first view of Germany was late on a dreary, overcast October day when, having passed through the English Channel, we anchored in the mouth of the Weser River. As the sun rose the next morning, I had my first view of Europe and Germany, a very impressive one, with the great ships, the *Berlin*, the *Columbia*, and the *Europa*, all docked in the vast Bremerhaven harbor, one of the best in Europe.

I was told by Germans we met while cycling through Germany that the student demonstrations we saw were organized by the Communists. The Nazis were later to use Communist activity as justification for their own, more effective, organization. In Berlin I was impressed by the gaiety and high living of the great city, then the largest on the Continent.

The year 1930, as I later learned, was a turning point for Adolf Hitler. By March 1930 the Nazi party had reached a membership of 210,000. Aided by economic collapse and a rise in the unemployed to 3 million, the Nazi party vote in the national election rose to 6.4 million in September 1930 (compared to 810,000 in 1928).

More than five years later I returned to Germany, when I was studying at Oxford as a Rhodes Scholar. The year 1936 was also marked by important gains for Hitler, including the unopposed remilitarization of the Rhineland. A German Rhodes Scholar friend invited me to visit his family estate near Berlin, and since my transit through Berlin coincided with the annual German Rhodes Scholars dinner, I was asked to attend.

At the dinner were forty German Rhodes Scholars, plus a distinguished group of guests: a former minister of agriculture, Hitler's finance minister Count Schwerin von Krosigk, the young Prince of Hanover, who had just come from Oxford, and Albrecht von Bernstorff, diplomat and scion of a distinguished German family. Best known of the group was Joachim von Ribbentrop, later Hitler's ambassador to London and foreign minister. He had a pallid face and appeared ill at ease. I took an immediate dislike to him.

Ribbentrop, a businessman in wines, came from the minor aristocracy and had married the daughter of a big champagne dealer. Ambitious, arrogant, vain, he was one of Hitler's worst choices for high office. He had, however, won Hitler's confidence as a foreign policy adviser in competition with the Foreign Office and was named ambassador to Great Britain. At dinner, to my surprise, I was seated next to Ribbentrop. Alas, I can recall nothing of importance of our conversation. He appeared contemptuous of our whole group and probably found me, at twenty-four, of no interest. Later I was told that Count Krosigk had castigated the younger Rhodes Scholars for being out of touch with their country.

My two-week visit with the Oppens took me to their Junker estate in the Mark of Brandenburg. This was a marvelous opportunity to observe firsthand the way of life of this special breed of Germans who had come as the Teutonic Knights in the tenth century to defend the eastern ramparts of Germany against the Slavs. The Oppens had for six hundred years cultivated their five thousand acres of land, three thousand of which were at Dannenwalde, or Dane's Woods, the family seat. Little did I or they realize that time was running out for them. Before the Soviet army took Dannenwalde in 1945, the family sought refuge in Hamburg. The manor house was used by the Soviet army as a hospital but soon burned, presumably by accident. My friend Harald and his brothers were all killed in action, and the parents had meanwhile died. I kept in touch with the remnants of the family during their dark days in Hamburg and sent them CARE packages regularly. When I and my family came to Bonn in 1963, the surviving members of the family did everything they could to make us feel at home, including us in weddings and family occasions. It was a real case of casting bread upon the waters.

After 1936 I was not to visit Germany again until just after war's end. On graduating from Oxford in 1937, I entered my chosen profession of oil exploration and became an independent oil producer in Texas. Alarmed at Hitler's threat, I joined the war effort in 1941, serving first on the War Production Board and later on the U.S.-U.K. Combined Raw Materials Board. In 1943 I joined the U.S. Navy as a Lieutenant (j.g.) and spent the last year of the war in the Pacific as naval liaison officer to Gen. Curtis E. LeMay, commanding general of the Twenty-first Bomber Command, who was conducting the bombardment of Japan from Guam with some 850 B-29 aircraft.

After the war I decided that a career in government service would be more challenging than geology and entered the State Department in a junior position as assistant to William Clayton, under secretary for economic affairs. Clayton, a fellow Texan, had created the world's largest cotton trading firm and was a man I greatly admired. Appointed by President Harry Truman as coordinator for aid to Greece and Turkey to carry out the Truman Doctrine, I came to Berlin in 1947 to sell Greek tobacco to the occupation authorities but met few Germans. In 1949 I became assistant secretary for Near Eastern, South Asian, and African affairs, and I later served as ambassador to Turkey. At the beginning of the Eisenhower administration in 1953, I resigned and returned to private life, resuming my profession as an independent oil producer.

I chafed at being out of government, however, and when John F. Kennedy was elected president in 1961, I readily accepted the invitation of the newly appointed Secretary of State Dean Rusk, an old friend and State Department colleague. I served first as councillor and chairman of the Policy Planning Council. When Chester Bowles was replaced as under secretary by George Ball, I was promoted to under secretary for political affairs. In both of these positions I had many contacts with German officials and was intimately involved with U.S.-German relations.

My work was made much more interesting by several direct assignments I was given by the president: once to negotiate with Moise Tshombe, prime minister of the Congo, now Zaire, another time with Ramfis Trujillo in the Dominican Republic, following the assassination of his father, Gen. Rafael Trujillo. President Kennedy always clearly explained what he hoped could be accomplished. He gave you the feeling that he was relying on you, giving you a strong incentive to do the best you could for him. In advising me how much we should let the new Dominican government offer the Trujillo family for their ill-gotten sugar properties, he cautioned, "Keep it low, like you were buying them for yourself."

Kennedy once kept me behind after a meeting to ask me why a certain big Texas oil man (I assumed he meant H. L. Hunt) did not pay taxes. He didn't flinch when I replied it was because he took advantage of our liberal oil tax laws, as his own father had done in partnership with a prominent independent oil producer in San Antonio. During a meeting on Vietnam, knowing I had administered the Greek-Turkish Aid program, he asked me why we were able to defeat the Greek guerillas. I listed in my reply some eight or nine factors. He immediately noted the important role played by Tito in denying sanctuary to the guerillas, saying, "That's just what I've been telling them about Vietnam."

But I grew restless in the vast Washington bureaucracy. I had enjoyed being ambassador to Turkey and wanted to have my own mission again, this time in Western Europe. The first European opening that appeared was Germany, and I was elated. Walter Dowling was completing a distinguished tour of duty there, and I was offered the post. I had hoped to have several months to prepare for my assignment, but when Dowling required surgery just weeks before President Kennedy's planned visit there, I was told to go immediately. On May 15, after settling my personal affairs as best I could, I flew to New York and caught the evening plane to Frankfurt.

Although I had visited wartime England and North Africa in 1943 as a civilian, I had no contacts with the war against Hitler's forces. My military service had been entirely in the Pacific against Japan. As a consequence, I had encountered neither Nazi forces nor the terrible suffering they had inflicted on the Europeans they had fought and conquered. I was shocked to learn of Nazi atrocities after the war. I could not relate these events to the Germans I had known as a young man. But by the time I arrived in Bonn in 1963, these wartime memories had receded into the background. The Germans I met in the government and in the Bundestag in Bonn, as well as the business leaders I saw in Frankfurt, Stuttgart, and Düsseldorf, had all been carefully vetted for Nazi connections. Occasionally it would surface that some individual had served in the German army or had joined a Nazi youth organization, but few had escaped the postwar screenings. Most Germans I associated with were as repelled by Nazi excesses as was I. The Nazis had disbarred many from opportunities in private life and others had been imprisoned.

A valuable contribution toward my ambassadorship in Bonn came from membership in the Bilderberg Group, organized by Prince Bernhard of the Netherlands. In 1954 Bernhard became the first chairman and leading spirit of the group. Membership included leading government officials, businessmen, and academicians, all dedicated to improving relations between the United States and its European allies.

I was a founding member of Bilderberg, the American members of which came largely from an organization called the Committee for a National Trade Policy. Other American Bilderberg members over the years were Dean Acheson, Dean Rusk, C. D. Jackson, Henry Kissinger, and Cyrus Vance.

The European Bilderberg participants constituted a select group. Some later became heads of government, including Helmut Schmidt of Germany; Guy Mollet, Réné Pleven, and Valéry Giscard d'Estaing of France; and Harold Wilson, James Callaghan, and Margaret Thatcher of England. Discussions of world problems with such a group provided valuable insights into European thinking—and useful contacts.

Bilderberg also included a number of leading Germans who later provided me valuable assistance: Fritz Berg, spokesman for German business as head of the *Bundesverband der Deutschen Industrie*; Otto Wolff von Amerongen, head of a leading steel firm; Carlo Schmidt, a distinguished constitutional lawyer and SPD deputy who also served as deputy speaker of the Bundestag; and Fritz Erler, the SPD's principal spokesman for defense and foreign affairs. Until his death in 1967, Erler was of great help as my principal SPD contact on foreign policy. These Germans and others gave me a good start in Germany.

Conversations reported in this volume are quotations from or paraphrases of memorandums prepared usually by myself, occasionally by a reporting officer present. I have provided all references to aid serious scholars who would like to see the precise texts, which are available among my papers in the Georgetown University Library in Washington, D.C. It was my custom in seeking information from key officials to either call on them in their offices or invite them to lunch with me alone at the embassy. Germans, I found, were inclined under such circumstances to be very frank, even about themselves. I had developed a technique over the years for recalling long conversations (two to three hours) almost verbatim with the help of just a few words jotted down inconspicuously from time to time on a small piece of paper. This avoided the appearance of taking verbatim notes, which would have made my informant more cautious. After the meeting, I immediately dictated the conversation while it was fresh in my mind.

Acknowledgments

During my years in Bonn, my secretary carefully kept in a special file classified documents which I could not, under security regulations, take with me when I resigned. When I left Germany, these files were sent to the Department of State in Washington, D.C. When I asked for them there a few years ago, I found the entire file intact as I had left it. My work on this volume has been greatly facilitated by the cooperation of the department's historical office, whose reviewers generously declassified most of those papers I wished to use.

Valuable assistance has also been provided by friends and former colleagues who are recognized German scholars: Dr. Martin J. Hillenbrand, former ambassador to Germany, now Dean Rusk Professor at the Center for Global Policy Studies at the University of Georgia; Robert Gerald Livingston, former foreign service officer in Germany, now head of the American Institute for Contemporary German Studies of the Johns Hopkins University; Professors Richard Hunt and Thomas Schwartz of Harvard University; the distinguished German scholar Manfred Goetemacher of the Free University of Berlin; Professor Karl H. Cerny of Georgetown University; and Professor Robert Herzstein of the University of South Carolina. Their help in checking my interpretations and filling gaps in my memory has been most helpful. I am particularly grateful to Professor David Schoenbaum of the University of Iowa for his editorial assistance.

I would also like to express appreciation to Lord Blake, distinguished British historian and provost of Queen's College, Oxford, for his overall appraisal; to Philip Wolfson, former foreign service officer stationed in

Germany, who did research in the State Department Archives; to Ambassador Fritz Caspari, former German foreign service officer, for recollections of a meeting in Berlin in 1936; to Barbara Harding, who provided translation; to Alison Raphael, who helped edit the book; to my secretary, Katherine Masyn; to my former secretary, Linda Fauteux; to Peggy Smedley, Catherine Forman, Miriam Schoenbaum, and Jeffrey Ostler for their assistance in typing; and to Michael Kelly for compiling the index.

I am particularly indebted to former high commissioner in Germany John J. McCloy, the most respected of the Americans who dealt with postwar Germany, for writing the Foreword for this book.

I accept full responsibility, of course, for all the opinions expressed herein.

1

Background

These memoirs cover the period May 1963 to April 1968: the last six months of the chancellorship of Konrad Adenauer, the three years of Ludwig Erhard's government, and a year and a half of Grand Coalition government under Kurt-Georg Kiesinger.

The end of the Adenauer era, which covered the extended period 1949–63, was marked by the formalization of Adenauer's long-time collaboration with President Charles de Gaulle through a Franco-German treaty of cooperation signed in January 1963. Erhard greatly strengthened cooperation with the United States, focusing on the so-called Kennedy Round of European-American tariff negotiations, East-West relations (particularly German reunification), and the movement toward European unity.

Johnson's abandonment of the MLF (multilateral force) in favor of a common nuclear planning group in late 1964; difficulties over German payments under the offset agreement with the United States that reached a climax in September 1966; the increasing American preoccupation with the Vietnam War; and an apparent U.S. preference for détente with the Soviet Union over reunification of Germany resulted in a shift in German attitudes toward a more independent, self-reliant stance. Erhard's domestic standing suffered from a mild recession that prompted a tax increase and declined further due to Erhard's inability to obtain from Johnson any relief from Germany's offset obligations. Erhard also suffered from the efforts of his traditional rival Adenauer and other German "Gaullists" to undercut him, which led to his downfall in 1966.

Kurt Kiesinger took a strong turn toward a closer alliance with France, distancing himself from the United States. But he too was weakened by the continuing recession and by disagreements between the coalition partners, particularly over an election reform that proposed to substitute majority voting in the English or American style for proportional voting and so threaten the viability of third parties like the Free Democratic Party (FDP). Controversy had also arisen with the United States over the terms of the nuclear nonproliferation treaty consummated between the Americans and the Soviets in 1968. Kiesinger did, however, join the United States in a renewed, though again unsuccessful, effort to overcome French resistance to British membership in the European Economic Community (EEC), more popularly known as the Common Market. The most important German foreign policy initiative under the Grand Coalition was Brandt's formulation of Ostpolitik, which was later realized under his chancellorship.

On the international scene, the United States continued, with Erhard's support, to search for détente with the USSR. The era's successes included the ban on atmospheric nuclear testing and the nuclear nonproliferation treaty, although the latter was not then ratified by Germany. The period was one of relative calm in U.S.-Soviet relations; the two governments engaged in a series of negotiations, some of which were partially successful. Since the United States still held nuclear superiority, no one really expected the Soviets, despite their brutal invasion of Czechoslovakia, to initiate hostilities against Western Europe.

American involvement in the Vietnam War continued to grow: a peak of 550,000 troops were sent to war in early 1966. The pressures on the Johnson government resulting from this unpopular war and attendant financial burdens, which were not covered by increased taxation, cast an increasing cloud over the administration and German-U.S. relations. Johnson's popularity plummeted, and he made the fateful decision not to seek reelection in 1968.

Germany is today a divided country; West Germany, the Federal Republic (FRG), had in 1986, 60.734 million inhabitants, including 4.7 million foreigners. East Germany, the Communist German Democratic Republic (GDR), occupied and largely controlled by the Soviet Union, had 16.8 million. Since 1937, when Germany as a whole had a population of 67 million, German territory has been reduced by 20 percent. West Germany now includes more than 14 million refugees from Germany's eastern territories and the GDR expelled in the aftermath of World War II. The large influx into the FRG from the GDR was halted only in 1961 by the building of "the wall." Sixty-four percent of the subsequent population increase in West Germany has come from foreign workers, principally Turks. Since 1978, however, the overall population of West Germany has declined, and it is expected to decrease by 3 million more by 1990.

What about relations between the United States and Germany? Gordon A. Craig (1982), a leading American historian of Germany, argues that the most important similarity between the two countries is that both, for long periods of their history, were "outsiders in world politics." Isolation was imposed on Germany in 1648 following its defeat in the Thirty Years' War; Americans chose this course in emigrating from Europe. Both countries, as a result, developed a feeling of uniqueness that was accompanied by xenophobia. According to Craig, both also followed strikingly parallel but different courses in developing national unity, which came only at the end of the nineteenth century and was accomplished along with a centralization of power and an economic resurgence.

Craig sees, however, a striking difference in the reaction of the two countries to the European Enlightenment of the eighteenth century. The American reaction was political—the establishment of a constitutional system based on popular sovereignty—whereas the result in Germany was to strengthen the existing authority, customs, and tradition, with an emphasis on morality and self-improvement. Germans became not only unpolitical but apolitical. One important result was that German foreign policy was left to the state, whereas American foreign policy, when it became acceptable, was recognized as an expression of the will of the American people and their moral excellence, if not superiority. German foreign policy displayed more continuity, American greater influence by ideology. The attitude of both countries changed markedly after the Second World War, particularly regarding their perception of uniqueness.

Americans are still deeply influenced by their participation in two world wars against Germany, during both of which they suffered heavy casualties. And yet German blood is estimated at approximately a quarter of American blood, and most Americans were raised with contemporaries of German descent. Few Americans, however, retain a German identity or loyalty. The Founding Fathers seriously considered accepting German, which has roots similar to English, as the national language. After both wars Americans gradually overcame their enmity toward the Germans and did what they could to help Germany recover. Americans who visit Germany today usually feel at home there, perhaps as much as in any other country in Europe. They sense the German reaction against militarism that has led Germany to renounce nuclear weapons. Most Americans today would identify Germany as one of the United States's most valuable allies. From any perspective, I believe Germans have become good Europeans.

In polls taken in 1957, when memories of the war were still fresh, 37 percent of Germans polled said they liked Americans, whereas 24 percent said they did not. By 1965 these figures had become 58 percent and 13 percent, respectively; by comparison, those who liked the British in 1965 were 46 percent, and the French, only 39 percent. In polls taken irregularly over the years 1953 to 1983 on the question, "With which of these countries should we cooperate as closely as possible?" positive responses for America peaked at 83 percent and were most recently 79 percent. Figures varied downward only slightly in between except for a low of 69 percent in 1956. The Soviet Union began with 18 percent in 1953 and was 38 percent in the latest poll, not going lower but reaching short-lived highs of 52 percent and 49 percent in 1970 and 1971. France's most recent rating was 66 percent, whereas Britain's was 50 percent. These figures speak for themselves, but the recent U.S.-French comparison, 79 percent to 66 percent, is, I believe, of particular interest. (Noelle-Neumann and Neumann 1967, 543–44.)

In spite of efforts by the Kiesinger government in 1966 to reduce Germany's dependence on the United States, Germans continue to make it clear in many ways that they depend on Americans for their basic security. During my time as ambassador there, Germans reacted sharply to any inference of reduced U.S. interest in the Western alliance, any threat of reduction in U.S. troop strength in Germany, and any evidence of waning U.S. support for reunification. The bonds between the two countries developed since the last war have not, in my judgment, deteriorated significantly even today. Peace marches are made by idealistic young people on particular issues. Occasional terrorist attacks against our military bases notwithstanding, there has never been any widespread "Yankee go home" movement.

My attitude toward Germans on my arrival as ambassador was friendly, and it was even more so when I left five years later. As a result of my academic training in geology and physics, subjects in which Germans excelled, I had great respect for German accomplishments in science. I respected their industry, the high standards they applied in whatever they undertook, and what I perceived to be their determination to put behind them the errors of the Nazi period and to earn world respect. The Germans seemed to me to possess a basic integrity that made them good allies and good people to do business with. I also knew their reputation for sometimes being dogmatic, stubborn, and overly meticulous. Some foreigners considered them a little stiff socially and unduly conscious of rank.

I determined to give the Germans I would deal with every chance to prove their sincerity, and I was not disappointed. Each of the three chancellors I dealt with had long experience in practical politics. They were, as individuals, quite different, but I always felt that they treated me fairly and openly. Adenauer was occasionally tricky; he never deliberately misrepresented matters, but he could be expected occasionally to conceal, to hedge on critical issues, or to allow ambiguities to creep in. Sometimes he presented us with surprises. I fully appreciate, however, that a head of government has a special responsibility in the decision-making process, since his decisions are final, and I am willing to give him the benefit of the doubt. Erhard and Kiesinger I always found friendly, forthcoming, and reliable. At the ministerial level, I invariably found openness and candor. I was fortunate to have most of my dealings with Gerhard Schröder as foreign minister, and with his under secretary, Karl Carstens. Both were amicable, straightforward, and honest. Neither ever attempted to conceal a difference or deceive me.

Soon after his election in 1960, President John F. Kennedy was challenged at a summit meeting in Vienna by Soviet Party Secretary Nikita S. Khrushchev and was confronted with the Berlin Wall and the placing of nuclear weapons in Cuba. Kennedy, with the strong backing of Secretary of Defense Robert McNamara, sought the support of America's NATO (North Atlantic Treaty Organization) allies in building up the conventional forces of the alliance in order to make possible at least a limited defense in the event of a Soviet invasion. But the U.S. advocacy of "flexible response"— graduated progression from conventional to tactical to strategic weapons, as opposed to immediate nuclear retaliation—alarmed our allies, who feared that the Soviets might not be deterred. By 1967, however, after six years of American efforts, NATO formally committed itself to a deterrence policy that included both a "flexible response" and a "forward strategy."

Since West Germany's army has become the largest European army in NATO and is located on the front line separating NATO and Warsaw Pact forces, it plays the key role in NATO strategy and in the allocation of U.S. military assistance and support. German deployment is closely related to that of American forces in Germany. A large percentage of the six to seven thousand U.S. tactical nuclear weapons stored under U.S. control in Germany are for use by German forces subject to joint U.S. and German approval. (Their number was decreased after NATO's INF decision in 1979 by unilateral withdrawal of 2,400 warheads.) This force is under the "two key" system, which resulted from a decision taken by the Bundestag in 1958 on Adenauer's initiative. Ironically, though, in view of the more recent deployment in Germany and withdrawal of Pershing II intermediate-range missiles, Adenauer refused at that time to accept American medium-range missiles capable of striking the USSR, even though they had been accepted by other NATO members.

Secretary of State Dean Acheson (1963, 247–60), one of the principal architects of postwar Europe, wrote cogently on European defense at this time. Acheson cited the failure to think through an agreed solution to the defense of Europe and the United States as the principal difficulty facing the alliance. This depended on the ability to solve other key strands—economic and political policy. Although NATO strategy has adapted to changing circumstances, it had never, Acheson said, had an adequate long-range plan, and it had not solved the problem of the placement and control of nuclear weapons.

A sound plan, according to Acheson, would require an increase in size and a clarification of the function of non-nuclear defense forces. It would also need a definition of the term "when necessary" for the use of nuclear forces that went beyond the "trip-wire" and "pause" theories of the past. The ultimate purpose would be to deny the Soviet Union the capacity to impose its will on Europe by conventional force.

Acheson considered possible the buildup of a conventional NATO defense of Europe without weakening the credibility of the U.S. nuclear deterrent. But he believed a European nuclear deterrent neither possible nor desirable, nor did he believe that multinational forces or nuclear "sharing" offered a solution. Acheson thought the creation of an agreed master plan, based on intimacy and confidence between the contributors of the nuclear and non-nuclear elements, and the forces to carry it, was the only solution.

Fritz Erler (1963, 95–106), foreign affairs spokesman for the German Social Democratic party, deplored the crisis within NATO and urged the strengthening of Western unity, Atlantic solidarity, and the European Community. Although Erler rejected supranational institutions, he felt that the European Community must strengthen its inner structure, so far blocked by de Gaulle, in order to enlarge its membership and develop its relations with the rest of the world. Erler proposed merging the Coal and Steel Community with the Common Market and strengthening the European Parliament. Success in the Kennedy Round of trade negotiations and in obtaining Western agreement on the political aspects of East-West trade, he wrote, would help greatly.

Erler deplored France's withdrawal of forces from NATO and the blocking of British entry. He also regretted undue reliance on nuclear weapons and urged strengthening non-nuclear defenses as part of a strategy of controlled, flexible response and good area deterrence. The alternatives were suicide or capitulation. He favored giving the NATO Council greater political authority. Major military decisions should be made on the basis of commonly agreed strategy approved by a military body with representation by all members and with competence over the whole military potential of the alliance. The decision-making process must be credible. Erler believed Europe's goal to be full partnership with the United States, which would make possible its proper contribution to world policy.

Long before I departed for Germany, the U.S. government had recognized the Federal Republic as a key NATO ally. Broad U.S. goals were to continue to build cordial and close relations with Germany based on equality, understanding, and a respect for each other's views and interests. We recognized a close coincidence in our respective national interests upon which we hoped to capitalize. But we also understood that we must keep in mind our historical and geographical differences, particularly those created by the long German border with Communist Eastern Europe. The United States, by contrast, was separated from Europe by the wide Atlantic Ocean. We also could not ignore the fact that Germany had recently lost a bitter war against the Western democracies and the Soviet Union.

Berlin played a special role during this period. Since it emerged as a ruin from World War II, Berlin has been a focus of East-West tensions, the vortex of the varied forces at play in the recovery and reorganization of Europe and the creation of a new balance of power between East and West. It has served as the crucible in which the wills of the NATO and Warsaw Pact countries have constantly been tested.

The U.S. government was fully aware of the special situation created by the division of Germany, especially the isolation and separation of Berlin. We believed that the eventual reunification of Germany was essential for lasting peace in Europe and that the problem of a divided Berlin was inseparable from that of reunification. We wanted to make clear to the Germans our sincere interest in these related issues and our support for a solution based on national self-determination. On the other hand, we did not want to get ahead of them, to be "more German than the Germans." We understood the need for caution: to avoid unnecessarily antagonizing the Soviets, arousing the suspicions of Germany's former enemies, or giving the Germans false hopes.

In the meantime, Americans remained committed to defending Germany under the NATO guarantee. To prove this to the Germans, as well as to the Soviets, it was the firm intention of the United States to maintain its brigade in Berlin and its force of some 200,000 to 250,000 troops in Germany proper. In order to protect Berlin, the United States and the European allies were determined to preserve their special rights there, recognizing the extensive ties between the western sectors of Berlin and the Federal Republic, which was responsible for the welfare of the city, its budget, and its representation abroad.

The United States also had a fundamental interest in good Franco-German relations. The rivalry between these two key European nations had been a fundamental cause of the two world wars. Despite the grave issues created in the early 1960s by France's reluctance to fulfill its NATO responsibilities and its insistence on dealing with the United States and Europe separately, the U.S. government still wanted to encourage Germany to maintain a close relationship with France. We were also committed to reducing the so-called technological gap with Europe and to the development of science and technology as a common resource. Germany loomed large in this effort since we had entered into agreements with the German government for the development of cooperative defense and atomic energy projects, as well as space research, urban planning, air and water purification, and noise abatement.

One consistent policy during my tour of duty as ambassador to Germany was to support German initiatives in improving relations with the East, both with the USSR and with other Warsaw Pact countries. Eastern Europe had always had a strong attraction for the Germans. In 1963 the Bonn government was making efforts not only to increase its substantial trade with the East but to exploit this politically to further détente between East and West as well as German reunification. Détente and reunification were seen by Germany's leaders as complementary goals, and I encouraged them in this policy. The West Germans also desired to help East Germans attain a higher living standard and greater freedom. They hoped to minimize the human effects of the division between the two Germanies. This hope would assume even greater importance as a result of Willy Brandt's efforts as governing mayor of Berlin and later as foreign minister and chancellor.

My support of a liberal policy toward developing better relations with the East was consistent with my view that we must, by all steps available, even small steps, seek to further the creation of a real, not a phony, détente. This was, I believed, a necessary first step if we ever hoped to reduce the hostility between the Soviet Union and the United States and the other Western democracies, which constituted the only threat to our security.

I delivered an address on this question on February 19, 1964, in Bonn. I recognized that many people of authority and influence in Washington not only questioned the feasibility of détente but were also unsure what role the Germans should play in seeking it. Particularly in the light of the division of Germany, which could not be healed without Soviet approval, could the Germans be trusted? Henry Kissinger, then at Harvard, was often cited among those who were uncertain on this point.

Despite German vulnerability, the hope of any early progress in German reunification was so slight, and the possibilities of a direct Soviet threat against Germany so great, that the Germans had every incentive to be cautious. Soviet harassment of Berlin access or the imposition of new hardships on the East Germans were always available to the Soviets as policy instruments. The delicate situation created by the division of Europe resulted from a war Germany had started, and that principally involved the German people. We could not expect to make progress with the Soviet Union on East-West issues without the full cooperation of the West Germans.

We must, I thought, guard against the creation of any German tendency toward "throwing in the sponge" via a movement toward neutralism. This would decide the future of Europe in favor of the Soviets. It would no longer be possible to organize a credible defense of Western Europe, and Germany would be at the mercy of the Soviet Union. We had also to be constantly on the alert for any restructuring of inter-Western European alliances, as was then being advocated by de Gaulle, for the purpose of eliminating the United States as a European power. But the best way to avoid such eventualities, I felt, was to work closely with the Germans on the basis of full reciprocal trust and confidence. I believed that we should make every effort to convince the Germans that this was in fact our policy.

The United States also looked to Germany, as one of the leading world trading nations, for help in U.S. efforts to liberalize the world trading system. The impending Kennedy Round negotiations were the most important initiative the United States had taken to this end in many years. Because of its heavy dependence on exports, Germany, I believed, shared our goals of reducing tariffs and other trade barriers. I also understood that Germany's commitments to the Common Market and its own special interests, for example with respect to protection of her uncompetitive farmers, resulted in political limitations. Nevertheless, the United States had great expectations of German support in trade matters, particularly from Ludwig Erhard, who as chancellor had always staunchly advocated the free enterprise market system. Much of my early effort in Germany was directed toward this end. The government also hoped to get Germany to increase its growing assistance to the developing countries, thereby relieving the United States of some of the burden it had borne since the war.

As strong supporters of NATO, under whose command the German army of 450,000 troops would fall in the event of war, Americans expected full cooperation in NATO affairs. But I was fully aware of the limitations the Bundestag had imposed on the German military budget and of German reluctance to see a revival of militarism. Germans were hesitant to seek careers in the armed forces, and there was an attitude of caution toward dependence on nuclear weapons or any increase in Germany's NATO role, for fear of arousing a reaction on the part of Germany's wartime enemies. Naturally, the attitude of the German government and people toward our own 200,000 to 250,000 troops in southern Germany was an important factor, as was their logistical support and their help in minimizing the foreign exchange burden on the United States of U.S. dollar expenditures in the Federal Republic. In 1963 it was clear to me that the Germans wanted our troops there and would be willing to make considerable sacrifices to assure this.

The United States attached great importance to disarmament efforts and looked to Germany for support. Germany was not, of course, a nuclear power and had no desire to be. The immediate goals of the United States, when I arrived in Germany, were to finalize the Limited Test Ban Agreement and a nonproliferation treaty. Again ironically, considering the strength and vehemence of West Germany's antinuclear movement, the reluctance of the federal German government derived mainly from its hopes of participating in the expected boom in the world nuclear power industry, in which Germans already had a recognized expertise. The Federal Republic was also sensitive to any hint of Western or Third World recognition of East Germany that might weaken the Western case for reunification. We hoped to work with the Germans in overcoming what was then believed to be an aggravating "technological gap" between the United States and Europe. We believed that Germany, which had always been in the forefront of the physical sciences, could help reduce the lag.

I was determined to persuade our country to accelerate the reentry of Germany as an equal member of the family of nations—as long as this continued to be justified by German performance. If Germany had, indeed, done the best it could to recover from its defeat and help other affected nations complete their recovery, this should be recognized by the international community. Recognition would provide the Germans with the incentive to try to complete their expiation for the Nazi era by making a greater contribution to the unity, well-being, and common defense of Western Europe. To deny Germany this recognition would be a disincentive. Later, in the main auditorium of Heidelberg University, in the presence of Chancellor Erhard, I developed this theme in the most important of the many speeches I made while in Germany.

In 1963 I saw Europe and its relations with the United States as being in a state of flux. The great architects of postwar policy had produced extraordinary results, culminating in the creation of NATO, the Common Market, and Euratom, the joint West European nuclear agency. But the reemergence of French nationalism, restrictive trade, and the difficulty of controlling nuclear weapons had almost halted the movement toward European unity and Atlantic partnership that was their ultimate goal. In many respects, the organization of the West was at a crossroads.

1963

May 16	The Bundestag approves the Franco-German treaty
June 22–26	President John F. Kennedy visits Germany
July 25	Draft Nuclear Test Ban Treaty initialed by the United States, the USSR, and Great Britain
October 16	Ludwig Erhard elected federal chancellor under a coalition of the CDU/CSU and FDP
October 18	Government Declaration by Chancellor Erhard
November 9	German-Hungarian trade agreement concluded; trade missions established
November 22	President John F. Kennedy assassinated; Vice President Lyndon B. Johnson assumes the presidency
December 17	First treaty on visits by West Berliners into East Berlin signed

2

Arrival in Bonn
May 1963

I arrived in Frankfurt to take up my duties as ambassador to the Federal Republic of Germany on May 16, 1963. As I descended from the plane I was confronted by a battery of cameras and microphones assembled by the German media. Taking out my short arrival statement (USIS, Bonn, press release 2734, June 4, 1963), I expressed appreciation for the great honor President Kennedy had done me in naming me ambassador to Germany. These words were not just pleasantries; I really felt them. I referred to my early visits to Germany and said how much I welcomed the opportunity to renew German friendships. I looked forward to living in Germany and laboring in the interests of German-American friendship, which was already deeply rooted and was important not just to our two nations but to the future of world peace. I expressed particular interest in the welfare of the people of West Berlin and reiterated American support for German reunification. I explained that my first duty as ambassador was to prepare for the forthcoming visit of President Kennedy, which would confirm the strong ties between our countries.

In Bonn the next morning, although I had not yet officially presented my credentials to President Heinrich Lübke, West Germany's head of state, I made courtesy calls to the two top officials at the Foreign Office, Karl Carstens and Gerhard Schröder, who would play an important role in my mission.

Karl Carstens, state secretary or, in our terminology, deputy secretary of state, has always been a favorite of Americans; after studying in five German universities he did graduate work in law at Yale. I had known him for several years through attendance at Prince Bernhard of Holland's Bilderberg meetings. When I was appointed under secretary for political affairs by President Kennedy, he had sent me a welcoming telegram. After service in the war and setting up his law practice in Bremen, Carstens entered politics as representative of his city with the federal government in Bonn. After serving as state secretary and as deputy minister, he entered the Bundestag in 1972 and quickly became Parliamentary leader of the Christian Democratic Union (CDU). In 1979 he was selected president of Germany by the Bundesversammlung, or federal convention. A man of integrity and goodwill, he helped steer us through many difficult situations.

Gerhard Schröder also started out in life as a lawyer and attended three German universities as well as the University of Edinburgh. Schröder entered the Bundestag as a CDU member in 1959. He served as minister of interior 1953–61, minister of foreign affairs 1961–66, and minister of defense 1966–69. Had he not suffered a heart attack he might himself have gone on to the presidency of Germany.

Schröder was a most pleasant and reliable man with whom to do diplomatic business. This was fortunate because he was my normal point of contact. Always half-smiling, low-key, slightly detached, he gave me his views on any subject with complete candor. As was characteristic of German high officials of that era, it seemed to me that he always told me the whole story from the German viewpoint, holding back little. By thoroughly exploring in advance the problems likely to cause trouble between our countries, we succeeded, I believe, in avoiding many crises. On only one occasion did I find him ruffled. Knowing that he would be resentful, I met him at the airport on his return to Bonn to report actions we had taken, without advance notice to Germany, to supply Israel from U.S. stocks held in Germany during the Six Day War, which began on June 5, 1967. Schröder met me in a reproachful mood but accepted my explanation in good grace, never losing his half-smile.

On May 18, 1963, I presented my credentials to President Heinrich Lübke. Lübke, whom I got to know well and grew fond of, was a kind, friendly man who made every effort to please. His background and experience in agriculture had given him little preparation for his presidential responsibilities; limited as they were. Adenauer presumably chose Lübke for the presidency because he was sure Lübke would not use the position as a base for a power play.

I was to have many meetings with Lübke during the next five years, always at his request. Although he wanted to be helpful, Lübke had the habit of bringing up matters during our meetings over which he had no authority and little understanding. Some of his positions were naive and at variance with the policies of his government. Hans Herwarth von Bittenfeld, a senior foreign service officer, explained this tactfully and asked for our forbearance. I usually parried innocuously with the president. After the first meeting or two, however, I did not report the substance of our conversation to Washington to save Lübke embarrassment.

One of my first duties was to make my calls on the Bonn diplomatic corps, starting with its dean, the papal nuncio. He was an amiable man but so bland that I could never recall anything he said, even when he presided over our official meetings. These calls were tiring and time-consuming affairs, since the various embassies in the new improvised capital of Bonn stretched from Plittersdorf at the south end of town to Cologne about thirty miles away.

My key colleague was the British ambassador, Sir Frank Roberts, who had arrived only a few weeks before me. Our countries, of course, had a strong community of interest in Germany. Roberts had been private secretary to Foreign Minister Ernest Bevin in 1947–49 and was one of the outstanding British diplomats of his era. I first met him when he was deputy high commissioner in India in 1949–51. Before being posted to Bonn he had been ambassador to the Soviet Union. Our respective positions could easily have brought us into competition, and they did, but in a friendly way. We have often joked about our rivalry to visit more German cities and make more speeches.

Next in importance was the French ambassador, Roland Jacquin de Margerie, and his successor, François Seydoux Fornier de Clausonne. Margerie was an attractive and able French career diplomat who left Germany in 1965 to serve in Paris as counselor of state. I enjoyed my association with Margerie, who reflected none of the well-publicized French-U.S. rivalry over Germany occasioned by the Franco-German treaty of reconciliation. I hoped to defuse any tendency to assign to us anti-French policies and always tried to make it clear to him that we welcomed the rapprochement between the two countries.

Soon began the interminable receptions and dinner parties that, although usually pleasant and undoubtedly helpful in establishing personal contacts, constitute a great burden for a busy diplomat. Most ambassadors in Bonn represented small countries with little serious business to transact with the Germans. Many posts were pure sinecures and their occupants political associates of their heads of state, who had rewarded them for services rendered. Others were political exiles. Many had little to do except entertain and be entertained and were sticklers for protocol. This meant that at formal dinners I usually ended up sitting between the same few wives of diplomats in my same relative position of rank. Although I could get by in French, which is widely spoken in diplomatic circles, many spoke no language I knew.

I hope someday the diplomatic profession will, like private business, lighten its entertainment baggage. My wife and I were to entertain 14,875 people at the embassy during our five years there (see Appendix 2), and this with almost no visiting congressmen. Since Bonn was a small, isolated town with no night life or sights to see, it was not a popular European port of call for American dignitaries. Our visitors were seldom a burden, since most were interesting, had a reason for being in Germany, and were most appreciative of anything we did for them. I did not envy the level of entertainment forced on my American colleagues in the larger and more socially active capitals—London, Paris, and Rome. No social group in Bonn corresponded to those in the major capitals, who considered ambassadors fair game and pressed them to accept their invitations and to include them in embassy parties.

My many visits to German cities were all pleasant occasions, both for myself and for my wife, who usually accompanied me. We were invariably received with warmth and courtesy. Interesting sightseeing was arranged, and the personal contacts and friendships that resulted made our five years in Germany rewarding. I regret that in a serious memoir it is impossible to express appreciation to the many persons involved. Some idea of their number can be obtained from the embassy contact list of twelve hundred individuals.

I was deeply indebted during my tour of duty in Germany to the highly professional and dedicated support by the fine foreign service officers of the staff of the embassy and consulates general. I have always been a staunch supporter of our foreign service, with which I was intimately associated for twenty years in a wide range of posts both in the State Department and abroad. I felt myself one of them and believe I was so considered.

I was fortunate to have as my deputy for four of my five years an outstanding career officer, German expert Martin Hillenbrand. After leaving Bonn, Marty served as ambassador to Hungary and later to Germany. He was succeeded in 1967 by Russell Fessenden, one of our most experienced officers, and Minister Coburn Kidd, who had served

well as head of the political section, departed for the important consul
generalship at Hamburg. He was succeeded by James Sutterlin, whose
German experience covered most of the postwar period. During most
of my stay in Germany the economic minister was Edward Cronk, one
of the few professional economists in the foreign service.

3

I Meet with Adenauer
May–August 1963

Until he relinquished his post in October 1963, there was no question that Chancellor Konrad Adenauer was the dominant figure in postwar Germany. Although he had begun to lose authority in 1959 and was a lame duck by the time I arrived in Bonn, Adenauer held firmly to the levers of power to the last. He refused to give up even after he was replaced by his economics minister and nominal deputy, Ludwig Erhard, and still attempted to control events by private conniving and daring leaks and pronouncements to chosen journalists.

Adenauer's last years involved so many battles within his party and with his coalition partners that almost everyone was happy to see him go. They were fed up with his authoritarian style and his unchanging approach to the Cold War. And yet in polls taken from 1962 on the German people consistently regarded Adenauer as the one German who had done most for their country. In 1962 he topped Bismarck for this honor for the first time by 28 percent to 23 percent. Five years later, Adenauer's margin over Bismarck had grown to 60 percent to 17 percent.

Adenauer was born in 1876 in Cologne, the son of an army officer who had retired to become a low-level civil servant. Two circumstances of his background strongly influenced his whole life: his fervent Catholicism and his heritage, as a Rhinelander, of strong attachments to neighboring France.

After desultory attendance at the Universities of Freiburg and Munich, young Adenauer returned to Bonn, becoming an assistant in the office of the Cologne public prosecutor. He joined a leading Cologne law firm and, more importantly, became a member of the Rhineland Catholic Center party. At age thirty, he became assistant to the Ober- burgermeister, or mayor. In spite of his stubborn and offensive manner, he was elected Oberburgermeister at age forty-one. After the Allied victory in World War I Adenauer performed his duties well, despite ups and downs with the British, who came to Cologne as the Allied occupation force. Adenauer emerged from the war as one of the leading political figures in West Germany and served as chairman of the Prus- sian State Council through the Weimar Republic.

When Hitler was appointed chancellor in 1933, however, Adenauer's fate under the Nazis was sealed; he had snubbed Hitler during the general election. Adenauer fled Cologne to avoid assassination. At war's end, the liberating American army brought him a message from Gen. Dwight D. Eisenhower asking Adenauer to take over the administration of Cologne. By July 1948, when the Allies allowed the Germans to draw up a constitution for a West German state, he was elected chairman. A year later, the West German state came into existence under the new Occupation Statute. In the elections held in August 1949, the Christian Democrats, in coalition with the small Free Democratic party, headed by Theodor Heuss, defeated the Social Democrats by a small margin, and Adenauer, at age seventy-three, was elected chancellor. Adenauer would dominate the new state for fourteen years.

Adenauer was an early supporter of the Schuman Plan, which, with strong backing from Jean Monnet and other leaders, resulted in the European Coal and Steel Community and eventually the Common Mar- ket. But Adenauer's lack of enthusiasm for German reunification be- came increasingly obvious. He admitted that he was willing to sacrifice the unity of the Reich for the unity of Europe. He openly espoused the concept of a "little Europe," based predominantly on Christian Dem- ocratic West European states. Later he drew increasingly close to Gen- eral de Gaulle and France, signing the Franco-German treaty of reconciliation of January 1963. Adenauer believed in European unity and opposed nationalism. He was particularly concerned over a pos- sible revival of militarism and nationalism in Germany. "I don't know what will become of Germany if we don't manage to create Europe in time," he once said.

Adenauer's domestic strength grew, and in 1957 he led his party to a benchmark triumph when he won the only absolute majority yet in a West German general election. He also enjoyed almost unqualified support from President Eisenhower and Secretary of State John Foster

Dulles, who is said to have created the Adenauer myth. But 1957 marked Adenauer's peak. From then on, a series of domestic and foreign challenges eroded his strength, and his support declined both at home and abroad. The election of a new Democratic administration in Washington and his own reduced majority at the West German elections of 1961 indicated that his time was finally running out.

Adenauer's relations with President Kennedy were never easy. Theodore Sorensen, in his biography of Kennedy, writes: "Adenauer was no longer considered our principal European advisor, and important differences arose between the Chancellor and Kennedy over how to negotiate with Khrushchev and deal with de Gaulle. Kennedy once remarked, 'I sense I'm talking not only to a different generation, but to a different era, a different world'" (1965, 559). Kennedy found Adenauer hard to please and hard to budge; his government was seen as vulnerable to leaks to the press. The young president had to give him repeated assurances of our love and honor. Yet, according to Sorensen, "Kennedy had a genuine liking and a deep respect for Adenauer. He admired what he had accomplished and enjoyed his wit. Although Adenauer never seemed to feel fully confident of Kennedy, he respected the firm U.S. stand at Berlin in 1961 and at Cuba in 1962" (559).

Contrary to American hopes and preferences, Adenauer also questioned British entry into the Common Market, proposing instead that the British "be permitted to enter only as associate members." Adenauer said further, apparently as a calculated insult, that changes in the German diplomatic representation in Washington would soon take place. Ambassador to the United States Wilhelm Grewe of Germany, a scholarly and competent professional, was, sadly, caught in the crossfire. Although Kennedy is reported to have respected Grewe as an ambassador, he and his staff tended to blame Grewe for misunderstandings— even almost a breakdown in diplomatic relations between the two countries. I felt sorry that Grewe was recalled.

Adenauer's image was damaged further by his acquiescence in the so-called Spiegel affair in October 1962, when Defense Minister Franz Josef Strauss misled the Bundestag about the arrest of journalist Conrad Ahlers in Spain over a claimed leak from the Defense Ministry. Adenauer's trip in 1963 to the United States, which had included a visit to Vice President Johnson's Texas ranch in which I participated, had given him no advantage, only momentary publicity.

Henry Kissinger in his *White House Years* attributed to "the bright young men who ran the Kennedy administration" the urging of "greater flexibility toward the East" (1973, 502). Kissinger believed that this helped produce a domestic upheaval in Germany, reversing the position of the Social Democrats from opposition to Adenauer's uncompromising pro-Western stance to one of criticism of the government for jeopardizing German ties with America. Kissinger saw in this a disquieting effect on Germans leading to fear of U.S. disengagement from Europe.

Kennedy made his first overture to the East in 1961 and followed it in June 1963 with a dramatic appeal for détente. Meanwhile Schröder, and then Brandt as foreign minister, pursued an Ostpolitik unimaginable in the Adenauer years, seeking normalization of relations with Eastern Europe and even East Germany. It was not until Richard M. Nixon assumed the presidency in 1968 that Washington began to question seriously where this might be leading.

What was more on our minds when I arrived in Bonn was West Germany's special relationship with France. Like many Europeans, Americans were surprised and concerned by the Franco-German treaty of cooperation signed by de Gaulle and Adenauer on January 22, 1963, during Adenauer's official visit to Paris. Adenauer's great respect for de Gaulle and his desire to use their friendship to bring Germany and France together were well known. On numerous occasions Adenauer had acted as de Gaulle's apologist, justifying French policies that challenged the United States and frustrated Europeans working for greater unity. In a letter to President Kennedy, Nikita Khrushchev compared de Gaulle's influence over Adenauer to the Russian peasant who caught a bear barehanded but could neither bring it home nor make the bear let him loose.

The treaty came so soon after de Gaulle vetoed British entry into the Common Market that his move had the aura of German approval, or at least acquiescence. The U.S. government had been particularly disturbed by the anti-American implications of the press conference in January 1963 at which de Gaulle pronounced his veto. We were concerned about the effect of the treaty on German relations with the United States and on NATO, from which France was in the process of disengaging. The State Department raised these issues with the German government.

The initial draft of the treaty before referral to governments for ratification can be summarized as follows:

The foreign ministers of the two countries, who would supervise the execution of the program, would meet every three months, as would ministers of defense and education. Chiefs of staff would meet every two months. Other representatives of the two Foreign Offices would meet monthly to assess current problems, without disturbing normal channels. Each government would create an interministerial commission to coordinate cooperation under the treaty.

In foreign affairs the two governments agreed to consult in order to reach insofar as possible an analogous position in European community and political problems, East-West relations, NATO, developing countries, and economic questions. Defense policies would be coordinated in the areas of strategy and tactics, exchanges of personnel, procurement, and civil defense. In education, each country was to emphasize training in the other's language as well as student exchanges and research.

The treaty appeared far-reaching, but it primarily detailed bureaucratic procedures which imposed onerous burdens and were difficult to carry out. Amid widespread criticism of the treaty, particularly from the United States, Schröder and his predecessor, Heinrich von Brentano, were appointed to work out a preamble that specified that West Germany's rights and obligations under its various multilateral treaties with the United States and its West European allies would not be adversely affected. The preamble also stipulated that the treaty would be implemented in such a way that the Federal Republic would continue to pursue such objectives as strengthening NATO and improving relations between Europe and the United States in cooperation with its allies. Finally, the document made appropriate references to the goal of German unity, the future integration of West German forces in the common defense of Europe under NATO, and the lowering of tariffs as the intended goal of the Kennedy Round negotiations, then in progress.

The Bundestag passed the preamble on May 16, 1963, the day I arrived in Germany. The Federal Republic and its friends breathed easier. On July 3, 1964, de Gaulle impaired the pact by failing to advise the FRG in advance of a major move toward the Soviets. The reduced importance of this treaty took a considerable toll on Adenauer and contributed to his final removal from power in October 1963. It also undoubtedly helped create Adenauer's need to defend de Gaulle, something I would encounter in all of my meetings with him.

Kennedy welcomed the historic reconciliation between France and Germany. But he did not hesitate to proceed with MLF (multilateral force) negotiations, an important issue between the two countries, with Germany the principal European beneficiary. De Gaulle opposed it, of course, but Kennedy was careful to leave the door open should the French wish after all to enter.

The question remained: What attitude should the U.S. government take toward the Atlanticist-Gaullist struggle going on in Germany which would so deeply involve the Erhard government? Many in Washington had been aroused, for good reason, by de Gaulle's stubbornness and anti-American nationalism. The tendency in such a situation, was to "fight back." I originally held this view myself. I believed, however, that we should not inject this issue into our bilateral relations with Germany by demanding that they take a position similar to ours vis-à-vis de Gaulle as a price for our support. They knew our position on de Gaulle well enough, and we also had to understand their dilemma. The issue involved both an acute internal political problem for Erhard and a wider challenge to Germany and France to end their traditional rivalry as a contribution to peace in Europe. United States Ambassador Charles Bohlen reported from Paris on March 2, 1963, soon after taking his post: "Insofar as Franco-American relations are concerned, I see very little that can be done to improve them. . . . I can see no particular moves that we can make beyond going on with day to day questions and matters as they come up" (1973, 502). A corollary of this, I concluded, was that we had little incentive, in our bilateral relations in Germany, to attempt to influence either France or German relations with France.

Our stated policy was that we welcomed a Franco-German rapprochement and had no desire to force Germany to choose between France and us. The French government and its embassy in Bonn appeared, however, to believe the contrary; it characterized our position, and in particular my position, in discussions with the German government, as being competitive with the French and even anti-French. De Gaulle himself was reported to have made such a comment.

To allay French doubts, I made every effort both publicly and privately to support the Franco-German rapprochement, and when François Seydoux Fornier de Clausonne became France's new ambassador to Germany, I invited him to lunch alone in order to tell him so. His surprise that I would have him to lunch for just the two of us indicated the suspicious attitude of the French toward our motives. The conclusion I reached from an analytical approach to the U.S.-French-German triangle was simple and, to me, clear. The greatest postwar step toward a peaceful, unified Europe had been the Franco-German accord. This had been created by two elderly heads of state who had done more than anyone else to mold postwar France and Germany. I often said publicly that had this accord not been reached, it should have been a major U.S. policy objective, perhaps our most important objective in Europe. It was our best hope of avoiding another Franco-German war such as those of 1870, 1914, and 1939.

I granted that we might have been able to cash in some of our credit with Germany to score points against de Gaulle. But I doubted this would succeed, given the age and inflexibility of the men involved. In fact, I reasoned, the adverse aspects of their rapprochement from our point of view derived principally from the uniqueness of each man. The specific impact of their personalities would recede with the coming of their successors, whereas the cooperation between the countries would probably survive. There was also the chance the relationship between the two might sour.

Because American relations with Germany were so good, the French had little chance of seriously endangering them, even if they tried. The Franco-German treaty called for consultation, but the Germans were free to go their own way in such important matters as Britain's entry into the Common Market. I thought that Germany and France's working together in harmony provided a comforting background for both countries. It also gave other Western European countries greater confidence that they could live together in peace, the traditional origins of wars having been "defused." Franco-German cooperation, even union, provided hope for eventual West European unity. In all, I considered French-German cooperation worth the gamble and believed that the United States should support it openly.

With concerns like this in mind, I made my first official call on Adenauer May 20 at his modest office in Bonn's Palais Schaumburg (airgram, Amemb Bonn, memcon 2465, May 20, 1963). At his suggestion, I came alone. Although I probably would have chosen to do this in any event, his request showed his wily streak. Our conversation, including time for interpretation, lasted two and a half hours. I was impressed by his composed, ramrod-straight bearing. Tall and thin, his head appeared abnormally small, his nose hawklike, his eyes quizzical. Though eighty-eight and scheduled to retire as chancellor in five months, Adenauer was still in control of his remarkable faculties. He represented a defeated country, but Adenauer was a world leader, on a par with others of that period of great statesmen: Winston Churchill, Charles de Gaulle, Robert Schuman, Alcide De Gasperi, and Joseph

Stalin. I report our conversation fully because it represents a record of what was on his mind at the time.

Adenauer had requested that our meeting be devoted to President Kennedy's forthcoming meeting and plunged immediately into this subject. He said that during the president's recent visit in Washington with Fritz Erler, foreign policy spokesman for the opposition SPD, there had been talk of a Kennedy address to the Bundestag. This raised certain problems on the German side, he said. It is true that since 1963 a number of heads of state, including President Ronald Reagan and President François Mitterand of France, have addressed the Bundestag in Bonn. But before then it had never been done, not even when President de Gaulle had visited Germany the previous autumn, and Adenauer claimed that it would set a potentially undesirable precedent. He also said that it could be embarrassing for the president to have to make a speech that might, even if it did not offend any members of the Bundestag, offend the Soviet Union.

As an alternative, it had been suggested that Eugen Gerstenmaier, Speaker of the Bundestag, give an official reception for the president to which all members would be invited. But Adenauer feared that this had the disadvantage of exposing the president to embarrassing questions. In addition, the plans for the president's visit were by now fairly firm and left little time available.

Adenauer favored a third proposal. He noted that as many members of the Bundestag as desired could attend the president's scheduled speech at the historic Paulskirche in Frankfurt on June 25. Gerstenmaier could preside. The chancellor added that many members of the Bundestag would be present at his dinner for Kennedy in Bonn and probably at the president's own dinner as well and would be able to meet Kennedy and talk with him.

I told Adenauer that I thought he had reached a satisfactory solution. As a former member of Congress, the president greatly respected parliamentarians and would wish to meet as many of them as possible while in Germany. The plans for his visit to Bonn, however, had reached an advanced stage, and there was insufficient time to arrange for a major new meeting or reception. So I agreed that, whether they belonged to the sponsoring German-American Society or not, as many parliamentarians as would like could attend the ceremonies in Frankfurt.

I then raised the question of the length of time that the president would meet with Adenauer. I pointed out that Kennedy wanted to see the chancellor for as long as he thought necessary to complete their discussions, to which Kennedy attached great significance. But Kennedy would also need time to confer with his aides and consider telegrams that would follow him from Washington. I wondered whether it might not be possible to reduce the time that had originally been scheduled, perhaps by arranging for simultaneous translation.

Adenauer replied that he did not wish to have simultaneous translations during that portion of the meeting when he talked with Kennedy alone. He did not specify how much time or what subjects this would include. He appeared reluctant to give up any of the time planned, since he had a number of topics he wished to take up with the president: Berlin, Germany as a whole, the Franco-German treaty, NATO, European problems, the Soviet situation, and certain economic matters. After a little polite pulling and hauling, Adenauer finally agreed to delay their morning meeting and allow earlier adjournment of their afternoon meeting if circumstances permitted.

In a deadpan way, I raised the delicate question of a possible meeting with Vice Chancellor Erhard. Adenauer's disparaging view of his successor was already well known. I said that the president was interested in discussing certain technical economic problems in Bonn, particularly U.S.-German trade and the Common Market. In light of Erhard's great interest in these questions, I asked if it could be arranged for the president to discuss such matters with him. Adenauer pointed out that arrangements had been made for Kennedy to be with Erhard in Wiesbaden and Frankfurt and that this should afford adequate opportunity for any discussions. He provided no opening for further discussion of Erhard's inclusion in the meetings with him or in a separate meeting. I did not pursue the matter further.

Adenauer said he also had a number of questions to raise with Kennedy with respect to Berlin. One had to do with the constitutional status of the city. West Germans considered the city a constituent state of the Federal Republic, and their constitution so stipulated, though the United States and other countries did not believe it comparable to the other states, given the peculiar legal situation conferred on both East and West Berlin by agreement between the wartime allies. But contrary to the American position, Adenauer noted, West Berlin's mayor, Willy Brandt, appeared to believe in its full constitutional equality with other states, especially when he needed more money from Bonn.

A second question had to do with Kennedy's arrival ceremonies. Adenauer expressed puzzlement that four national anthems—American, British, French, and West German—were to be played. Which would be played first? I responded that we too were unhappy with the length of the opening ceremonies and the playing of all the national anthems. I would look into this.

Adenauer then expressed concern that both Kennedy and Brandt, the president of the United States and the mayor of West Berlin, but not Adenauer, would speak at the arrival ceremonies. Given the contested status of the city, he feared that the East Germans and others who would be listening would not understand the exclusion of the West German chancellor. Adenauer felt that it was important that he should speak, too. I replied merely that I would convey his views to the president.

Adenauer and I were at least able to confirm his role in the ceremonies at the city hall in West Berlin. As he understood it, there would be a speech by the speaker of the West Berlin Parliament, welcoming the president, followed by a response from the president himself. Then there was to be a speech by the chancellor, thanking the president for his visit on behalf of the Federal Republic, and an invitation from Brandt to sign the city's official guest book. The West German chief of protocol, who was present during the entire meeting, concurred that this was his understanding. I assured him that it was also ours.

Adenauer then said that he had heard that George Meany, president of the American Federation of Labor, had proposed that Kennedy speak to an international trade union congress, which by chance was meeting in Berlin at the time of Kennedy's visit there. Adenauer considered this inappropriate on the grounds that it was an international meeting. He did not want to give the impression that he was against labor unions, he said, even though about half of German workers were not union members. But he thought it would be preferable for Kennedy to address German workers at a plant. I replied that this matter would also be taken up with the president. With respect to the purely American part of Kennedy's visit to Berlin, involving American troops, houses, and so on, Adenauer did not intend to participate. But he expected to be present at the airport to bid Kennedy farewell.

Adenauer then turned to the Franco-German treaty of friendship. He wanted the U.S. to understand that his primary objective in the Franco-German treaty was to prevent the recurrence of a Franco-Russian alliance like those in the past. I replied that a Franco-German rapprochement was something we desired as much as he. Our concern was that the basis for agreement between the two nations not become a fait accompli that would complicate or obstruct bilateral relations with us or in such multilateral councils as NATO and the EEC. It was our hope that matters affecting Europe as a whole could be worked out jointly in the multilateral context.

Adenauer came back at me very sharply on this point. Advances in Soviet rocketry in the late 1950s had already made the reliability of the American nuclear deterrent, and the American nuclear umbrella over West Germany and Western Europe, a major issue between Washington and the European capitals. It should be no surprise that he, as a lifelong believer in Franco-German cooperation, echoed de Gaulle's skepticism. Adenauer wanted to know, for example, whether we had consulted Germany and France about the nuclear cooperation between the United States and Britain that Kennedy and Prime Minister Harold Macmillan had recently agreed to at their meeting in Nassau? After all, said Adenauer, Macmillan had also visited de Gaulle but had not mentioned that he would seek either submarine-based Polaris missiles from Washington for Britain's independent nuclear arsenal or U.S. help in creating an MLF. It was the announcement that Macmillan and Kennedy had agreed on these points that precipitated de Gaulle's press statement opposing British entry into the Common Market.

I responded that the Nassau meeting was basically intended to solve a bilateral Anglo-American problem: our inability to supply the British with the Skybolt missile we had earlier agreed to make available but had then cancelled. The solution to this problem, I argued, was in a sense strictly bilateral. The proposal for an MLF at this time was largely a result of circumstance, but it could also be seen as a gesture to compensate the other members of NATO for our Polaris offer to Britain. In any event, I said, the MLF was clearly a proposal without validity unless it was acceptable to other NATO members, including the Germans. We had immediately discussed the Nassau agreement with the Germans before finalizing any of its details. It would have been better if we had been able to engage in talks with all concerned before making the proposal public, I acknowledged, but it is not always possible to control the precise timing under which such matters arise. I told Adenauer that our concept of the way allies should deal with one another was to discuss a new matter quietly with all concerned and then to seek decisions within a multilateral framework in a give-and-take manner, with everyone sitting around the table.

Adenauer countered by defending de Gaulle. It was necessary that de Gaulle revive confidence in France before he could accomplish anything else, he said. De Gaulle had first to renew the pride of the French army and then to solve the problem of Algeria. These were great achievements. I answered that other European nations had made comparable progress since the war without injecting a nationalistic element into their relations with one another. Adenauer responded that the Germans did not want to incur adverse reactions from Europeans who were still suspicious of them and so found it better to keep quiet about their own army and economic progress and merge unobtrusively into the European context.

My reply to this was that other countries which did not face Germany's problems—particularly Belgium and Holland, but also Italy and now Britain—had accepted the "European idea." Adenauer retorted that the other European nations, particularly Belgium and Holland, and not France, had rejected the results of his efforts in 1961 to form a European union. He acknowledged that de Gaulle had changed his proposal somewhat by including the existing European Community institutions, whose successful operation required unanimity. But he still insisted that it was not de Gaulle's fault that it had failed. He himself had told General de Gaulle that he favored both the MLF and Britain's entry into the Common Market, Adenauer insisted. De Gaulle assured him that he also favored Britain's—I assumed ultimate—entry. Adenauer considered de Gaulle to be not nationalistic, as he understood the distinction, but simply patriotic.

Our long meeting then ended. Adenauer had reacted characteristically in many ways. He showed clearly his dislike of Erhard and his uncertainty about his position vis-à-vis Brandt in Berlin. The jockeying between the two, including their positioning during the car ride with Kennedy, went on right to the end of the visit. Adenauer's defense of de Gaulle and his resentment against the closeness Kennedy and Macmillan had displayed at Nassau were also evident. His explanation that he sought the Franco-German treaty to prevent de Gaulle from entering into a treaty with the Soviets and his protestations that de Gaulle was not the obstacle to European unity were not convincing to me. Adenauer's affinity for the aging French president, undoubtedly the only remaining postwar leader whom he viewed as a peer, came through clearly as his last great obsession. He did not realize that his cherished treaty with de Gaulle was to fulfill their expectations for only six months, until both parties agreed to disagree the following July.

Later, during President Kennedy's visit, Adenauer told me that he would like to talk privately with me. I made an appointment to call on him July 12, after the Kennedy visit. As our discussion evolved, it became apparent that his principal purpose was to express his deep distrust of the German labor movement, which he feared was under Communist influence. This led, of course, to an indictment of the opposition SPD, which had labor support. (Airgram, Amemb Bonn, memcon A-120, July 16, 1963.)

Adenauer began by affirming that Germany should be a part of the West. This had been his aim during fourteen years of political activism. Only when one has lived under a dictatorship, he said, can one realize its effect and appreciate freedom. Adenauer told me that he had never known Hitler but thought that the Nazis succeeded because contemporary politicians and army leaders lacked courage. The support of certain businessmen was also vital to Hitler's success, he added. His own objective since the fall of Hitler had been to save personal freedom in Germany against the Communist threat of the Soviets.

Adenauer considered that the Social Democrats were from the beginning against Communism, but not—unlike the Catholic Center party—as a matter of principle. The power of the state over the individual could be resisted only on the basis of ethics, not on an economic basis, as the Social Democrats believed. The Christian Democratic Union was born of this concept, which Adenauer told me, was the same view held by John Foster Dulles: "We were very close together on that." Adenauer believed that the Socialists and the National Socialists had much in common. He said that the CDU had, beginning with the occupation, been determined to cooperate with the big three: the United States, the United Kingdom, and France. In doing so, they had had to fight the SPD every step of the way. Under Herbert Wehner's leadership the SPD appeared to be changing, Adenauer acknowledged.

He recalled that Kennedy had told him during his visit that it was easy to distinguish between the Republicans and the Democrats in the United States but that in Germany he could not differentiate between government CDU and opposition SPD members. He had not wished to argue this with Kennedy; since Kennedy was in a sense a guest of all the German parties, he felt that it would have been inappropriate. But he wanted me to know the real situation. It was necessary to look not just at leaders but the people "on the back benches" and the mass of their supporters.

He did not mean to imply that all CDU members were good Christians and that the SPD represented evil, Adenauer explained, but rather to point out a basic difference in perspective. The SPD relied on the labor unions, who got their money from an international banking arrangement. This led them to say things they did not really believe in. Adenauer acknowledged that the CDU got most of its money from business and was therefore vulnerable to being called capitalist. Before the war, he continued, both free and Christian trade unions existed in Germany. The British and American occupying forces had prohibited National Socialist labor unions, permitting only a Socialist union and no free or Christian Democratic unions. He believed that the Americans had approved this because they did not understand the situation and that the British had done so because a Labour government was in power.

In his opinion trade unions had too much power. It was not the workers who determined when strikes took place, he pointed out, but only the people who voted in union elections, which were not secret. Since the voters constituted a minority, he regarded this as undemocratic. He noted that Germany had 22 million workers; of these, only 6 million belonged to trade unions and only 5 million were active members. Yet the union bosses decided for everyone in it.

Adenauer considered that the Metal Workers Union was in basic control of the West German Trade Union Congress, the DGB. This union consisted of 1.8 million strongly organized members. He had been advised by people in whom he had confidence that the DGB was Marxist. He knew George Meany, he repeated, and was certain that Meany's views differed greatly from those of Otto Brenner, leader of the Metal Workers Union. Adenauer expressed fear that if the SPD gained power these Marxist elements would gain control of the country. This, he said, was the great danger facing Germany and Europe as a whole.

I had already learned of Meany's deep distrust of the German labor movement for its ties with the Communist bloc labor unions. Ludwig Rosenberg, the chairman of the DGB, advised me that Meany had broken off all contact with him and the German unions because they had sent visiting delegations to Eastern Europe. He implored me to explain to Meany that German labor was not pro-Communist and to urge Meany to be more cooperative. This I was, unfortunately, never able to do.

When I met Rosenberg at a rally in Dortmund in July, he informed me that, though a few labor leaders favored nationalization of industry, it was not a DGB objective. He and others, though not a majority, also favored a shift in the ownership of the means of production. But his choice was the creation of a profit-sharing fund that would equalize the share the workers received in strong and weak industries.

Changing the subject somewhat from organized labor and its reliability, Adenauer expressed the view that the Western allies had contributed greatly to Hitler's success. He recalled that when Hitler moved troops west of the Rhine, Britain had advised France not to react. In fact, he pointed out, we now knew that Hitler would have withdrawn had he been challenged. Adenauer told me that he had predicted war if the French troops did not come, since Hitler would realize that he could take whatever he wanted. But Adenauer also referred reassuringly to a recent German poll that revealed how little Germans now thought of Hitler. Compared to their views of himself and Bismarck, only 5 percent of the people thought that Hitler was the man who had done the most for Germany, and only 3 percent thought that Hitler was the politician who had done the most. President Kennedy had asked him who was the greatest German, Adenauer reported. It was only then that he had been struck by the fluctuations in public attitudes on this question over the past one hundred years.

Concluding with his favorite subject, Adenauer said that he had supported Franco-German reconciliation since 1918, including the period of the Weimar Republic, because he believed it to be absolutely essential for both countries. In order to appreciate de Gaulle, he added, one must remember that the French army was against him because he lost Algeria. This was why de Gaulle felt he must show that France was being treated on a par with the United Kingdom.

I asked Adenauer whether he had any questions or concerns about the forthcoming Harriman-Hailsham test ban negotiations in Moscow. I pointed out that the limited test ban proposal made by Khrushchev in East Berlin came as a surprise to us, that we were unclear as to the status of the proposed, rather ambiguous, linkage with a nonaggression pact. Our policy on this remained the same as expressed by Secretary Dean Rusk in Ottawa—namely, we would not make any commitments in this field without consulting our NATO allies. Adenauer responded that he was not the least bit concerned about the conduct of the Moscow talks. He added that he had not discussed the subject of French inclusion in the test ban with de Gaulle.

Nonetheless, by the time I met again with Adenauer in July, the principal issue on the international scene was the partial nuclear test ban treaty. On July 23 Kennedy advised Adenauer that we were close to signing but would make no further commitments without consulting our allies (memorandum, P. M. Cleveland, Amemb Bonn, Aug. 1, 1963). Kennedy hoped that West Germany would be among the first to sign. After asking me to express his thanks to the president for his consideration, Adenauer returned to the question of de Gaulle, who still seemed uppermost on his mind. He said that he did not want always to be in a position of seeming to defend de Gaulle, but he did not have the feeling that the Americans were really aware of the problem de Gaulle faced.

Adenauer said that de Gaulle had spoken highly of Kennedy during the French president's recent visit to Bonn but had noted that the United States and Europe had markedly different evaluations of the nuclear issue. For example, Adenauer explained, Europeans found it difficult to believe that if the Soviets attacked Western Europe and exploded a few symbolic hydrogen bombs over the United States, the U.S. government would be willing to risk the destruction of America that would result from a full nuclear conflict with the Soviets. Adenauer himself had already made this point to former Secretary of State Dulles. Dulles had replied merely that the Americans would be braver under such circumstances than the Europeans thought.

In April, a month before I arrived, Adenauer had made one last attempt to bar Erhard from succeeding him as chancellor but failed to sway the CDU Executive Committee. Adenauer had been forced to submit his resignation, which he did with a characteristic lack of grace. Adenauer was little in evidence in Bonn during the summer; as usual he vacationed in his beloved Cadenabbia on tranquil Lake Como, from which he had returned only in March. Apart from the Kennedy visit, which was a great success for Kennedy but not for Adenauer, whom he overshadowed, this isolation was broken only by de Gaulle's visit to Bonn and Adenauer's own farewell visit to the general at Rambouillet.

At final goodbyes in Bonn, Eugen Gerstenmaier, president of the Bundestag, congratulated Adenauer on being the first German chancellor in a hundred years to retire of his own free will, which was not exactly true (Prittie 1979, 114). Willy Brandt, his political opponent, said in his final tribute, "He made the free part of Germany an ally of the West, lent powerful impulses to West European unity, . . . devoted himself to Franco-German reconciliation. . . . Even his political opponents of yesterday are conscious that Germany is poorer from the loss of a man who set standards" (ibid., 116). The Adenauer era, which had lasted fourteen years and had launched Germany on the road to democratic statehood, had ended. With the emergence of Erhard as chancellor, the period of transition leading to a new era had begun.

4

Impressions of Erhard
May–August 1963

Ludwig Erhard undoubtedly made the greatest individual contribution to the remarkable West German economic recovery from World War II that contemporaries acclaimed as the *Wirtschaftswunder*, the economic miracle. Always overshadowed by the better-known Adenauer, who neither knew nor cared about economics, he finally succeeded to the chancellorship despite Adenauer's efforts to isolate, ridicule, and, in the end, block him. After a good start, however, he lost ground steadily until his coalition collapsed and he was unceremoniously ejected from office. Like all Americans serving in Germany, I liked Erhard immensely. He was loyal, straightforward, and unpretentious. I enjoyed my three years of association with him and felt sorry for his decline and fall. I thought he deserved better.

Erhard's origins were humble; his father, a north Bavarian, left his farm to open a haberdashery in 1897, twelve years before Ludwig's birth. Erhard was a good student at the Nuremberg School of Economics, and after graduation he served at the prestigious Institute of Market Research until he was forced to leave because of his refusal to join either the Nazi party or the Labor Front. He ran his own market research office until his reputation as an economist led to his discovery by the American occupation authorities, to whom he would always give credit for his later success. He was chosen director of the U.S.-British Bizonal Council, the most responsible position held by any German during the occupation. Committed to a free market approach, Erhard ended rationing and price controls two days after the Allies announced currency reform in June 1948. These events led to Erhard's greatest accomplishments. Under his direction, 12 million refugees were settled, 7.7 million jobs were created, the national income grew by four times, and the German mark became one of the strongest currencies in Europe. Germany's economy surged ahead of its European rivals, where it remains today. Erhard's economic successes made the CDU under Adenauer almost invulnerable to attacks by the opposition SPD. But Adenauer began to attack Erhard in public in 1956 over a minor matter of changes in the bank rate.

Countess Marion Dönhoff (1982, 108) has traced the transition from Adenauer to Erhard excellently in *Foe into Friend*, in which she points out the striking differences between the two men. According to Dönhoff, Adenauer used power in an authoritative way. Since he had the authority, leadership meant making the decisions. For Erhard the role of leadership was to persuade, since he believed people acted according to reason and their own best interests. There were great expectations of Erhard, as a liberal following a conservative. Dönhoff perceived that U.S.-German relations had come under increasing pressure during the latter part of Adenauer's regime, as discussed elsewhere. De Gaulle considered Erhard an Anglophile, and the German government under Erhard was unable to prevent itself from being drawn into the increasing tension between France and the United States. The key issues were support of NATO, the role of the force de frappe, and whether Europe should speak with one voice within an Atlantic community or be the "Europe of fatherlands" de Gaulle thought he could dominate.

When Erhard succeeded to the chancellorship on October 18, 1963, his parliamentary majority was higher by twenty than Adenauer's had been in 1961. He was at the peak of his popularity. His inaugural statement to the Bundestag focused rather on more of the same that Germans enjoyed than on any new departures: a strong currency and stable prices, aid to farmers, and social justice at the European as well as the German level. Predictably, he also endorsed existing policies on reunification, West Berlin, NATO, and defense, with increased emphasis on military cooperation with the United States. But if Adenauer could be characterized as a Gaullist, Erhard was clearly an Atlanticist and a Greater European, favoring a wider Common Market and an open door for trade.

I first called on Erhard on May 27 while he was still vice chancellor and economics minister (airgram, Amemb Bonn, memcon A–2459, May 27, 1963). As chancellor-designate, he was in a key position. He had always been friendly to the United States. I wanted not only to establish friendly personal relations with Erhard but to sound him out on current critical issues within the European Community, particularly the key questions of British entry and the troublesome problems created by de Gaulle.

Erhard received me warmly. He had an attractive smile and light blue eyes. I was impressed by how short he was. Like many Germans, he was overweight and stocky with a round, cherubic face. His hair was neatly parted. As usual, he was smoking a cigar. Erhard spoke little English, although he could both speak and understand more than he would admit. Erhard commented that the prevailing atmosphere in Germany appeared favorable, both for my arrival in Germany and for President Kennedy's forthcoming visit. I said that the president would welcome an opportunity to talk with him while he was in Germany, particularly on certain economic questions. Erhard replied that he did not know whether it would be possible to arrange for confidential discussions. He undoubtedly knew that Adenauer would do everything he could to foreclose such a meeting.

Erhard did not share de Gaulle's "European vision." He had, however, the impression that it might now be possible to make some "barter deals" with the French. It was Erhard's impression that, although continuing contacts between Britain and the EEC were desirable, the time was probably not yet opportune for further serious negotiations on British entry. The British Labour party had already adopted a negative position on British entry, and the Conservatives would hardly dare to engage in such negotiations until after the next British election.

He pointed out that Germany opposed the idea of one power dominating the European Community. He felt that the final shape of Europe was not yet clear but that it would not just happen as a result of economic cooperation. It required a deliberate "political act." The most serious difference between France and Germany, as he saw it, was that the French wanted to develop and cement the Common Market to their own advantage while continuing to play a dominant role in the EEC's relations with the associated African states.

In contrast, Germany desired a liberal and outward-looking community. It was time for the community to consider its external relations, he said, to avoid isolating itself from the rest of the world. Erhard felt sure that most of the European Community members agreed with the German view. He was confident that things would improve significantly after 1966, when Common Market rules would permit majority rather than unanimous voting of the EEC's six members. Erhard said that none of the countries concerned could afford a failure of the Kennedy Round negotiations and that all had worked hard in Europe to achieve its objectives. He was unsure, however, whether the results, particularly on agricultural matters, would altogether please the United States.

I acknowledged that this possibility was well recognized in Washington but stressed the importance of outward-looking European trade policies, for which the Kennedy Round negotiations were vital. The administration feared that failure could lead to a revival of isolationism in the United States. Erhard replied that these were precisely his views. He had considered warning the French in Geneva of the dangers of renewed American isolationism but had refrained from doing so since he feared this might be what the French desired.

Erhard then referred to another subject he considered important—the transfer of sovereignty by the EEC-member state to the EEC Commission. He believed that commission personnel, who were chosen for technical and administrative ability, should not and could not be permitted to make what are essentially political and policy decisions.

At the close of our conversation, I raised the issue of the U.S.-German offset discussions, which were about to resume shortly and would haunt Erhard throughout his term as chancellor. In accordance with their existing agreement the Germans were committed to offset the continuing foreign exchange cost of maintaining U.S. troops in Germany. Would the German government be able to continue finding sufficient U.S. military equipment to buy and be able to pay for it, I asked him. Erhard could not answer this with complete certainty, since it was the responsibility of the defense minister, but he stated that he hoped it would be possible. He knew that the German defense effort had to be increased and that heavy equipment must be purchased from the United States. He was also fully aware of the importance of German purchases to the U.S. balance of payments.

I emphasized the great importance of this to Washington, noting that we were then running a balance of payments deficit of over $3 billion a year, which at the time seemed to us a lot of money. I hardly needed to point out that the cost of maintaining U.S. troops in Germany was a major factor in our deficit and that our troop levels would continue to be an inevitable target in the U.S. Congress to the extent that their cost was not offset. Erhard agreed, but pointed out as well that the actual trade balance between the United States and Germany favored the United States. This would be an important consideration in the

Kennedy Round, particularly if Europe should close itself off from trade with America.

Before leaving, I could not fail to raise the quantitatively minor but politically troublesome matter of the "poultry war." When my confirmation as ambassador came before the U.S. Senate, this had been the principal question raised by the influential chairman of the Foreign Relations Committee, Sen. William Fulbright of Arkansas, a major chicken-producing state. Erhard replied that he realized fully the great political importance of this matter in the United States and would see how he could help.

I left my meeting feeling satisfied and looking forward to the time when Erhard would assume the chancellorship. His naturally friendly attitude toward the United States would make it easy to deal frankly with him. We could expect every consideration for our point of view. I realized that we must in turn try to protect him from the accusation of being too pro-American. He seemed a little incautious in this respect. I also searched for evidences of the weaknesses in Erhard that Adenauer had been only too ready to point out.

When I called on Erhard again at his request on June 20, he raised other questions that provided interesting clues to his attitudes and apprehensions on the eve of assuming the chancellorship (telegram, Amemb Bonn to Secstate, 3544, June 20, 1963). I said that I had heard of the possibility of agricultural questions being removed from politics in Germany by agreement among the three major parties.

Erhard confirmed that some consideration had been given to this, but doubted that such an agreement would ever be possible. In the past, the parties had been able to agree only on protection for farmers, he said, and Adenauer was unwilling to take any initiative on agriculture at all. But Erhard insisted that, once he was chancellor, he would do something serious about the European grain price problem that so favored inefficient French and German farmers and so discriminated against productive overseas producers. Jokingly, he asked that we not, for the time being, reveal his position on agriculture since it might affect his chances of being elected chancellor. He declared in all earnestness that he could not honestly support the Kennedy Round unless, at the same time, he was willing to do something about Germany's agricultural problems.

Erhard then told me that he had requested my visit because he wanted to raise a rather sensitive matter, which he hoped would not be misunderstood. Rather like Adenauer, he began by pointing out that the difference between the two political parties in Germany was considerably wider than was the case in the United States. Although in some respects the CDU and the SPD had come closer together in recent years, they still had considerable ideological differences, he emphasized. He was no enemy of the SPD and was certainly not reactionary, he added, and he hoped that I would not see any personal motive behind what he was about to say. But there was, he said, considerable speculation in German political circles concerning the U.S. government's attitude toward German domestic politics.

Speaking frankly, Erhard told me that the question had arisen as to whether the U.S. government and President Kennedy had a preference for the SPD and regarded the CDU as only a caretaker government to tide things over until the next election. Again like Adenauer, he referred to Kennedy's scheduled talk in Berlin before a labor audience. While he considered the union leadership moderate, Erhard regarded the unions themselves as one-sidedly SPD. As a result, he said, some in CDU circles feared that the general public might interpret Kennedy's appearance before this group as an endorsement of the opposition.

I assured Erhard that we had no intention of taking sides in internal German politics. It was a matter of general policy to maintain strict neutrality as between other countries' anti-Communist, nonextremist parties. We sought to maintain contact with all elements in a country except the political extremes. Over the years we had maintained such a close and effective relationship with the West German government that we had no conceivable reason for deviating from this general policy of neutrality. We had not proposed that President Kennedy address the International Trade Union Congress in Berlin because it was predominantly SPD but because we considered labor important to West Germany's economy and society and believed that unions are important institutions in a democracy. Erhard answered that it would be helpful if the speech could somehow be balanced by another of the president's German speeches to make it clear that he had no party preferences.

When I met Erhard again, after the Kennedy visit, I told him that the president had expressed regret at not having been able to talk more with him on the general question of foreign aid (telegram, Amemb Bonn to Secstate, 875, July 13, 1963). Kennedy believed it highly important that Western industrial nations increase and improve the terms of their aid to developing countries and had noted a recent decrease in German aid to India. He believed that this was no time for the West to let down. The performance of the other Western countries would have an important influence on foreign aid decisions by the U.S. Congress.

Erhard admitted the validity of Kennedy's comments, but his reply was rather oblique and not encouraging. Although there would be no firm decisions on foreign aid before he assumed the chancellorship in August, he said, his first task was to put Germany "back on a firm economic basis" and to stop inflation, which would require rigid budgetary control. He assured me that the Federal Republic would, of course, continue to provide foreign aid, but Erhard regretted that it had not been started earlier, when "we could afford it."

These first conversations with Erhard were for the purpose of "touching base" with him as a key minister, a friend of the United States, and the next chancellor of Germany. They would be on an entirely different basis when he succeeded to power. In the meantime my next important initial contact now shifted to Berlin and Willy Brandt.

5

Introduction to Berlin
June 1963

Since the end of World War II the Four Powers—France, Great Britain, the United States, and the Soviet Union—have accorded Berlin special treatment. As a result of the occupation treaties and the subsequent division of the city, the three Allied ambassadors—British, French, and American—were in theory the government of West Berlin. With the passage of time and the Federal Republic's assumption of responsibility for meeting Berlin's large budgetary needs, the area of authority exercised by the Western Allies gradually receded. The city came to be governed as part of West Germany for most practical purposes, with the notable exception that the deputies sent to Bonn by Berliners could vote neither in the selection of the chancellor nor on substantive legislation. The three powers did, however, provide the only basis for security the isolated city had, for which the respective military forces there acted as hostage. The Federal Republic, the governing mayor, the senate, the three Allied military commandants, and the three Allied ambassadors had to work together.

A mayor and city council initially had to cope with the former capital's many acute problems under the direction of a Kommandatura, composed of the representatives from the four occupying powers. This civilian administration rationed food during the early period of reconstruction, supervised the removal of rubble, and enforced Allied law. Then came the Cold War between the Soviets and its wartime allies, which resulted in Berlin's division between East and West. During the 323-day Soviet blockade of West Berlin that began in April 1948, the

Allies delivered over 2.1 million tons of food to the city's three western sectors.

In 1950 about 30 percent of West Berlin's labor force was out of work. Berlin's population had many more people in the age group 50 to 65 and far fewer under the age of 21 than West Germany as a whole. Unemployment in West Berlin was also 30 percent higher than in West Germany. As late as 1955, when West German unemployment had dropped to 4 percent, it was still in excess of 8 percent in Berlin. Major efforts were required to develop transportation, schools, utilities, and industry. Special incentives in the form of subsidies to compensate for increased production costs were offered to industries who rebuilt or moved to West Berlin.

On November 30, 1948, the division of Berlin was institutionalized by the establishment of a separate city council in the Soviet sector and the cutting of telephone communications. Berlin became two cities, although the border continued for some time to be open to visitors from either side. In order to overcome this division and isolation from West Germany and to assure a continued healthy economy in West Berlin, the *Senat*, or governing body of the three Western sectors, took several drastic measures, including family benefits to raise the birthrate. Every effort was made to create employment in research and high technology as well as the emerging service industries. Efforts were also made to revitalize Berlin to boost morale and to attract tourists and Germans inclined to move there through encouragement of the arts, the opera, the Berlin Philharmonic, the ballet, and by such new educational institutions as the Free University. Before the Wall divided the city, Berlin had been promoted as a meeting point between Eastern and Western Europe. Great efforts are still being made to perpetuate Berlin as an international art and conference center.

I was fully aware of Berlin's importance before I came to Bonn as ambassador. I recalled my first visit to postwar Berlin, when I had been quartered in the requisitioned home of a professor, and remembered how uncomfortable I felt seeing his books and files still in place. I was appalled as I made my way through the ruins to dine in a restaurant in the basement of a destroyed mansion. I pitied the grim, gray figures of German workmen, struggling in the mist and snow to rid the city of rubble. What a change from the metropolis of glittering cafés, music, and dancing I had seen as a student at the peak of Berlin's prewar prosperity.

I had made another visit just before the erection of the Wall in 1961 and had found in West Berlin few damaged buildings or empty former building spaces. The rubble had been removed or piled in neat mounds. The U.S. mission had arranged for my wife and myself to visit East Berlin, which presented a sickening sight by comparison; countless buildings remained gutted by bombs and bullets. Little improvement could be seen beyond the pretentious boulevard of shops and apartments that was conceived by its architects as the Stalin-Allee but is now known as the Frankfurter Allee. Only the massive new Soviet embassy seemed built to last. Few people walked the streets. Our driver told us that this was typical and that four hundred people a day were going over to West Berlin. The Soviets made an incalculable mistake in continuing their punitive measures of dismantlement and exploitation rather than trying to make Berlin a showcase for the pretended accomplishments of the Communist world.

John F. Kennedy assumed the presidency on January 20, 1961. He had been well briefed on Germany and Berlin before his historic meeting with Chairman Khrushchev in Vienna in early June. Khrushchev's attempts to bully the young president made a strong impact on Kennedy and led to his well-publicized American military buildup in Europe, the acceleration of NATO strategic planning, and sharp exchanges with the Soviets. No national emergency or general mobilization was declared, however, as occurred in 1958.

On August 13, 1961, with East Germany hemorrhaging from the exodus of up to three thousand inhabitants a day to West Germany (total until the stoppage 3.3 million), including many highly trained professionals, Khrushchev began construction of the infamous Berlin Wall, which was to have an indelible effect on Berlin. Rightly or wrongly, the Allies did not protest vigorously against the erection of the Wall. In fact it was almost the only means available to the Soviets to stop the escape of East Berliners, and its construction ushered in a period of greater toleration of West Berlin by the Soviets.

After the erection of the Wall on August 13, 1961, Secretary of State Dean Rusk and Soviet Foreign Minister Andrey Gromyko held intermittent, inconclusive talks on Berlin, as the Soviets tested the Allies' will to hold their position in the city. Starting on February 8, 1962, the Soviets attempted systematically to harass civil and military Allied air traffic with Berlin. The United States made a strong protest, calling the Soviet measures totally unacceptable. Although the issues raised by the Wall remained serious, they were largely subsumed by the Cuban missile crisis in October 1962. When the Soviets saw that Allied resolve on Berlin could not be broken, they abandoned disruptive efforts except for harassment of Allied convoys on the Autobahn, which started soon after my arrival in May and lasted until November 1963.

I returned to the State Department in 1961 as head of the Policy Planning Council. In accordance with my understanding of its long-range planning role, I had declined to participate in the day-to-day work of the Berlin task force, which had been set up to handle operational problems created by the Berlin Wall and the subsequent challenge to Allied air access. Policy Planning had, however, made a contribution by developing the concept of a Berlin access authority. According to this plan, an international agency would be created with representatives from both East and West but with a majority from neutral nations. This agency would make all major decisions regarding access by the occupying powers. The idea was given a fair hearing but never achieved acceptance.

Since the late 1940s Berlin-related matters of common interest to the three Western occupying powers and the Federal Republic had been run by the Bonn Group of subambassadorial officials from the respective governments. Over the years the group had established efficient procedures and understandings. The officers knew one another well, were in frequent contact, and acted almost independently. Obviously, the three ambassadors were consulted on important matters, many of which were referred to their capitals, but there was no regular procedure for higher-level consultation. From what I learned I thought it would be appropriate to organize regular meetings of the ambassadors plus Under Secretary Carstens of the German foreign office.

On June 3 I made my first visit to Berlin, which had been a high priority since my arrival, departing from Bonn on the evening of June 3 with my aide and other embassy officers. The trip marked, incidentally, the last use of the embassy's two-car ambassadorial train, as a result of a congressional economy decision. From my briefing I knew the location of the eight Soviet divisions surrounding Berlin out of the twenty-one in East Germany and how close our train came to those we passed during the night. We were met at the suburban station in the American sector early the following morning by Maj. Gen. James Polk, the American commandant in Berlin, and U.S. Minister Arch Calhoun. Polk was tall, erect, and wiry, as befitted a cavalry officer, and had a warm, friendly smile. We were to have a long and pleasant association in Germany, lasting through his assignment as commander of U.S.

Ground Forces Europe. Calhoun, an able, alert, career foreign service officer, represented the embassy in Berlin. (Memcon, USCOB and U.S. Mission, Berlin, June 4, 1963.)

At American Headquarters Polk described the practical problems he faced with Mayor Willy Brandt and the Berlin Senate in carrying out his difficult assignment. The main problems hinged on the limitations the Berlin authorities placed on the responsibilities of the three commandants and their recent tendency, presumably with Brandt's approval, to take independent actions without consulting the Allies. I pointed out that we must permit the Germans as much latitude as possible on minor matters but that on basic issues we could not allow them to weaken the Allied position. We were in Berlin only because of certain legal statutes that must be maintained.

Various staff members described the current situation in East Germany, whose regime was said to be facing its greatest problems since 1953. The internal political situation in the GDR had deteriorated, and the economic situation was grave as a result of a disastrous winter and a decline in exports. Food would have to be imported in the face of strong Soviet pressure to balance the East German economy. The reliability of East German troops was considered good.

Polk found no clear pattern in Soviet policy toward the city but said that the Russians continued to probe for weak spots to ensure that the Berlin problem "was kept alive." He confirmed that the Soviets were trying to narrow the rules governing Allied rights of air access with a possible eye toward turning air traffic control over to the East Germans. It was generally agreed that West Berliners were particularly interested in greater security of access arrangements and that they favored the concept of an international access authority. They also wished to reduce the harsher impacts of the Wall. Under Brandt's leadership, the West Berlin government was trying to establish a new dynamic for the city. Meanwhile, pressure came from the Berlin CDU to make Berlin a full German state, with Allied presence on the basis of a contract with Bonn.

Following the briefing, I paid a short visit to RIAS, the radio station in the American sector, which broadcasted a daily diversified U.S.-sponsored program to East Berlin and East Germany. The East German government could do little to stop its people from listening. The station provided an accurate picture of what was going on in West Germany and the world and boosted the morale of the Germans under Communist control. RIAS had a dedicated staff that had survived great hardships.

I was also taken on a tour of the Wall. It was not just the disruptive squalor of the hastily built structure or the pitiful looks of the East Berliners one could see on the other side that left an impression. It was what the Wall represented for East Germans. They could not visit or receive fellow Germans or relatives from the West. They could not travel as tourists or to professional meetings, except within the Soviet bloc. Pictures taken of me at the Wall show a grim face. I was not acting. I felt grim. East Germany seemed to me like one vast prison.

During my five years in Germany I gave attention to the possibility of negotiating with the Soviets to stabilize the situation in Berlin. I approached this question from a number of directions during the regular talks I held with the Soviet ambassador to East Germany, Peter Andreyevich Abrasimov. At no time, however, did I receive any encouragement. The Soviets remained opposed to any new agreement on Allied presence in Berlin and complained constantly of alleged illegal West German activities there, such as Bundestag committee meetings. President Kennedy and President Johnson nevertheless continued their efforts to relieve tensions with the East.

There was, however, a sequel that I believe should be recorded here. Starting in 1970 the Nixon administration made a determined effort to obtain a treaty on Berlin. It was led by my able successor, Ambassador Kenneth Rush, who had assumed his post in 1969 after the brief ambassadorship of Henry Cabot Lodge. After difficult and protracted negotiations, often involving heads of governments, a quadripartite agreement on Berlin was finally reached on September 13, 1971. The agreement did not change the basic legal position of the Four Powers, but it did stabilize the status quo and legitimize a kind of agreement to disagree. The Allies considered that they had obtained improved access rights and enhanced security for the people of West Berlin. For their part, the Soviets could claim new influence over Allied activities in West Berlin.

In practice, questions of harassment were now left to be negotiated between the two Germanies, but it was assumed that the Allies would continue to take serious problems to the Soviets. Despite constant bickering, access arrangements since then have worked reasonably well. The main source of ongoing controversy concerns the ties between the Federal Republic and West Berlin, which have increased substantially and which will undoubtedly continue to engender frequent Soviet protests.

6

First Contacts
with Brandt
June 1963

The most important duty of my introductory visit to Berlin was, of course, my first meeting with Willy Brandt, who received me for the traditional signing of the Golden Book at the Rathaus Schöneberg. Brandt was later to serve as foreign minister and as postwar Germany's first Social Democratic chancellor, but he was then the city's governing mayor. His attractive smile and engaging manner had already made him a favorite with Americans. In 1974 Brandt resigned from the chancellorship as the result of a scandal involving personal and security matters. But his strong appeal among leftwing circles led to his political resurrection as the perennial head of his party and to his global recognition as an international elder statesman.

Herbert Ernst Karl Frahm, the name Brandt used for his first thirty years, was born in 1913 in the old Hanseatic city of Lubeck, son of a working woman. Willy Brandt was Frahm's nom de guerre during the Nazi era. Brandt was one of that generation which suffered in an atmosphere of deep frustration after Germany's defeat in World War I and what was to Germans the onerous Treaty of Versailles. As a young man Brandt opposed the rising tide of Nazism, became a left-wing Socialist, and in 1930 entered the Social Democratic party. He soon demonstrated his leadership in political circles and became an accomplished speaker.

Brandt rose steadily within his party and in 1952 became a member of the Berlin City Parliament. It was in large part his skillful handling of the West German response to the 1953 worker uprising in East Berlin, and the 1956 demonstrations in West Berlin in support of the Hungarian uprisings, that led to his election as governing mayor of Berlin in 1957 at age forty-three.

During the ensuing years Brandt achieved recognition as the symbol of the brave resistance of his beleaguered city. He developed a reputation for hard work, a willingness to listen to and consider opposing views, and loyalty to his supporters. He showed an ability to cope skillfully with difficult situations and displayed an unflappability and an iron will in times of crisis. During this period he began to rely heavily on his close assistant, Egon Bahr, whom many found equivocal in his orientation to the West. Brandt was also tempered by his bitter rivalry with the relentless Adenauer, leader of the CDU.

The American ambassador's special role in Berlin conditioned my relationship with Brandt as governing mayor. Later, when he became foreign minister under Chancellor Kurt Georg Kiesinger in the CDU/CSU-SPD Grand Coalition in 1967, our respective roles changed, allowing a more informal working relationship.

In the five years I worked with Brandt, he was always relaxed in our official discussions and appeared to be firmly oriented toward the West and friendly to Americans. He was good company for a convivial evening. He and his attractive and popular wife, Ruth, seemed a happy couple. I never encountered any difficulty in communicating with him. When misunderstandings appeared, we faced them squarely. Although I sensed that some of his advisers questioned U.S. and Allied policy, I never doubted his sincerity in fulfilling the unusual relationship that bound the United States and Berlin. But he always represented something of an enigma to me. In spite of his open and friendly manner I often found it difficult to penetrate his detachment. I sensed that he was more complicated than he seemed.

When we first met, Brandt, like all Berliners, had only recently gone through the excruciating experience of the Wall. He still deeply resented that neither the Adenauer government nor the United States and the other Western allies had offered effective resistance. The Allies had not protested officially for four days, and Adenauer had not even interrupted his reelection campaign in West Germany to visit the city. General Lucius D. Clay, whom President Kennedy later sent to Berlin on a special mission, gave comfort to the Berliners, who remembered him for standing firm during the Berlin Blockade. But nothing tangible resulted from his presence in the city.

One incident that would later affect my own right to visit East Berlin as ambassador had incidentally arisen during this period. Shortly after the Wall went up, a senior official from our embassy in Bonn had refused to show his identification during a visit to East Berlin, on the theory that the flags on his official car were self-evident confirmation of his right to be there. Only after a show of U.S. tanks at the checkpoint was he rescued from the Soviet sector by a police escort. U.S. officials subsequently felt obliged to maintain this precedent and continued to refuse to show their identification. As a result, they were not allowed into East Berlin.

When I met with him on June 4, Brandt was friendly, turning on his well-known grin-cum-smile. I felt the celebrated charisma that had helped elevate him to world prominence. I opened the conversation by describing the powerful impression made on me by the Berlin Wall. Brandt opened by reviewing the course of West Berlin morale since August 1961, moving from the initial shock generated by the erection of the Wall to the major disturbance triggered a year later by the tragic death of a young man named Peter Fechter, who had bled to death in sight of West Berliners after being shot while trying to escape from East Berlin. This psychological crisis had now been overcome, Brandt felt, and morale was generally stable and satisfactory.

Brandt described the health of the Berlin economy as good but remarked that it could be better. While the index of West Berlin industrial production was only about 180, compared to over 300 in West Germany, its recent rate of growth had exceeded that of the Federal Republic. The current overall lag was explained by Berlin's slow start. In 1948, the year of the West German currency reform, Berlin industry was still producing at less than 20 percent of what it produced in 1936, whereas West German production had already recovered to 85 or 90 percent of its 1936 level.

Brandt believed that the West Berlin industrial index might eventually reach West German levels, but only if Berlin industrialists overcame their somewhat cautious and conservative attitude and made far larger investments in automation. He also pointed out that West Berlin had developed a much more diversified industrial production than before World War II, when the city had manufactured primarily electrical equipment, machinery, and women's clothing.

The movement of people into and out of West Berlin did not seem to concern Brandt. City authorities, he said, had no wish to turn West Berlin into a ghetto by interfering with the normal flow of population. During 1962, the influx of workers from West Germany had, in fact, reached gratifying proportions. He was sharply critical of the policy

West German authorities had followed with regard to East German refugees. While there was still unemployment in West Berlin, most able-bodied refugees had been sent to the Federal Republic, whereas welfare cases had been retained in Berlin, aggravating the city's demographic problems.

I asked whether the local housing situation constituted a major obstacle to persons wishing to settle in the city. Brandt doubted it. He pointed out that Berlin had more large apartments available than other German cities, though small units were still hard to get. Moreover, adequate funds were available for new construction, with most of the new building financed directly or indirectly by the city government. The housing industry had produced 20,000 to 22,000 dwelling units per year, in addition to new office buildings, factories, cultural edifices, and the like. Brandt emphasized that building capacity could be increased through modernization and the use of more rational methods. But the construction industry was chronically reluctant to invest in the major new equipment necessary for more rapid efficient production.

With reference to the search for improvements in the overall situations of Berlin and Germany as a whole, Brandt dismissed as thoroughly unrealistic the idea prevalent in some quarters that the East German economy would collapse, sparking fundamental political changes, if the West firmly refused credits or other forms of assistance. He found it highly improbable that the East German economic situation would get completely out of control. For reasons of prestige and power politics, the Soviets could not afford to allow a collapse of the economy, let alone of the Communist system itself, and would presumably do anything necessary to shore up East Germany. Furthermore, an aggravated economic crisis would provide a ready pretext for even more stringent political control. It would thus lead not to liberalization, in Brandt's view, but in fact produce the opposite result.

Brandt inclined toward a different approach. He thought that efforts to improve conditions in East Germany might be regarded as an area of joint interest between the Soviet Union and the West. There was already evidence of differences between the Soviets and the East German regime since the early years, when the Soviets simply gave orders. Khrushchev, he recalled, had recently told a Western visitor that the East German Communists behaved at times like adolescents whom one would like to spank. Even though the East German regime was their unhappiest partner, however, the Soviets had to allow it a certain latitude.

Brandt was certain that the Soviets were increasingly embarrassed by the East German "museum of Stalinism" and that they were somewhat sensitive to the human effects of Germany's total division. Although they could never allow themselves to be pushed out of East Germany, he believed they might at least welcome the increase in productivity and living standards that would permit political liberalization and greater stability. Under such conditions, they might then gradually reduce their military presence and immediate responsibilities in the area, allowing an East German Communist regime to acquire a more managerial character and tolerate greater mobility across the borders. A lessening of the Soviet grip on East Germany might in turn produce conditions under which the two parts of Germany could begin to grow back together. Although I did not say so, I was skeptical.

In line with his long-range concept, Brandt favored a certain measure of Western assistance, such as an increase in short-term credits to finance intra-German trade. But the Western side had to be careful in its efforts to establish contacts and restore some movement between the two parts of Germany, he warned. Such approaches must not appear to be aimed directly at the reunification of West and East Germany.

I asked whether he thought credits to the East German regime would directly benefit people in East Germany, and he appeared to doubt this. Chairman Walter Ulbricht of East Germany and the Soviets could not afford, for the time being, to permit more liberal conditions and greater production of consumer goods, since industrial production in East Germany continued to fall short of plan goals. Brandt also seemed relatively unconcerned about the possibility of formal East German annexation of East Berlin. For all intents and purposes, East Berlin was already treated as part of East Germany, he argued. I replied that such a change in the pattern of our access to East Berlin would produce a new, serious situation, which might interfere with Soviet activities in West Berlin. I thought it likely that the continuation of their activities in the West was of greater importance to the Russians than our patrolling in East Berlin.

Brandt admitted he was impatient with the prevailing legalistic approach to the issue of diplomatic recognition. Since he was not a lawyer, he said, he found it difficult to appreciate the fine distinctions between de facto and de jure situations. Meanwhile, the West Berlin police were forced to stand idly by at the sector border as people were killed by order of the Communist regime, and American soldiers had to acquiesce to interference by East German border guards whenever they tried to exercise their right to visit East Berlin. As far as Brandt was concerned, this too was a form of recognition, even if it differed from the classic diplomatic definition.

After my meeting with Brandt, I toured the installations of the Berlin brigade, our contribution to the defense of the city. It was, in a sense, a hostage to the city's exposed situation, assuring our involvement in any ensuing conflict. The officers and men of the Berlin Brigade understood well that a few thousand troops in the combined Allied forces in Berlin could never withstand attack from the eight Soviet divisions encircling the city. They nonetheless considered service in the brigade a great honor, and their morale and readiness were high.

The following morning I attended Polk's USBER (U.S. Brigade Berlin) staff meeting and took a USBER helicopter to view the Berlin sector and zonal borders. The Wall snaked through the former dividing line between East and West Berlin like an ugly scar, punctuated at intervals by towers with armed border guards. Beyond lay a strip of plowed land that was raked regularly to detect footprints. Police dogs prowled the area, ready to stop any trespasser.

Before leaving Berlin, I received James Conant, the distinguished chemist and former president of Harvard, who had been our last high commissioner and then our first ambassador in Bonn, now on a temporary appointment at the Free University. Low-key and self-effacing, Conant was highly respected by Germans, and his months in Berlin were a great help in our efforts to boost morale there. Together we visited the rector of the Free University, which the United States had been instrumental in founding. I was to have many future contacts with the university and to witness the sad politicization that took place there as part of the worldwide wave of student unrest beginning at Berkeley.

At the residence I received forty-five representatives of the Berlin press corps. The meeting evolved into an informal press conference on Berlin and U.S. policy toward Berlin and Germany. I was to find that the Berlin press were highly sensitive to the nuances of policy changes, reflecting the vulnerable position of the city and its complete dependence on the Allies.

Following my return from Berlin, the first luncheon meeting of the Bonn Group at the ambassadorial level was held in my residence. Frank Roberts, Roland Jacquin de Margerie, and Karl Carstens all agreed that such meetings would be helpful and that we should schedule them on a monthly basis. Indeed, they continued for the duration of my five years in Bonn. They not only contributed, I believe, to a better understanding of Berlin matters, but toward the four men improving their working relationship.

I deferred one last official visit for a later trip, but it, too, was part of my formal responsibilities in Berlin. Now nearly forgotten, Spandau prison for Nazi war criminals was one of the last remnants of Four Power rule. Since 1946, each of the occupying powers ran the prison a month at a time, the United States having been allotted April, August, and December. On April 23, 1964, I exercised my right as ambassador to inspect the prison. By 1964 the prison was kept in service only to house the remaining three major war criminals sentenced by the international military tribunal in Nuremberg on October 1, 1946. These were Rudolf Hess, who had been Hitler's deputy, Baldur von Schirach, the Nazi youth leader, and Albert Speer, who had been minister for armaments. Speer and Schirach were later released from Spandau on September 30, 1966.

The purpose of my inspection was to determine the state of the prisoners' health and treatment and to see whether they had any complaints or requests. As inspector I was to interview each man separately after examining his cell and personal effects. Under prison rules, the prisoners were supposed to be addressed only by their prison numbers. However, I found this too inhuman, and, even though I was accompanied by the British, French, and Soviet commandants, I used their names. By tradition, the inspector did not raise personal or political questions.

Of the three, Speer—who was bucking for early release—was the most forthcoming and ingratiating. His daughter, well known in the Berlin American community, had once approached me in her father's behalf at a reception. Under Secretary of State George Ball once told me that she had also sought his help in obtaining Speer's release. Speer told me he was primarily interested in having more books, and a better lamp to read by.

Hess has always been accorded particular attention because of his senior rank and his spectacular wartime flight to Scotland. At the time of my inspection, he was not permitted a watch because of Soviet objections, his books were censored, and he was not allowed facilities to make tea or coffee. Only in 1966 was he allowed a daily, rather than weekly, bath. Hess was then feigning insanity and said nothing that would hurt his game. He looked gaunt and somber, with deep, dark, staring eyes. Nothing of his personality came through. He had two small rooms, each perhaps ten feet by six feet, in one of which, like the other prisoners, he kept a metal footlocker for his meager personal effects. When he opened it for my inspection, the officer's uniform hanging inside was identified as the one he wore when he parachuted into Britain.

Schirach made no effort to impress me. His appearance was sullen, and his requests, if any, were too trivial for me to recall. All of the prisoners expressed a desire for more time outside, where each had a garden. I was told that, when the prisoners were permitted to go outside, Hess and Schirach were often together. But they refused to associate with Speer, whom they considered as from a lower social class, leaving him to garden alone. After the release of Speer and Schirach, the three Western allies decided Hess should be released as well. Apart from humanitarian considerations, Spandau is a large and expensive prison for one man. The Soviets, however, remained adamant, and Hess died there.

Another experience which provided a grim view into the German past was my visit to the Berlin Document Center, which contained Nazi party membership records, SS personnel files, and other government documents, 14 million in all. When Berlin was threatened, they were all packed and moved by land toward Bavaria, where they would have been destroyed but for the timely arrival of invading Allied forces. After the war, the material was used for prosecution of Nazi war criminals and to screen candidates for West German government jobs. Even today visa applications are checked from time to time against personnel files in the Berlin Document Center to ensure against unrestricted admission to the United States of former SS officers. Though it was never America's intention to assume permanent custody of these records, the United States also hesitated to turn them over to the Federal Republic. The opportunities both for conveniently losing or misplacing papers and for blackmail were obviously great.

7

The Kennedy Visit
June 22–26, 1963

The high point of my activity during my first weeks as ambassador to the Federal Republic, of course, was President Kennedy's first and only visit to Germany, June 22–26. His tour, which also included Ireland and Italy, was a benchmark in the history of German-American relations. Theodore Sorensen has said that Kennedy's purpose was "to talk to their publics in the wake of de Gaulle's charges against the U.S." Kennedy was concerned with overall U.S. relationships with Western Europe, which he considered of greatest importance "to us and, I hope, to the people of Europe." On his return Kennedy felt that he had accomplished this objective, particularly with young people, and that he had placed the United States in a position "to get more done." (Sorensen 1965, 579.)

It was because of Kennedy's visit to Germany that my own arrival in Bonn had been advanced. The visit had been the subject of intense planning by the embassy over many months. I was determined to travel to every place Kennedy would visit and meet with every official he would meet. Kennedy drove himself hard and was known to be a tough taskmaster. Since he was to be in Germany only ninety-one hours, every moment had to count. In addition to Bonn and neighboring Cologne, Kennedy's itinerary included Frankfurt, Wiesbaden, and Berlin. For security reasons he had chosen to stay in Bonn at the home of the deputy chief of mission and in Wiesbaden at the Von Steuben Hotel, the U.S. Air Force's guest house.

During his visit Kennedy was to meet Adenauer, Lübke, Brandt, and Erhard. He was to be received by the mayor of each town he visited, attend a mass at the Cologne Cathedral, address the Bonn embassy staff, be given a dinner by and give a dinner for Chancellor Adenauer, hold a press conference, visit army units, lunch with U.S. military officials, and make a major address at the Paulskirche in Frankfurt, the site in 1848 of Germany's first democratic constitutional convention. In West Berlin he was to speak at the labor convention that made Adenauer and Erhard so apprehensive, visit the Wall, speak at the city hall, and address remarks to a select audience at the Free University. Unfortunately, the American interpreter's German translation of Kennedy's speeches was not equal to the occasion, and it was necessary to borrow Adenauer's interpreter for the president's speeches in Frankfurt and Berlin. With his skill, he made Kennedy's words come to life with remarkable results.

No negotiations were involved in Kennedy's meetings with Adenauer and other officials, only what are called in diplomatic parlance tours d'horizon of current issues. He had met them all before and conversed with them with ease. The key events from the standpoint of policy impact were the speeches at the Paulskirche, the West Berlin City Hall, and the Free University, to which considerable thought had been given both in Washington and Bonn.

The subject of the Paulskirche speech, to which most important German officials and leaders had been invited, was "Partnership with Germany and a United Europe" (Kennedy 1964, 113). Kennedy opened with a tribute to German democracy, which he recalled had been cradled in a historic meeting of the Frankfurt Assembly at the Paulskirche in 1848. The European and American revolutions and search for liberty and freedom were parts of one common movement, Kennedy said. The interdependence of our age was reflected in our common efforts within the framework of the Atlantic partnership, the strengthening of NATO, the building of Europe, the expansion of trade, and assistance to developing countries.

The object of our common policy, Kennedy continued, was to create a new social order founded on liberty and justice in which men are masters of their fate and states the servants of their citizens, working toward a better life for all. To achieve these goals we must seek a world of peace in which people live together in mutual respect and regard. "Let it not be said of the Atlantic generation that we left ideals to the past, nor purpose and determination to our adversaries," he declared. The audience responded enthusiastically during the speech and applauded strongly at the end.

Kennedy's address on the steps of the Rathaus in Berlin on June 26 before an audience crowded into the Rudolph-Wilde-Platz—the so-called Ich bin ein Berliner speech—attracted the greatest attention (ibid., 98). The use of the phrase "I am a Berliner" resulted in a great psychological coup. One of the young embassy wives had helped the president learn to say the phrase in German at a party in Wiesbaden the evening before he went to Berlin. From my vantage point behind Kennedy I could see clearly the excitement of his audience, which was estimated at 100,000 to 150,000 people; they filled every bit of space in the Rathaus square and the streets leading into it. Kennedy held them in the palm of his hand from his opening to the final climax. He was at his oratorical best, his timing perfect. As he repeated in his characteristic manner his expression, "Let them come to Berlin," the crowd roared back in approval. One could feel the tension—the developing bond between the slight figure of the young man and the Berlin citizens of all ages and walks of life who had come to pay him tribute. These people had experienced the ravages of war and knew that their freedom, even their lives, depended on the faraway nation Kennedy represented. They were not disappointed; they came away with greater confidence in their future through confidence in him.

Later that day, speaking at the Free University to intellectuals, Kennedy addressed the subject of "The Defense of West Berlin and West Germany" (ibid., 113). He characterized the objectives of the Free University as turning out "citizens of the world" who could comprehend the sensitive tasks facing free people and who were willing to commit their energies to the advancement of a free society. Kennedy quoted Goethe as believing that education and culture were the answer to international strife. He applauded the Free University for having maintained its fidelity to truth, justice, and liberty.

Justice required, Kennedy said, that we of the West keep contact with the East and try to improve the lot of their peoples, to show them how democracy works. The reunification of Berlin and Germany was part of the reconstitution of a larger Europe, Kennedy affirmed. The Eastern states were unable to match the pace of modern society and its intellectual ferment, which required human initiatives and the diversity of free minds. This ferment was apparent in the new Europe of the West and would have an increasing attraction for the East. To succeed, however, the West must increase its strength and unity.

In their bland joint communiqué at the end of the visit, Kennedy and Adenauer expressed agreement on continued close collaboration to develop a genuine community among the nations of Europe in close partnership with the United States; to strengthen participation by the developing nations in world trade; to pursue controlled disarmament and the cessation of nuclear weapons tests to help avoid a dangerous arms race; to strengthen NATO common defense planning and the joint operation of defense forces; and to use their best efforts to create the proposed MLF. They also reaffirmed the right of self-determination under the United Nations Charter and German reunification in peace and freedom, including the freedom of Berlin. Here they would seek to counter the inhuman effects of the Wall and try to reduce the tension it created. Their overall goals remained peace and freedom.

Kennedy's visit to Germany in 1963 has been acclaimed widely as one of the most successful state visits on record. It removed some of his own reservations about Germany, and it endeared him to the German people. He was indefatigable throughout and he mastered all of his briefing material. Although a hundred key Germans were at the dinner Kennedy gave at the Embassy Club in Bonn, he had some flattering comment to make to each, indicating his understanding of each man's position.

As a result of the visit, there was a remarkable outpouring of admiration and affection for Kennedy on the part of the German people, particularly the young. This charming, jaunty, youthful American aristocrat, with his ready smile and wit, provided a sharp contrast to the dour octogenarian Chancellor Adenauer and his chubby successor-to-be, Ludwig Erhard. Kennedy's barrage of inspiring statements embodied his idealism, his unbounded optimism, and his hope for the future. Delivered in his effective staccato tempo with his charming Boston Irish brogue, his speeches enthralled his audiences. I was sitting next to Kennedy in an open car as we drove from the airport to Frankfurt. Tens of thousands of Germans of all ages lined the road, waving banners, and shouting welcomes. As the car went past, their faces lit up. Individually and collectively, the Germans were having a love affair with young Jack Kennedy. He had demonstrated his friendship for the Germans and his appreciation of their postwar efforts at rehabilitation. This success served as a long-lasting lubricant for the subsequent day-to-day conduct of U.S.-German relations and gave me great confidence in the outcome of my tour of duty.

Only five months later, in the aftermath of the president's assassination in Dallas, an unprecedented outpouring of grief swept Germany. The Germans felt that they had lost one of their own. By the thousands they stood by candlelight in silent tribute in churches on dark autumn evenings. For months afterwards, I was to spend much of my time attending ceremonies dedicating monuments and structures in his honor all over the Federal Republic—here a bridge, there a road, at another place a statue. Germans of that generation would never forget Jack Kennedy.

Many flashes from the Kennedy visit still come to mind: Adenauer and Brandt in Berlin jockeying for precedence with respect to the president in a contest that Brandt won; my being shoved bodily by Gen. Chester Clifton, the president's military aide, so I would displace the French minister in Berlin, who Clifton thought was hogging the limelight by standing directly behind the president as he began his speech at the Rathaus; Kennedy inspecting an infantry division near Frankfurt with its full complement of troops, transport, weapons, and equipment stretched out in formation behind it and the brigadier general who commanded it alone out front, receiving the president's salute; Kennedy scowling in defiance at the Berlin Wall; hearing the roar of the Berliners in front of City Hall, then feeling the letdown of the crowds at Tegel airport as the president ended the visit that had lifted the whole German nation to such emotional heights. Words were not needed that evening as I returned to Bonn with Chancellor Adenauer and other German officials.

8

Military and Economic Questions May–October 1963

In view of the importance of NATO defense to U.S. security and the significance to the Federal Republic of the over 300,000 American military personnel there, it was natural that I pay our U.S. and NATO command headquarters in Germany an early visit. Commanding officers for Ground, Air, and Armed Forces Europe were all located in Germany, in Wiesbaden, Stuttgart, and Heidelberg, respectively. In their NATO capacities they reported to Supreme Allied Commander Europe (SACEUR), at this time my friend Gen. Lyman (Lem) Lemnitzer, who was based in Paris. The U.S. ambassador in Bonn was responsible for political relations between the German government and U.S. military units in Germany, which were, except for the Berlin brigade, all assigned to NATO. My simulated rank was that of a four star general.

I have always enjoyed working with military men, having served in the navy during World War II and later in the Air Force Reserve. I spent the last year of the war on Saipan and Guam as naval liaison officer for Gen. Curtis LeMay, who commanded the Twenty-First Bomber Command, the B–29s, in the air war against Japan. Generals Jimmy Doolittle and Toughy Spotz were often in our headquarters. I attended the morning briefings of Commander-in-Chief Pacific Forces (CINPAC), Adm. Chester Nimitz. I like the frankness and friendliness of service people, their crisp thinking, their acceptance of orders from above and responsibility for giving orders below.

Many outstanding U.S. officers were stationed in Germany during my stay there. When I arrived, the commanding officer of Armed Forces Europe (USAREUR) was Gen. Paul Freeman, low-key, efficient, open, and friendly. He was succeeded by another competent officer, Gen. Andrew O'Meara, and in turn by Gen. David Burchinal. I had served with Dave in the Pacific B–29 air war and had observed his progress through a distinguished career in the air force.

Because I enjoyed their company and wanted to get to know these officers under informal circumstances, my wife and I invited the key commanders and their wives each year to spend a weekend with us at our embassy residence in Bonn. Here we closed the gates and, although we had one official meeting, spent time at the swimming pool, by the barbecue pit, and dining together. These weekends remain among our most pleasant memories of our Bonn years.

An American ambassador's authority has been given various interpretations under different presidents, but it derives mainly from being the personal representative of the president in a country and head of the "country team." American officials stationed abroad under such circumstances will I found accept loyally the leadership of an ambassador who exercises it in a proper way and will cooperate as a group to work out internal differences and present a common front to the host country.

In a large embassy like Bonn, on the other hand, a variety of Washington agencies are represented in addition to the State Department. Their own varied and often conflicting objectives inevitably affect the loyalty and career dependence of their embassy representatives. Problems arising from divided loyalties and interests are usually resolved with a little patience. But important issues arise in cases where, as in Germany, there is a large Central Intelligence Agency (CIA) representation and military commands of several hundred thousand.

The question of conflicts with the CIA is simplified in Germany by the fact that most intelligence-gathering activity is directed against third countries, particularly the Soviet bloc. Because of West Germany's location and the close cooperation developed between the German and U.S. intelligence in the postwar period, this process operates smoothly within mutually accepted guidelines. In addition to intelligence from the East, the German government permits the United States to carry out numerous broader functions in Germany.

Only occasionally did CIA activities in Germany raise serious problems with the West German government or with me as ambassador. I had elected to be fully informed as to these activities and made it clear that, in case I raised objections in important matters that could not be reconciled, both the CIA station chief and I would inform Washington of our respective views and transfer the problem there for a final decision. Many issues were better decided in Washington, where broader aspects could be taken into account and where honest differences in views between officials in Bonn were less likely to create personal issues and leave hurt feelings. My general approach was for an orderly decrease in U.S. intelligence activities in Germany; some of these activities were holdovers from postwar problems that had meanwhile ceased to exist.

No such serious unresolved issues arose, to my recollection. In one case, the Munich intelligence staff was found to have been overzealous in arranging for a group of German high school students to report on a visit they had made to the Soviet Union. In the face of protests from parents, such projects were discontinued. Another time in Berlin I requested the CIA to give up a cover position in the U.S. mission there that supervised contacts with students and representatives of developing countries. I respected the professional competence of the top CIA official stationed in Frankfurt and his representative in Bonn, with whom I kept in close contact.

The relationship of the ambassador with the heads of U.S. military missions in Germany created different problems in that the ambassador had no command authority in purely military matters. At the same time, the ambassador held responsibility for political matters, including significant issues arising with the German civil authorities, which necessitated frequent consultations and interventions. These ranged from minor matters of infraction of German law by our military personnel to important questions of force levels, troop deployment, and the functioning of the offset agreement. These questions were usually settled amicably with the help of our local consul generals and the able USAREUR liaison officer stationed in the embassy.

The military commanders, having spent a lifetime in working out their command and collateral relations within their services, were usually reasonable and cooperative. This applied to all of the many joint issues that arose out of the serious stoppages of U.S. Berlin convoys in 1963 on the autobahn through East Germany. I did take issue with what appeared to me a low-level Pentagon-initiated attempt to sell to the Germans for cash an interest in our line of communication (LOC) across France. But this was largely on the grounds that it was not ours to sell; in any event, the French did not think so.

Only one incident involving a military matter was ever considered sufficiently important to make a full dress referral to Washington. Early in my stay in Bonn, the question arose as to whether the United States should make helicopter flights over East Berlin. The U.S. position had always been that, due to the quadripartite responsibility for Berlin, the Allies had this right, even though they had not exercised it regularly. When the question of renewing the flights was raised, I took the matter up with the recently activated ambassadorial Bonn Group. All representatives confirmed their belief that we did have the right and that it should be used. The French, however, agreed only on the basis that they be allowed to concur in how it was done.

When U.S. helicopter flights resumed, the Soviets reacted sharply, scrambling fighter aircraft from their closest fighter base to intercept them. The helicopters were withdrawn too quickly, however, to permit attack by Soviet planes. Particularly in view of the Soviet inability to intercept the helicopters, it was clear that the newly resumed flights, in plain sight of East Berliners, were a major embarrassment to the USSR. It seemed to me that we had forced the Soviets into a dangerous situation. Was it worth risking conflict to fly helicopters over East Berlin just to exercise our right to do so? It seemed to me, under the circumstances, that flying the helicopters showed weakness rather than strength. Their quick withdrawal made it obvious we feared Soviet interception. If a Soviet fighter succeeded in knocking down one of the helicopters, it might trigger a broader armed conflict with the Soviets, perhaps even a world war.

When I asked the military about the mission of the helicopters, apart from proving our right to fly them, they replied that it was for photographic intelligence of a Soviet radar installation on top of a building near the Tempelhof airfield. To prove its importance, they sent a full delegation of intelligence officers to Bonn with supporting photographs and charts. They made a skillful and spirited case for their helicopter flights.

There it was, they said, the small radar that could, in the event of hostilities, detect our incoming flights. They maintained that we needed to keep our photography up-to-date in order to evaluate the radar frequency and thus be able to jam it. When I inquired, I found that photographs taken over time had shown no change. I asked why it could not be photographed by regular aircraft landing or taking off from Tempelhof? Having been in naval intelligence during the war, I thought I knew enough about the issues involved to conclude that the helicopter flights were not worth the risk. The air force and I presented our cases to our respective bosses in Washington and awaited the result. As it turned out, Washington decided against the flights and the air force yielded gracefully.

But along with military issues, economic issues loomed large on my arrival in Bonn. Substantial German-American business ties had antedated World War I. American cotton supplied the Bremen market; American oil companies, particularly Esso, Mobil, and Caltex, furnished petroleum to German refineries and marketed their products; Ford and General Motors's Opel were among Germany's largest automobile manufacturers. IBM had achieved a virtual monopoly in advanced computers. Since American policy had strongly influenced the development of the postwar German economy, our respective business methods and philosophy were closely attuned.

In 1963 American investment in West Germany stood at $1.8 billion, exceeded only by investments in Britain and Canada. Meanwhile, West German investment in the United States, as typified by Hoechst, the large German chemical firm, was rising too. American trade in German manufactured products, led by such firms as Siemens and Krupp, was substantial. Heads of U.S. and German companies had developed a high degree of rapport. Most West Germans showed little interest in socialism, and business proceeded on the basis of classical free-market competition. Worker participation on corporate boards in the steel and coal industries on the basis of a policy of codetermination were the exception and had little impact on laissez-faire capitalism.

The correct relationship between American diplomats and American business abroad is a much-discussed subject. Having come to the State Department from a business background, and having served on the boards of a number of companies other than my own, I felt at ease with businessmen and wanted to help them in every legitimate way. Before leaving for Bonn, I made a point of getting to know the chairmen of important American firms doing business in Germany, assuring them that they and their representatives were always welcome in the embassy. During my five years in Germany, I regularly attended the periodic meetings arranged by the embassy economic section for top representatives of German subsidiaries of American firms.

Many of our firms, particularly the older multinationals, tend to avoid relations with the U.S. government altogether. In part, this derives from business's traditional suspicion of government and the fear that requests for government assistance abroad could result in unwanted interference. Many American businessmen abroad are also suspicious of State

Department personnel, some of whom they consider antibusiness. Other firms fear that the embassy will provide embarrassing information to U.S. tax or antitrust authorities. American businessmen and the embassy economic section usually have a good rapport, but since most political officers, including ambassadors, have had little business experience, company men are inclined to distrust their judgment in business matters.

Embassy personnel also often fear that if they help one American firm, they can be criticized by its competitors or blamed if their advice turns out to be wrong and the company incurs a loss, endangering their careers. Indeed, I am sure that some embassy personnel feel that the companies are trying to use them to their own advantage. Unfortunately, businessmen often see the hesitancy of the officer to help as representing laziness or indifference.

There is also a real question about how well served an established U.S. firm might be by assistance from its government. An American company usually operates through a local subsidiary often staffed entirely by local nationals. The Singer Sewing Machine company had a thousand employees in Turkey when I was ambassador there in the late 1950s, not one an American, and the chief executive officer was an Armenian. Many U.S. subsidiaries are not even regarded as foreign firms, an image the parent company seeks to create. If the U.S. government intervenes openly in a matter affecting the firm, its local image is jeopardized. Even if the embassy intervenes privately with the host government, there is some danger that the reaction might do more harm than good. After all, the host government sees the subsidiary as, in this case, a German company employing German nationals, even though it might be wholly American-owned.

As an example, I recall the day I was called on by the head of a German refinery owned by a U.S. refining company, himself a U.S. citizen, as the result of an invitation I had extended him at a social occasion in Munich. "We've been operating our refinery in Bavaria for twenty years, so I thought it was time to pay a call on the ambassador," he told me. Indeed, this was his first such visit. Our discussion revealed that the firm had done well in Germany and appeared not to have needed any assistance from the embassy. If so, I assured him, he had pursued the right course in going his own way. But he did mention in passing that he was having a bit of trouble with the Bavarian government over a tax matter. He was considering employing a well-connected local from an aristocratic family to advise him. Since I was apprehensive about this particular man's background, he asked whether I could have our consulate general look into the matter confidentially and see whether a better adviser might be available. This was done, and the report confirmed that the company's original candidate would be a mistake. Several more suitable candidates were suggested, and one was hired with good results.

In another instance, I was able to intervene on behalf of McDonnell-Douglas, the St. Louis–based aircraft manufacturer, and the Boeing Company, both of whom were negotiating with Lufthansa, the German government-controlled airline, for intermediate-range aircraft for domestic use. Lufthansa was interested both in what eventually became the Boeing 737 and the Douglas DC–9, neither of which was yet in production. I was in touch with both companies. The British government was meanwhile pressing the merits of the BAC 111 made by the government-owned British Aircraft Corporation. The sale was worth $35 million. A rather amusing incident occurred at a dinner given in Cologne by the German Rhodes Scholar Association, which both I and my British colleague, Sir Frank Roberts, attended. Called to the phone, he came back smiling and chuckling. "I believe this call is for you, George," he said. It was Donald Douglas.

As it happened, the negotiations were at an acute stage, and the U.S. embassy had heard rumors that the British were putting pressure on the German government, although not, according to Frank Roberts, on a political basis, by pointing out that if they missed the sale they might, because of the loss of foreign exchange, have to reduce the level of their forces in Germany. At this point, I called Ludger Westrick, Chancellor Erhard's chief of staff and a good friend of the United States, and asked to see him as soon as possible. He received me within half an hour, and I explained the situation. I told him that although the embassy had assisted both companies we had not taken sides, leaving it to Boeing and McDonnell-Douglas to sell their product. We would have accepted any decision Lufthansa made on merit, but we could not accept losing the sale to the British as the result of political pressure. After all we had done for Germany, I said, Americans would never understand this. Westrick picked up the phone and asked for Herman Abs, honorary chairman of the supervisory board of Lufthansa. Westrick explained the situation, making it clear that he was speaking for the chancellor. The West German government, he told Abs, took no position on the sale but expected Lufthansa to make its decision entirely on commercial grounds. Boeing got the contract in February 1965.

On another occasion, the chairman of Mobil Oil Company, Albert Nickerson, was having trouble with Gelsenberg, a German oil-marketing company with which Mobil had an oil supply contract. Hans-Guenther Sohl, chairman of Gelsenberg's advisory board, was a good friend and hunting companion. With the approval of Nickerson, who I knew would be in Germany, I invited Sohl to join us for dinner at the embassy. After setting the stage for the two, I sat back silently after dinner and let the guests work out a long-sought agreement between their companies.

These are examples of how I believe an American ambassador can assist American companies. Preferential treatment must clearly be avoided. But beyond this, one should give any reputable American firm all reasonable help. The United States's already precarious balance of payments provided full justification. The British, who had experienced balance of payments difficulties from the end of World War II, set Americans a good example in the tenacity with which they supported their firms. American companies deserve no less. Criticism of favoritism can be avoided by giving help to all reputable U.S. firms, even when they are in competition.

At least one aspect of the embassy effort to help new American companies find business in German markets could certainly not be considered controversial. Working with the economic section of the embassy, the U.S. Department of Commerce organized many industrial fairs all over Germany to help American firms, which were often represented by husband-wife combinations. I attended these fairs, made speeches, and talked with our exhibitors. I recall one machine-tool fair in Essen where $30 million worth of orders were placed with American firms, later leading to more. The climate for American business in Germany, which has always been good, was rewarding in those years both to American companies and to the American economy.

In view of the importance of the U.S.-German business relationship, I addressed it in many public appearances. In a speech to the German business community in Frankfurt on October 20, 1964, I defended American business against the fairly common accusation at the time that the United States was attempting to dominate German industry. Although cumulative American investment in the Federal Republic was substantial, I noted that it nonetheless constituted only 4 percent of all West German investment. Only thirty U.S. subsidiaries in West Germany employed more than one thousand people, and that of the Federal Republic's eighty-five largest firms, only three—Esso in tenth place,

General Motors in eighteenth, and Ford in thirtieth—were American subsidiaries. The point was not whether American industry benefited but whether the Federal Republic benefited from our economic presence. This speech was quoted widely in the German press without notably adverse comment.

In 1963 the principal economic issues facing the United States and West Germany concerned certain internal problems of the Common Market, preparations for trade negotiations scheduled for 1964, and various specific U.S.-German and U.S.-EEC trade problems, most of which have been with us ever since. These included antidumping measures and access to the European market. Starting in the immediate postwar period, the United States had taken the lead in attempting to stimulate world trade by liberalization through tariff reductions and removal or softening of nontariff trade barriers.

Under the leadership of William Clayton, under secretary of state for economic affairs, a determined effort was made to create an ambitious International Trade Organization for this purpose. Rebuffed by the U.S. Congress, a watered-down version, the General Agreement on Tariffs and Trade (GATT), was accepted as a compromise. This resulted in a series of negotiations toward trade liberalization, the most recent in 1963 being what we called the Dillon Round, after Treasury Secretary Douglas Dillon. This had resulted in an average cut in tariffs of 10 percent, to be realized over a period of years.

One of the principal problems U.S. negotiators faced lay in persuading U.S. trading partners to accept the principle of broad flat percentage cuts, which was questioned for high tariff items. Some countries posited that across-the-board cuts would result in insufficient reductions in such cases. Principal alternatives were to cut high-tariff items more or attempt to balance the various high tariffs remaining after the cuts. The challenge for the EEC, as seen by Washington, was to regain its momentum following the setback in "community spirit" caused by de Gaulle's veto of Britain's bid for membership. The reaction to this harsh and unexpected move had cast a pall over the immediate future of the Common Market.

The work of preparing for the forthcoming trade negotiations would take place largely in a committee created for this purpose. It was expected to be long and arduous. Since West Germany would play a key role among the six nations represented, the United States wanted to work with the German government to influence the committee's decisions. The most troublesome bilateral trade problem the United States faced at that time was the so-called poultry war. American producers had created a great furor when U.S. poulterers were largely eliminated from the lucrative German market by the high EEC-wide tariff levies on U.S. exports. In a curious twist of fate, it would be my first task as U.S. ambassador to Germany, one of our key allies in vital security matters, to do battle for the lowly chicken. I regretted that I was thus forced to use up some of my initial goodwill.

In talks with senior Foreign Office officials, I emphasized the importance the United States attached to the poultry issue, saying that it seemed symbolic of a misguided protectionist policy orientation of the Common Market. They replied that they thought we were overemphasizing the problem but that they recognized fully the importance of providing some relief to us on poultry and promised to help bring this about.

Soon after my arrival, I paid a courtesy call on Agriculture Minister Werner Schwarz (telegram, Amemb Bonn to Secstate, 3502, May 19, 1963). I assured him that I fully understood his difficulties in dealing with problems of German agriculture, which in many respects are similar to those faced by the U.S. secretary of Agriculture. Although both countries faced acute problems in the agricultural field, I hoped that these could be handled without jeopardizing common long-term trade objectives. I referred to the German farmers' insistence on high prices as a threat to continued progress within the EEC and its relationships with third countries, pointing out that there were other ways of assisting farmers than artificially high prices. I referred to the key importance of agriculture in the forthcoming GATT negotiations, the success of which depended considerably on solving the grain price problem in a way that would not impair the competitive advantage of efficient producers like, for example, the United States.

Schwarz acknowledged the inefficiency of German agriculture. In fact, as a result of normal economic forces, the farm population was diminishing. He warned, however, that this structural adjustment could not be forced by government edict. Farm discontent could become a serious problem, which Germany's Communist neighbors would exploit. Due to the handicaps of small farms, poor soil, and harsh climate, German farmers were entitled to government support. He refused to concede that there were means of supporting farmers other than artificially high prices.

I noted that Americans, too, had farm support programs, but that the

United States was willing to have these discussed in connection with the forthcoming GATT negotiations. The long-term objective of both countries should be the efficient allocation of productive resources and the promotion of world trade. The United States was willing to reduce tariffs on such commodities as automobiles, even though Volkswagen had already captured a large piece of our market. I reminded Schwarz of our heavy financial obligations for military defense in Europe, which we could not continue to bear if we could not export. To clinch my case, I showed him the morning press, reporting criticism in the U.S. Senate of EEC agricultural policies, which had caused some senators to threaten a substantial reduction in the U.S. aid program.

The Germans were also concerned with the numerous antidumping investigations underway in our country over alleged U.S. sales at lower than domestic prices. Although many products were involved, by far the most important was wide-diameter steel pipe. I knew that the Germans were sure to raise this problem with me, but since U.S. laws permitted almost no discretion, I could do little to satisfy them in the absence of new legislation. I knew that consideration was being given in Washington to an international approach to the antidumping problem, but this was of no immediate help to the Germans.

A particularly acute and not unrelated issue that I was instructed to take up with the West German Foreign Office almost immediately was the question of contracts by the German steel firm Mannesmann to supply the Soviets wide-diameter steel pipe—160,000 tons the first year—for the construction of an oil pipeline from the USSR to Vienna. Like the Reagan administration nearly twenty years later, the Kennedy administration was concerned that this pipeline would result in a dangerous dependence of Western Europe on Soviet oil supplies, which the Russians could use for political leverage. As instructed, I put great pressure on the Germans to cancel the pipe order. Otherwise, I said, I feared U.S. confidence in Germany would suffer. The German government acquiesced to our pressure, but very reluctantly because of the substantial loss to Mannesmann and to the German economy.

Later, colleagues in the Foreign Office advised me that the government had regretted giving in to the United States on this issue and was determined never to do so again. This reaction should have provided an important clue to the German position on the same issue when it arose during Ronald Reagan's first term; the same German company contracted to furnish large-diameter pipe and pumping equipment for the Soviet gas pipeline from the Urals to Western Europe. The Germans and other European suppliers predictably held firm, and after considerable acrimony, the United States backed down.

In light of the great importance of the Kennedy Round, I soon called on Under Secretary Rolf Lahr of the Economics Ministry. Lahr later became state secretary (economic) in the Ministry of Foreign Affairs (memcon, Amemb Bonn, May 21, 1963). He was thoroughly dedicated to trade liberalization and was well liked by Americans. He described efforts currently under way in Geneva to reach a compromise agreement on the basic rules to govern the forthcoming negotiations. He assured me that the Federal Republic was extremely anxious to see the Kennedy Round succeed and noted that some GATT agreements were required for the necessary preparations. With this in mind, Erhard was trying to reach some compromise between the U.S.-proposed equal percentage reductions for high tariffs and the European preference for larger percentage cuts.

Lahr said that it would be unfortunate if these efforts at compromise failed, since any delay would make it difficult for the Germans to get French cooperation in the Kennedy Round in exchange for other concessions they desired. Unfortunately, he said, the impression was growing in Europe that some U.S. tariffs were so high that even a full 50 percent reduction would leave them at protective levels, whereas 50 percent cuts in more moderate European tariffs would substantially increase trade. The United States should not give the impression of being unwilling to talk about the disparity problem.

I responded that we were prepared to deal with the disparity question as a special problem if the equilinear (equal percentage) approach was accepted as the basic negotiating principle. I pointed out that a 50 percent reduction in many high tariffs would be more important quantitatively in stimulating trade than a similar cut of a low tariff. There were, I admitted, doubtless cases where the reverse was true. The equilinear approach had been suggested to us originally by our European friends after the last round of tariff negotiations. We were surprised by the Common Market's hesitation to go forward on that basis.

In response to my question about the compromise proposals being considered in Geneva, Lahr replied that these included a formula that would cut high tariffs by a larger percentage than the lows and reduce all rates by 50 percent with a floor of 10 percent. This formula might be applied selectively to commodity areas where a wide disparity in tariffs existed, presumably leaving all others to straight equilinear treatment. This was, Lahr said, the general direction of thinking in Geneva.

But the complexity of the tariff issue was nothing compared to the growing problem of supporting American troops in Germany. Implementation of the so-called offset agreement between the United States and the Federal Republic was a difficult and persistent problem during the 1960s. Although it arose in a military context, I treat it here as an economic problem since its implications were mainly financial. The United States was experiencing a severe balance of payments problem caused or aggravated by the war in Vietnam, which necessitated strong measures.

The offset arrangement was initiated on October 24, 1961, in an agreement between U.S. Deputy Secretary of Defense Roswell Gilpatric and West German Minister of Defense Franz Josef Strauss. Its purpose was to ensure for the coming two years German procurement of U.S. military goods and services equivalent to U.S. military expenditures in Germany, which earned dollars for the German economy (office memorandum, Amemb, Bonn, May 29, 1963). The amount involved was about $650 million a year. The original agreement provided for German cost-sharing in U.S. research and development projects and German payment for American military procurement services in the United States; depot supply services and depot maintenance in Europe; sale of U.S. war reserve stocks prepositioned in Europe; U.S. storage facilities in Europe; and joint use of U.S. training areas in Germany.

On September 14, 1962, Strauss and Gilpatric agreed to extend the existing offset arrangements for calendar years 1963 and 1964, with German payments to be made in fiscal years 1964 and 1965. The Germans would not, however, make a firm commitment to the 1964 payments, in light of their adverse overall economic situation. This was our first warning of impending difficulties. After a domestic political crisis involving his role in the questionable arrest in Spain of a senior editor of the news magazine *Der Spiegel* and the major cabinet reshuffle that followed, Strauss was succeeded as minister of defense by Kai-Uwe von Hassel, with whom Gilpatric exchanged the new offset plans on February 25, 1963. On May 3, U.S. military expenditures in Germany for the calendar years 1961–62 were calculated to have been $1.375 billion, which we agreed the Germans had offset fully. But in these talks the Germans refused to agree to make more than $1 billion in payments during the U.S. fiscal years 1964 and 1965 and pledged instead only to make their best efforts to increase this up to a complete offset.

The annual renewals of the offset agreement during my tour in Germany were attended by hard, often acrimonious bargaining. The bad feeling was compounded by widespread misunderstanding of the purpose of the agreement both in Germany and in the United States. The German public tended to associate offset payments with reimbursements to the United States for stationing costs, which depicted our troops as mercenaries—which was onerous for both countries. Germans did not generally understand that they received a full quid pro quo from us in their purchases and that the only consequence was on the balance of payments. For their part, Americans often perceived German reluctance to make the offset payments as reneging on their obligations, though also without understanding clearly what the payments were for.

It was pointed out in my first briefings that the offset system was working well. Concern was expressed for future years, however, because the German defense procurement buildup was declining. Bundeswehr costs, which had risen from DM 14.9 billion in 1962 to DM 18.3 billion in 1963, were proposed at only DM 19.3 billion for 1964. There was also intense competition for military sales from France and Britain, as well as from German industry, which then as now needed the business and wanted the accompanying access to technology. The United States had every incentive, of course, to hold Germany to its offset agreement for balance of payment reasons and to assure German attainment of NATO force goals through arms and service purchases. I was advised that a team from the Defense and Treasury departments would soon arrive in Bonn to work out procurement programs with the Germans as well as to discuss cooperation in combat logistic plans. This proved, however, to be only the beginning.

On July 2 West Germany's Defense Ministry advised the United States that it had decided to cut its defense budget for 1964, possibly to DM 18 billion, below the 1963 level. Such a reduction would make it impossible to carry out any new procurement projects, and the Federal Republic would not be able to meet the full offset. The bargaining continued as Lyndon Johnson succeeded to the presidency after Kennedy's assassination. The Vietnam War increasingly made itself felt on the U.S. balance of payments, and our need for a full offset also increased. Because Johnson recognized Secretary of Defense McNamara as a tough negotiator and because sales of military equipment provided one of the best means of increasing our foreign exchange earnings, Johnson gave McNamara special responsibilities in this connection; McNamara took these so seriously that he often participated in offset negotiations directly.

As American thoughts turned increasingly to Southeast Asia, German thoughts turned increasingly to Eastern Europe. Trade with the East had traditionally been of greater importance to West Germany than to its Western allies. In 1962 German exports to the Eastern bloc countries totaled $503.9 million, approximately 40 percent of which went to the Soviet Union, whereas its imports totaled $533.9 million. Although only a small percentage of Germany's overall trade, it was important to the German economy and its political implications were even greater. To the Eastern countries, trade with the West was a part of their drive toward greater independence from the Soviet bloc, even though 70 percent of their foreign trade was with one another. To many Germans, it was a bridge to reconnect the halves of Europe, a means to ease the division of Germany, and even an instrument for making the East more dependent on the West and West Germany, thus leading to greater political cooperation (Gorgey 1972, 14).

In 1962 Bonn's new foreign minister, Gerhard Schröder, had expressed his intention "to ease the atmosphere and to further understanding of our mutual problems" (ibid., 13). He proceeded to use trade missions and trade agreements with Eastern Europe to this goal, beginning with a mission to Warsaw in 1963. Unfortunately, a series of adverse factors resulted in a decrease in both exports and imports between Germany and the East in 1964. The United States followed these developments closely in Washington and in Bonn. Although Americans took a generally benevolent attitude in the hope that German efforts to develop trade with the East could result in relaxed tensions, some Americans, and some Germans as well, feared the Federal Republic might go too far and use its trade missions as a base for establishing full diplomatic relations with Soviet bloc countries that Bonn had hitherto refused to recognize.

Washington was particularly interested in the strong effort made over the years by Berthold Beitz, general manager of the Friedrich Krupp company of Essen, to develop trade with Eastern Europe. Colorful, daring, and publicity-conscious, Beitz was to many a man of mystery who moved quietly across East-West lines and gained personal access to heads of state. In 1963 he made another visit to Poland and to the

Soviet Union, conversing with Khrushchev. I knew Washington would be interested in a report of what he had to say. On June 14, Edmund Kellogg, who as consul general in Düsseldorf had done an excellent job in developing good relations with the Ruhr industrial leaders, arranged for me to lunch in his residence with Beitz. Because our entire intelligence community was greatly interested in what Beitz had to report, the head of the CIA station in Bonn accompanied me. (Telegram, Amemb Bonn to Secstate, 3473, June 15, 1963, and embassy memcons, June 14, 15, 1963.)

Beitz reported that he had received the impression during his visit to Moscow that Khrushchev (who was thrown out of office shortly afterward) was depressed and worried. Khrushchev told Beitz that the USSR faced an emerging younger generation both in the Soviet Union and in the satellites that was impatient for the better things of life, particularly for more and better consumer goods, food, housing, and clothing. In the Soviet Union, the present generation was better educated than any previous one, but Soviets were fully aware of the disparities between their living standards and those of the capitalist world. Khrushchev felt that he could not ignore the craving within the USSR for greater personal well-being.

Beitz believed that the West, and particularly West Germany, could gain by assisting Khrushchev to fill this gap. He believed that satisfying some Eastern European consumer wants would lead to demands for more, and the resulting growing dependence on the West could provide us political leverage. Beitz added that, in his opinion, at least 10 percent of whatever was supplied should come from West Berlin. This would not only contribute to West Berlin's viability but would also provide opportunities to use supply as a weapon. He opposed, however, any insistence that trade agreements contain a "Berlin clause," identifying Berlin exports as such. West Berlin, he argued, was a German city and should no more be mentioned than Essen or Dortmund. Furthermore, the absence of such a Berlin clause would make it easier for the East to buy from West Berlin.

Beitz said that Khrushchev was also having troubles regarding trade with the satellites. But he emphasized that the West must remember that satellite maneuverability was limited and should not demand nor expect too much in the way of Western orientation in return for trade. Nor should the West initially expect much volume of trade, he added. Satellite purchasing power was limited, particularly since agricultural deficiencies, combined with the demand for goods produced by growing urbanization, gravely reduced agriculture as a source of foreign exchange. Considering the extensive activity of West German banks in Eastern Europe today, and the burden of East European debt incurred, it is interesting to recall that in those days Eastern Europe would not accept credit from West Germany. In sum, Beitz doubted that trade with the East was likely to increase more than 5 percent in the next few years. In reporting this conversation with Beitz, as desired, I attracted wide attention from the agencies in Washington by the tried and true technique of giving it a high security classification and requesting that its distribution be limited.

Beitz persisted in his efforts to promote East-West trade, particularly by Krupp, which was then the second largest steel company in Germany and a major manufacturer of heavy capital goods. He developed an ingenious barter arrangement with Poland that in a sense permitted Poland to export labor. But, though Beitz's plan for general East-West trade aroused widespread interest, it was never carried out.

Jean Monnet, distinguished French politician, philosopher, and statesman, had devoted his wartime efforts to Allied raw material supply. Direct, modest, with an incisive mind and a keen sense of how to get action when something important was at stake, Jean became a favorite of most Americans. From 1956 to 1973 he chaired the Action Committee for a United States of Europe, which included representatives of all non-Communist political parties and trade unions within the Common Market Six. After 1962 he concentrated on Britain's admission to the Common Market.

My first meeting with Monnet in Germany occurred when, on the invitation of Ludwig Rosenberg of the German Federation of Trade Unions (DGB), I attended a rally at which all non-Communist labor unions in Europe were represented (airgram, Amemb Bonn, memcon A–120, July 16, 1963). A loyal SPD member, Rosenberg pursued a typical career as a trade union official, rising in 1962 to the presidency of the DGB. He was a devoted member of Monnet's Action Committee. As a result of Rosenberg's leadership a pro-EEC rally was staged at Dortmund on July 11.

I had no departmental guidance, but it seemed to provide an opportunity to establish good relations with Rosenberg and to find out what the meeting was all about. I had already called on Rosenberg at his headquarters in Düsseldorf and had found him friendly and open. I also wanted to show sympathy for the German and European trade union movement. To my surprise, I found that I was the only ambassador in Bonn present and that behind the stage in shirt sleeves, masterminding the show, was Jean Monnet.

Rosenberg immediately ushered me onto the stage and introduced me to the assembled twenty thousand labor representatives from all over Europe. I was greatly impressed with Monnet for having pulled the rally off and also with the enthusiasm of those attending. They demonstrated to me quite clearly that they placed much more hope in a united Europe than any narrow nationalism. After hearing the speeches and talking with some of the labor leaders present, I concluded that the European labor movement was destined to be a strong pillar in the European movement and that we should encourage this and take advantage of it. I gave Monnet full marks for perceiving this and including the unions in his movement.

In a letter to Under Secretary George Ball on July 19, I addressed his proposition that Europe was in a "mess" and that prospects for European unity were poor (letter, McGhee to Ball, Amemb Bonn, July 19, 1963). I told Ball I shared his basic analysis. Although there were stirrings toward unity, such as the recent decision to provide for contacts with Britain through the West European Union, and new hopes for resolving the grain price issue, I agreed that de Gaulle had halted the European unity movement. This seemed to result from de Gaulle's highly personal view of the role of the nation-state, which was shared by few in France outside his own circle and by almost no one of any stature elsewhere in Europe.

But once de Gaulle had succeeded in making his position effective by exercising French rights under the Treaty of Rome, many people appeared to have "piled on" in support, either because de Gaulle's nationalistic view still had attractions, or because people tended generally to accept or even make a virtue of necessity. It could also represent the political instinct of opposition parties to oppose their own government or be because other partisan interests were being served. The one element I had worked hard to inject into President Kennedy's Frankfurt speech during his German visit was an open recognition that the movement toward European unity had reached an impasse. It seemed that this would heighten the message's sense of realism while reaffirming our ultimate faith and confidence in the unity-partnership concept.

I agreed with Ball that one of the principal objectives of our European unity policy was, in his words, to "tie Germany firmly to the West within the framework of a united Europe" and that this could be furthered by a bilateral German-French relationship. I believed, however, that other bilateral German contacts could also be useful in this respect, particularly with Italy and the Benelux and Scandinavian countries. But we had to recognize that a reservoir of anti-German feeling, particularly in England and Italy, remained and that suspicions in France and other countries had not yet been overcome.

Though I agreed with Ball that "nationalism is contagious," I did not believe that the infection had yet overcome the temporary immunization Germany had experienced through defeat. Although mutterings tantamount to incipient nationalism could be heard among certain intellectual and youth circles out of the mainstream, most responsible Germans considered themselves still in the process of being accepted once more into the family of nations. Germany had no plans or hopes for defense apart from that which the United States provided. Its tendency was still to "lie low," not to be conspicuous even in terms of strengthening its armed forces or economy, much less its possibilities of leadership. I agreed with Ball that Germany, if not anchored to the West, could again become an unpredictable force, but I did not believe that Germany was near breaking loose from her moorings.

Nor did I think that we could judge Erhard by his performance under Adenauer. Adenauer inevitably overshadowed him. I had frequently felt in talking with Erhard that he would like to have taken a certain action but that if it did not fall squarely within his competence as economics minister, Adenauer gave him no opportunity to act on his ideas. Although I doubted he would ever have great ability for foreign policy direction, I saw no reason why he should not, as President Truman had, develop into a good executive. I considered it too early to predict but believed Erhard could rely on Schröder as Truman had on Acheson, and I considered Schröder thoroughly competent to provide the direction of foreign policy. Both men knew that if they split, only the opposition SPD would gain.

I agreed with Ball that it was not enough to say that Germans "do not want atomic weapons," although I believed this to be true. A better statement was that Germany would be increasingly dissatisfied if it were unable to exert greater influence on decisions affecting atomic defense and other basic matters. No Germans were foolish enough to believe that they could have an independent defense, either conventional or atomic, or could threaten aggression.

What Germany sought, I believed, was assurance of a forward European strategy by us and others concerned in its defense. Even more important to Germany was our ability to convince the Soviets that this would be done to deter their aggression. The Germans wanted to participate in an MLF mainly because they understood that they could not get an important say in nuclear strategy unless they helped pay the bill. This involvement, moreover, would help achieve Ball's objectives of anchoring Germany to the West and Tom Finletter's goal of giving the alliance forward momentum.

I advised Ball that I would go further than he had in saying that there was no "inherent danger" of a German diplomatic adventure with Moscow, because of the realities of nuclear dependence, because this would endanger the continued presence of American forces in Europe, and because of the deep suspicions that it would arouse among Germany's Western allies. These disadvantages contrasted with the small chance of getting anything from the Soviets. For anything important, the Germans would have to pay a high price—maybe even detachment from the West. This, I believed, would keep the Germans away from Moscow for a long time.

I urged that we seek support for our European unity efforts among European groupings that cut across national lines, reporting that I had recently attended a rally in Dortmund of 23,000 delegates representing 12 million European workers. Once the British Labour party was in power contacts among European Socialist parties could be increased. Business groups also had a great incentive to participate, particularly if Atlantic partnership and trading opportunities with the United States could take precedence over a united Europe.

These private groupings, unfettered by the realities of political power, could perhaps establish better cooperation than governments. I did not believe that integration of foreign and defense policy in one European state was in sight. But I did believe that movement toward supranationality in trade and transport, power, taxation, social, and labor policy was inexorable. He thought that the pent-up force to achieve this would be released when de Gaulle was no longer on the scene.

I agreed with Ball that "Germany alone was the only European country capable of immediate constructive action" toward the unity-partnership concept. Our principal objective in Germany should be to see that Germany would continue to channel its energies within this framework. The most important contribution we could make was to influence Germany in this direction and away from the old competitive nationalism.

9

Nuclear Problems
May–July 1963

Control of nuclear weapons has always been a critical matter within the NATO alliance. When NATO was formed, the United States was the only member country possessing nuclear weapons and had a virtual world monopoly, exceeding considerably in strength the Soviet nuclear force, which had launched its own first intercontinental ballistic missile (ICBM) in 1957. By 1960 the Soviet force had increased greatly, and Kennedy made much of an impending missile gap in his campaign for the presidency. Although it has subsequently been established that there was no gap, he and Secretary McNamara started immediately after the election to fill the "gap" by building one thousand land-based Minutemen ICBMs, giving the nuclear arms race a big boost.

The so-called *force de frappe*, the independent French nuclear force whose intended deployment was announced in May 1963 by Defense Minister Pierre Messmer of France, was to consist of fifty Mirage IV bombers with a speed of Mach 2. They were to have a range of 2,500 kilometers without refueling, and to carry a fission bomb equivalent to fifty to sixty kilotons of TNT. The first plane and bomb were to be operational before the end of 1963 and were to be followed in 1968 by three submarines carrying forty-nine thermonuclear missiles with a range of 3,000 kilometers. At that stage the French force had no hope of hitting targets with precision.

In late 1963 Secretary of Defense Robert McNamara announced that the United States had over two thousand nuclear warheads, including five hundred ICBMs—the land-based Atlas, Titan, and Minuteman and the sea-based Polaris—and that the United States planned to increase the number of ICBMs to fifteen hundred by 1966. Between 1961 and 1967 the United States planned to augment the number of missile sites by tenfold, providing wide dispersion. The Strategic Air Command had more than five hundred bombers on air alert and quick-action ground alert. At about that time it was announced that the number of U.S. Polaris submarines, each with sixteen missiles, would be increased from sixteen to forty-one by 1967. The total number of U.S. nuclear warheads in ground and air weapons placed under NATO command, mostly in Germany, stood at six thousand.

As the nuclear forces of both superpowers grew, the basic concept of "massive retaliation" that had prevailed since the early 1950s was superseded by a policy of "flexible response," based on "graduated deterrence." This provided the United States with a choice of options to meet a threat of war and to fight the war if one broke out. The new strategy was coupled with U.S. help in increasing Europe's conventional capabilities, although Europeans were disturbed by the U.S. concept of using this conventional advantage, in the event of conflict, to achieve a "pause" in the battle by stopping the Soviet advance before either side crossed the nuclear threshold. McNamara announced the new policy to NATO in May 1962 without prior consultation.

One of the principal issues between the United States and West Germany when I arrived in Bonn was the MLF, the seaborne nuclear force originally conceived and proposed in the State Department in 1959. It was to be manned by mixed contingents from European NATO members, but principally by the United States and Germany. In 1961 President Kennedy indicated his willingness to share U.S. nuclear responsibility with a united Europe, and the MLF was represented as a step in this direction. To the Federal Republic, participation in the MLF meant for the first time a share of nuclear responsibility within NATO in a way considered acceptable to the other Europeans. It might be said that the MLF bought time for the development of a real policy of deterrence. The MLF continued to be a major concern in German-American relations until 1965, but interest was already waning in 1963.

As elaborated in a subsequent memo from Secretary of State Dean Rusk, the MLF was intended to provide a way for the two major non-nuclear European countries, West Germany and Italy, to participate in their own nuclear defense without encouraging national nuclear weapons proliferation, avoiding the precedents established by Britain and France. The project would support those proponents of moderate, democratic government in Germany who wanted to forestall pressures for a national nuclear weapons program. Former defense minister Franz Josef Strauss and others were already advancing views that portended eventual aspiration to German nuclear power. Not only did Strauss's CDU colleagues Gerhard Schröder and Kai-Uwe von Hassel believe the MLF to be essential, but even Fritz Erler, the defense and foreign policy spokesman of the opposition SPD, warned Americans that the Germans would not be content indefinitely with second-class nuclear status.

The State Department thought not only that the MLF would strengthen the alliance by reassuring the Germans but that it would create a closely knit force in which some major (and smaller) members could take part and have pride. It would give confidence to NATO members by associating them closely with the United States in owning, controlling, and manning a major nuclear force. The MLF could also provide some of the medium-range ballistic missiles (MRBMs) desired by NATO's military leadership and many Europeans to offset Soviet MRBMs threatening Europe without the disadvantage of concentrating them in Germany. The latter step would create political problems with other allies and run the risk of Soviet counteraction. It is ironic to note in retrospect how virtually the opposite arguments were advanced about twenty years later when Pershing 2 MRBMs were deployed in West Germany and sea-based deployment was generally agreed to be unacceptable.

The State Department argued that the MLF would provide a practical means of countering de Gaulle's proposals to create a French-organized Europe, which included German support for the force de frappe. It was believed that success of the MLF would destroy de Gaulle's strategy, whereas its failure would greatly strengthen his chances of success. It was also argued that the MLF would create a powerful alternative to British and French national nuclear forces or would itself lead to a common force into which they might eventually be drawn. It was thus supposed to promote European cooperation and unity within an alliance partnership, drawing the key European nations together in a real working force of major military, political, and psychological importance.

Supporters further argued that the MLF would show the Soviets how European and American resources could be harnessed in providing nuclear forces for the alliance while persuading Europeans of the futility of trying to enter the nuclear race as individual nations. It would confront the Soviets with another mode of nuclear deterrence that would be extremely difficult to counter. As an added benefit, it was claimed that the MLF was a means to share part of the heavy cost of nuclear weapons with our allies.

It had initially been proposed that the MLF be mounted in submarines stationed off the European coast. But because of technical difficulties, the concept was changed in favor of surface vessels off the coast or in canals, rivers, or harbors. It was understood that use of the MLF would require a unanimous decision from a committee of representatives from all the participating countries. In theory, the MLF would be created by a charter or treaty that would be open to all NATO members and would require ratification by the member governments in accordance with their constitutional requirements. An overall administrative organization would be created to operate the force. No one nation could contribute more than 40 percent of the installation and operating costs. The preliminary cost estimate was $500 million a year for ten years, plus a modernization cost over the period of $1 billion, at a time when American defense budgets were still in the neighborhood of $50 billion a year. The United States and Germany were each expected to contribute about 33.3 percent, Italy 15–20 percent, Britain 5–10 percent, and Belgium 5 percent.

Unsurprisingly, grave objections to MLF were voiced from the beginning both in the United States and in Western Europe. Many military leaders doubted the practicability of mixed manning. There was also widespread concern over any German finger on the nuclear trigger and disappointment that surface ships had been substituted for submarines. Adenauer tended to favor the MLF because it enhanced Germany's position in NATO and for the first time gave the Federal Republic a role in nuclear decision-making. While some Germans were unhappy with the abandonment of the submarine mode, Defense Minister Hassel was appeased by being given public credit for suggesting the use of surface vessels. The SPD's Erler was reported to favor the MLF because it ensured American control as an element of restraint. Other Germans were concerned about the principle of unanimous decision because it might allow a neutralist finger on the trigger and so prevent the weapon's use.

This was the general background of the ill-fated MLF when I arrived in Germany. Although I had participated in many discussions on it as chairman of the policy planning council and later as under secretary for political affairs, I had never had any direct connection with MLF planning before and had no firm convictions about it. Although I was initially impressed by the strong support it enjoyed from high officials in our government and in Western Europe, I became increasingly skeptical even before leaving Washington that the MLF was a "gimmick." By the time I arrived in Bonn, I sensed that support was cooling in both Washington and Bonn, where the main support presumably lay, and that the Germans mainly supported the MLF because they thought Americans wanted them to. At the same time, we were becoming concerned that they were not more critical.

On July 9 I sent the State Department our full appraisal of German attitudes toward the MLF, pointing out that Adenauer and Schröder backed it basically for political reasons (telegram, Amemb Bonn to Secstate, 91, July 9, 1963). Hassel, unsurprisingly, tried to make a strategic case for it as an MRBM substitute that would cover targets in Eastern Europe of special interest to West Germany. This would give Germans greater access to planning and control and would further a forward strategy and early employment of nuclear weapons. Nevertheless, I emphasized, there was an underlying skepticism on the part of other officials, the public, and the media.

Some never considered MLF credible irrespective of German views, given the uncertainty of Italian and U.K. acceptance, which was a must if Germany was to be included. If, as President Kennedy had indicated during his visit, our present position was a low-key holding operation, Adenauer and Schröder would stay with us. Hassel's stance, which was less certain, should be strengthened during Secretary McNamara's impending visit. I recommended several other steps to improve the standing of the MLF, pointing out the adverse results that might ensue, such as greater German reliance on the French nuclear force, if a feeling that MLF was dead were to grow in Germany.

On several occasions, I raised with the embassy staff the question of whether we should not as an alternative to MLF urge Washington to accept a policy of encouraging the Europeans to create an independent nuclear force and offering our help. I was concerned at the apparent slowing of the European unity movement and argued that a joint European effort to create and operate a nuclear force might give it new impetus. French intellectual and political activist Jean Monnet, who was highly respected in the NATO countries, had been emphasizing this point. The MLF, which then still seemed to find European approval, had the disadvantage of requiring unanimity to reach decisions. The United States had taken a strong position against national nuclear proliferation and had emphasized unified nuclear control, which was another way of saying that it wanted to remain in charge. Although

Kennedy and McNamara had left the door open, America had done nothing to encourage Europe to develop its own nuclear force. I was concerned that the Europeans, discouraged by our negativism, might seek a solution based on the force de frappe as a kind of "declaration of independence" from us.

I thought that a European force organized with American support could be more easily integrated into one command structure with our Strategic Air Command in Omaha. At the same time, it would be so small in comparison that no one would expect to operate it independently. I incidentally hoped that Britain, as a member and contributor to the force, would thus be encouraged to assume more European responsibilities. But my deputy, Martin Hillenbrand, whose judgment I greatly respected, and the political section of the embassy argued against me. Although the Germans thought it possible that President Johnson might be more receptive to such an idea than Kennedy had been, they had made their own position clear by opposing an Italian proposal for making the ultimate goal of the MLF a European nuclear force. For the Germans, the MLF was principally a way to get the United States inextricably involved in the defense of Europe, and they shared a general European fear of nuclear involvement without an American restraint. The SPD would undoubtedly oppose a European nuclear force. My colleagues thought it would be paradoxical for the embassy to propose a European move that the Germans opposed.

It was also pointed out that Italian Socialists would also oppose a proposal like mine and that it thus might split the Italian government. It would further meet with opposition from the Dutch, who were already lukewarm on the MLF. British Labourites, and perhaps even the Conservatives, would oppose it too, thus threatening British acceptance of MLF. In general, it was argued, the Europeans might see American support of a European nuclear force as a way to get itself out of European nuclear defense. In the end I gave in, and we did not send the State Department my telegram on a European nuclear force.

Slowly, support for MLF seemed to melt away. "Is this not a dead issue?" asked former Defense Minister Franz Josef Strauss, in a discussion I had with him over lunch (telegram, Amemb Bonn to Secstate, 658, Aug. 19, 1963). Strauss's main objection lay in the U.S. veto. I pointed out that Germany and the other MLF contributors would also have a veto. Strauss replied, however, that he favored a European nuclear force based on a combination of French and British nuclear capabilities, which could be coordinated with the U.S. nuclear force.

Arthur Schlesinger, in describing Kennedy's *Thousand Days*, attributes to Kennedy skepticism about the MLF, although Kennedy accepted the need to "reassure the Germans and show NATO that there were alternatives to Gaullism" (1965, 872). Kennedy saw Berlin and Europe as secure and did not want to divert attention from more serious problems elsewhere. He saw MLF as "something of a fake" and never considered abandoning the U.S. veto over its use. Nor could he see why Europeans would be willing to spend so much money on MLF with no real control. Germany wanted it only as a status symbol, a link with us, to provide nuclear equality with Britain and avert German pressure for an independent nuclear deterrent. We will come back to the MLF.

Secretary of Defense Robert McNamara's visit to Bonn on July 13 provided an excellent opportunity for a high-level exchange on military matters, including the partial test ban treaty with the Soviet Union, which was currently a high-priority item in Washington. Erhard had already let it be known that the treaty had been criticized in the cabinet and that the issue would probably come up when McNamara saw Chancellor Adenauer. Hassel later confirmed that a majority of the Cabinet had joined in the criticism and, for the moment at least, seemed opposed to German adherence.

At his meeting with Adenauer, McNamara tried to persuade him that the treaty was evidence of Western strength, not weakness, and proof of the increased military power of the West, particularly American and West German, in recent years (airgram, Amemb Bonn, memcon A–250, Aug. 2, 1963). Adenauer replied that he evaluated Soviet motives differently. As he saw it, the Soviet Union had been shifting its strategic military priorities from the West toward a more hostile China while trying to deal with domestic setbacks, including a bad crop the previous year caused by the shortage and reduced skill of labor. Russians could not be trained even as well as Italians, Adenauer added. As a result Khrushchev was obliged to become more friendly to the West. He naturally wanted something from the West in return in order to save face. Adenauer claimed that John McCone, U.S. director of Central Intelligence, had expressed a similar view when he was in Bonn a few months earlier.

In all frankness, Adenauer said, the Test Ban Treaty was no great success for the United States. It had been discussed that day in the Cabinet and there had been a great deal of criticism of it. He showed me a copy of a conservative German newspaper with an article concluding that the treaty was actually a gain for the Soviet Union. He feared that it would only increase Western complacency and would handicap the United States in the development of an antimissile missile. Adenauer was afraid that the treaty would result in recognition of the Soviet Occupied Zone. The term *state* used in the treaty was the most outspoken term that could be selected. If, as the treaty provided, one-third of the adherents called for a conference, a conference must be convened. This might result in the two Germanies facing each other, which would imply recognition. President Kennedy's visit to Berlin would be negated; the German people would be shocked. In these circumstances he hesitated to say whether Germany would accede to the treaty.

McNamara reassured Adenauer that the treaty did not imply recognition. The U.S. government had made this clear to the Soviets. By their own actions the United States and Germany could make this clear to the world. Adenauer repeated his grave doubts. He had asked what the United States would do if there was an attempt to convene a meeting as provided for in the treaty. Any such action taken under international law, he continued, implied recognition.

McNamara replied that the Soviets were behind in the development of an antimissile missile and that the test ban negotiations would leave the United States with an atomic technology that the Soviets would never be able to attain. He reassured Adenauer that the United States would under no circumstances take any action in its quest for reduced tensions with the Soviet Union that would have the effect of recognizing East Germany. Adenauer requested that Secretary of State Rusk make a clarifying statement to this effect that would have some immediate impact on German public opinion. McNamara agreed that the United States must continue to increase its strength and stressed that the treaty represented a wedge between the Soviets and the Chinese. It was essential that the Federal Republic accede to it, he said, in order to drive the wedge deeper.

McNamara presented one more problem to Adenauer. The United States, in light of its balance of payments problems, could not continue the present rate of military expenditures abroad. We had already taken concrete steps to improve our position, as recently reported by the president to the Congress. We appreciated greatly the assistance that Germany had rendered in the past through the offset purchases of military equipment. It was, however, absolutely essential that we receive as an offset the full amount of our dollar expenditures in Germany— $1.3 billion in the next two years, not the $1 billion that had been suggested by the Germans. Hassel replied that although $1.3 billion over two years was still the objective, he doubted if actual purchases that year could exceed $1 billion. After 1965 he felt that there should be a new intergovernmental agreement between the two countries regarding the future of the offset arrangement. McNamara emphasized once more that the United States wanted to leave its forces in Germany but would not be able to do so unless there was a continuing full offset agreement.

On July 25 the nuclear Test Ban Treaty was initialed by the United States, Britain, and the Soviet Union. Described as a first step toward the permanent and verified discontinuance of such tests in all environments, it provided for a prohibition by each signatory of all atmospheric tests or any others at any place under its control that would spread nuclear waste beyond their territories. The parties also agreed not to cause, encourage, or participate in such tests anywhere else. Nuclear tests for peaceful purposes were subject to approval by all original parties. Provision was also made for dealing with suspected violations and with withdrawal from the treaty, as well as with amendments, ratification, and accession to the treaty by the original states and other states.

Not being a nuclear power and knowing realistically that there was no way it could become one, the Federal Republic had no objections to the substance of the treaty, Adenauer's criticism notwithstanding. The only question on German minds was whether East German accession to the treaty would affect the country's eventual reunification. As always in those days, they strongly opposed any action that might seem to confer international legitimacy on East Germany. I understood this well, of course, and emphasized it in my exchanges with the State Department on the treaty.

On July 13 I had, on my own initiative, gone to London to lunch with Ambassador W. Averell Harriman, who was enroute to Moscow for the final treaty negotiations with the Soviets and with the British, who were represented by Lord Hailsham. I explained to Harriman the German viewpoint, emphasizing their sensitivity on the GDR accession issue.

On July 23 President Kennedy sent a message to Chancellor Adenauer through the embassy advising that we were close to a treaty and that we would not enter into any nonaggression arrangements without first consulting our Allies. The president hoped Germany would be among the first to sign. Minister Hillenbrand, who delivered the message, reported that Adenauer made no significant comment and that Schröder, to whom he repeated the message, seemed generally pleased. Schröder, however, wrote a letter that day to Secretary of State Rusk, asking that any accession clause exclude the possibility that the GDR would join. On July 24 Rusk replied that the United States believed it was important that all states, including Communist states, particularly Communist China, adhere to the treaty. Adherence to multilateral treaties had not, since the war, implied recognition.

At a press conference on August 3, Kennedy made it clear that the treaty in no way implied recognition of East Germany, and Rusk announced the next day that he would emphasize this in his testimony before the Senate Foreign Relations Committee (letter, Secstate Dean Rusk to Federal Minister of Foreign Affairs Gerhard Schröder, Aug. 4, 1963). Thereupon the Federal Republic publicly welcomed the Test Ban Treaty and eventually signed it.

The contretemps over the Test Ban Treaty was fairly typical of the way relatively minor problems between the United States and Germany could lead to fevered controversy and require elaborate explanations and reassurances before subsiding. I estimated that such issues of German confidence in the United States arose on an average of every two to three months and typically involved U.S. force levels in Germany, the reunification issue, American statements that implied any lessening of confidence in Germany, or the importance the U.S. attached to its relations with the Federal Republic.

Those issues, I considered, reflected both the insecurity and lack of self-confidence that the Germans still suffered as a result of their disastrous war and the importance to them of the United States as friend and protector. Each time such an issue arose, I resolved to restrain any impulse of annoyance. I felt responsible for answering all questions and for explaining U.S. policies patiently in order to relieve anxieties, even though this involved constant repetition.

To simplify this process, I developed the habit of making many speeches all over Germany to make clear the United States's position on key issues. In particular, I emphasized U.S. approval of the rapprochement between Germany and France. This policy involved more speaking appearances than would normally have been required and more than other ambassadors made, and I often wondered what the German government thought of it. One day after a routine meeting, Schröder detained me to volunteer that he was aware of my speeches and always read carefully what I said. He said that he found them very helpful and urged me to continue, which I did.

The question of an East-West nonaggression pact had been raised but wisely discarded in connection with the Test Ban Treaty. In statements on July 19 and again on July 26, 1963, Khrushchev, in conformity with the increasing interest in reducing tensions and seeking a detente, had proposed a nonaggression pact between NATO and the Warsaw Pact, the freezing or cutting of defense budgets, measures to reduce possibilities of surprise attacks, and reduction of foreign forces in East and West Germany. According to Arthur Schlesinger (1965, 916), Averell Harriman was convinced, during the test ban negotiations, that these were possibilities that should be thoroughly considered.

The Soviets saw obvious advantages in such measures in consolidating their hold on Eastern Europe. But Adenauer did not want these changes without progress toward reunification, and his desires influenced and reinforced U.S. skepticism over such relaxations, which some thought might lead to false expectations in the West. According to Schlesinger, Kennedy "hoped to maintain the momentum generated by the Moscow negotiations, but his primary concern was to get the [test ban] treaty through the Senate." Kennedy did not want to take any new steps that might interfere and "was skeptical that there was much in the non-aggression pact for the United States" (ibid., 917–18). Rusk, who also saw little advantage, took a negative position with Khrushchev when he was in Moscow in August to sign the Test Ban Treaty. The matter was not pursued further.

10

Return to Berlin
August 1963

One of my first official acts, only five days after presenting my credentials, was to send a message to the Soviet ambassador to East Germany, Peter Andreyevich Abrasimov, along the lines of similar messages sent by my predecessors on taking up their duties in Bonn (telegram, Amemb Bonn to Secstate, 3139, May 21, 1963). I advised him that President Kennedy, when appointing me U.S. ambassador to the Federal Republic, had entrusted to me, in matters of concern to the United States and the Soviet Union, the authority and responsibility exercised by my predecessor as successor to the U.S. military governor in Germany.

Although this was a routine matter, I had high hopes that I might develop a contact with Abrasimov that might be of value in working out problems between the Allied authorities in Berlin and the Soviet Union. I had heard interesting reports about Abrasimov, whose age was very close to mine. Born in Belorussia, he attended the local university and began a career as an electrician. Joining the Soviet army in 1941, he quickly became active in party work, which he pursued intermittently until 1956, when he entered the Soviet diplomatic service as minister-counselor to the Soviet embassy in Peking. He later served in Poland for nine years before coming to the GDR in 1962. He was a member of the Central Committee of the Communist party and had twice received the Order of Lenin.

Abrasimov obviously ranked high in his country and party, as his post in East Berlin confirmed. In a sense, he was the government of East Germany. Since we then had no representative there, I looked forward to receiving some impression of the Soviet role in East Germany through contacts with Abrasimov. Like other U.S. ambassadors who dealt with him during his long tour of duty, I found him an interesting and attractive individual, frank and open within the limits of Soviet custom. We were to have many involved and productive conversations and convivial luncheons. Although no important agreements were reached, there resulted a relaxation of tension and minor accommodations. I felt that I had developed sufficient rapport with Abrasimov to be able to appeal to him in a time of crisis.

Soon after sending my message in May, I asked our mission in Berlin to make the necessary arrangements for me to call on Abrasimov in East Berlin, as early as August if possible. He would presumably then return my call. One of the problems I faced in calling on him was to assure I did not have to show any special identification at the checkpoint.

All arrangements for these visits had to preserve the Byzantine protocol under which business was conducted between the Allied and Soviet authorities in Berlin. To avoid the impression that I entered East Berlin on Soviet tolerance, we could agree to my being escorted from the Friedrichstrasse checkpoint to Abrasimov only if our protocol officer then reciprocated by escorting him to me on his return. The Soviet protocol officer would see me through the checkpoint going and coming. If for any reason he did not, I would return to Abrasimov and demand that our original arrangements be honored. Serious consideration was also given to anything that might cause the West Berlin authorities to get the impression that Americans and Soviets were colluding behind their backs.

The negotiations for my visit continued until, on August 5, I approached the border between the two zones in my official Cadillac with the two American flags flying bravely from the front fenders. In the presence of the Soviet protocol officer, the East German guard raised the barrier without approaching my car, and I proceeded to the Soviet embassy. It was a huge sprawling structure of lugubrious Russian style, as befitted the importance of the ambassador. After our formal greeting, we proceeded to the luncheon that had been arranged. As would be the case with subsequent meetings, these were long and elaborate affairs. Drinks, which I took sparingly, were offered both before and during lunch.

Discussion on this occasion was not of great importance but might be of interest in shedding light on the problems uppermost in our minds. I went on the assumption that I was dealing with Abrasimov only as the Soviet representative in residual quadripartite German matters (telegram, U.S. Mission Berlin to Secstate, 141, Aug. 6, 1963). Abrasimov took the initiative in trying to put the conversation on the basis of broad Soviet-U.S. interests. Was it our opinion, for instance, that the Federal Republic could be persuaded to accept adherence to the impending Test Ban Treaty? I declined to address the question, responding merely that I was confident everyone would eventually sign the treaty except for the few nations whose negative attitude was already known.

He suggested that a successful Test Ban Treaty might presage the settlement of such other issues as the future of Germany and West Berlin. I replied that we were still unconvinced, despite many years of discussion, that the Soviet proposals for Berlin offered sufficient guarantees for vital Western interests there. The United States believed that both the Berlin and the German problem could only be resolved in the framework of reunification, in which the East German people were able to express their free will. In any event, I commented, we were not likely to solve the problem in this meeting.

My major pitch was that Americans and Soviets, together with the French and British, had a serious responsibility for minimizing friction in day-to-day matters affecting Berlin. We two could contribute by seeing that tensions were minimized. Would he use his undoubtedly great influence on the East Germans for this purpose? Abrasimov replied by disclaiming any responsibility for East Berlin, the capital of an independent state, recognized by fourteen nations. He was only empowered to deal with West Berlin, he said.

By no means did this relieve the USSR of its obligations under the quadripartite agreements of 1944–45, I countered. If the Soviets disregarded American rights in East Berlin, they could not expect us to protect theirs in West Berlin. I then protested East Germany's creation of "barred" and "security" zones in East Berlin. I asked for assurance that our commandant, who had not visited East Berlin in order to avoid incidents, would not be harassed if he visited the city. Soviet generals visited West Berlin without embarrassment, I noted. Abrasimov promised to look into these questions.

Abrasimov nonetheless pointed out that Soviet journalists were effectively barred from West Berlin by denial of residence permits. I answered that this did not interfere with their freedom of movement in West Berlin. He complained that Soviets were not free to develop their Lietzenburgerstrasse property in West Berlin, a damaged building whose space they needed. I countered that we were not free to rebuild our prewar embassy, which was within a barred zone in East Berlin. Abrasimov complained that Soviet artists and athletes were not permitted to appear in West Berlin without approval from Bonn, which they refused to seek. I promised to look into this.

We parted on a friendly basis. Though nothing concrete had been accomplished, and only specific minor issues raised, I liked Abrasimov. In time, I hoped, we could move on to more important matters and perhaps even solve some. I waved to the Soviet protocol officer as he left us after getting me through the checkpoint without my having to show identification.

I next saw Willy Brandt again October 4; there had been no serious problems in Berlin for some time, but our conversation was symptomatic of the ways the city continued to be a problem for us, for Germans, and, not least, for Brandt himself (memcon, U.S. Mission Berlin, Oct. 4, 1963). It was typical of the era that the conversation began with my giving the obligatory reassurance that, in recent talks in Washington, Vice President Johnson had assured Schröder that no U.S. troop withdrawals from Germany were envisaged. As a result of a shift in supply routes, however, some headquarters and service troops would be withdrawn from France. But I advised Brandt that we were not encouraged about the prospects for further agreements with the Soviets following conclusion of the Test Ban Treaty. There had been some preliminary talk about nonaggression agreements and confidence-building exchanges of observer teams to monitor movements of troops. But in ongoing bilateral discussions with the Soviet Union, the Soviets had linked the establishment of observation posts with their demand for withdrawal of Western ground troops from Central Europe, a proposal obviously unacceptable to the West.

The United States was also unprepared to consider a nonaggression agreement seriously unless the Soviets conceded significant improvements in Berlin. We were nonetheless relatively optimistic about chances for an agreement on nonproliferation of nuclear weapons. We were opposed to proliferation. The Soviets were opposed to it too—for example, to the MLF because they saw it as a way to put nuclear weapons in German hands. There was some hope that a treaty banning "bombs in orbit" might also be worked out with other, minor, bilateral U.S.-Soviet agreements.

I explained our view, which Brandt presumably shared, that the chances for progress on such problems as the Berlin and German questions were better in an atmosphere of détente. But we were not interested in concluding agreements just for the sake of détente. Rather, we hoped that détente would result from successful negotiations of genuine benefit to both sides, such as the Test Ban Treaty. We had no intention of lowering our guard vis-à-vis the Soviets or making concessions without receiving something in return.

I referred to a school of thought in the Federal Republic which appeared to fear that the German and Berlin questions might be passed over in a general relaxation of East-West tensions. According to this theory, tension was necessary as long as the Berlin question remained unresolved, and the West must link these problems to every discussion or negotiation with the Soviet Union. In my judgment, this view ignored the fact that the United States had no intention of forgetting the German and Berlin questions and believed that, from a tactical viewpoint, better progress might be achieved on these problems in an atmosphere of greater East-West relaxation. We would give full consideration to the German problem in all areas of negotiation in which it was actually involved, I said, but Washington could not, of course, be expected to do so in every sphere in which a bilateral U.S.-Soviet agreement might be possible.

I added that Schröder had received assurances in Washington that the Federal Republic would be fully consulted on future agreements with the Soviets, particularly those involving Germany and Berlin. Brandt's concern was that things not be treated in such a way as to support the Communist thesis that West Berlin was an entity independent of the Federal Republic. He pointed out that it had been standard policy for many years to extend to Berlin many West German laws and treaties, for example, ocean navigation or mining, which had no practical application in the city. Berlin's inclusion nonetheless served to strengthen its ties with the Federal Republic.

While there did not appear to be any significant change in the number of arrests, harassments, and interferences on the Autobahn, and what arrests there were seemed valid, Brandt left no doubt that the situation angered him. He reacted viscerally to the dangers, indignities, and unwarranted delays to which travelers were subjected. Though some interference might be due to inefficiency, he said, some was certainly due to organized harassment, and he was concerned that the situation might discourage travelers from using the surface routes to Berlin.

The day after I talked to Brandt, I met Axel Springer, the legendary postwar publisher whose publications constituted about one-third of the West German press, including the prestigious dailies *Die Welt*, *Bild Zeitung* (with the largest circulation in Germany), and the *Hamburger Abendblatt*. The son of a publisher, Springer was trained in journalism and founded his own firm at forty-five with substantial assistance from occupation authorities. A devoted German nationalist and patriot, he abandoned his early inclination toward German disengagement from the West after a visit to Moscow in 1958. Since then he had consistently supported a hard-line policy in dealing with the Soviets, defiantly building his firm's headquarters alongside the wall that separated the two Berlins.

Since my arrival I had wanted to sound Springer out and seek his cooperation. When I finally called on him in his modest but tastefully restored suburban home, he was in a relaxed mood (telegram, Amemb Bonn to Secstate, 1278, Oct. 9, 1963). One of his close business associates had, however, told us that Springer's attitude toward all East-West questions was influenced by his conviction that the United States and the Soviet Union had reached a secret bilateral agreement at Germany's expense. I had been authorized by the president to extend Springer an invitation to visit him if he came to Washington. But Springer said he had already cancelled plans for a visit, partly because of business obligations but also because he perceived a difference between his views and those of our government. I assured him that we did not consider differences between us to be a barrier.

In our ensuing discussion on the desirability of East-West negotiations, the most important issue being debated in Germany at that time, Springer assumed a rather defensive position. He and his colleagues were not, he said, "just cold warriors." He believed that we should always be prepared to talk with the Soviets and would, for example, have no objection to U.S. wheat sales to them, as long as no credits were involved. He was also not, as was often said, interested exclusively in Berlin. When he found that German ships were engaged in trading with Cuba during the recent missile crisis, he had published the fact in an effort to force them out.

His main preoccupation, he continued, was that the United States should not give the Soviets any assistance that could have the effect of bailing them out of their present difficulties, thereby freeing them to return to their former rigid position. If they were experiencing an adverse period, we should let their situation deteriorate further before making any real effort to help them. He also believed that any assistance involving concessions or long-term credit on our part should be accompanied by tangible political concessions affecting East Germans, Berlin, and reunification.

Springer said that Germany must pay for reunification in terms of economic assistance to the Soviet Union, presumably on a grant or long-term credit basis within the framework of a coordinated Western policy. Germany would, I assumed, bear the principal share of the burden, which would confront the Soviets with unified terms and conditions. Springer's approach, as he described it, impressed me as essentially patriotic and emotional. In essence, he was saying that the Germans, and particularly Springer himself, had done very well economically and should now be willing to pay out of their wealth to better the lot of their East German brothers. His proposal for large-scale assistance to the Soviets in exchange for improvements in East Germany was reported to be widely supported in Germany. Springer himself, however, admitted that the Soviet Union, in the present context, could grant no real political concessions like free elections, autonomy, or the right to a confederal relationship with West Germany.

I was to see Springer again from time to time. I had no serious concerns that he was working against U.S.-German cooperation; he continued, however, to indicate suspicions and reservations on particular issues—particularly regarding U.S.-Soviet relations.

A few months later, in December, I came away from talks with both Secretary of State Rusk and President Johnson in Washington with a clear impression of their deep desire to achieve a breakthrough in East-West relations. Springer and Erhard, meanwhile, had independently hinted to me at a new German approach to the problem through "generosity," a delicate way of saying that they thought German unity could perhaps be "bought" and that Germans would be willing to pay the price. The following March I met with the respected SPD mayor of Bremen, Wilhelm Kaisen, who suggested a massive Western aid program to the Soviets comparable to our Marshall Plan for postwar Europe. This had struck me as particularly interesting coming from a Socialist leader who had known Lenin and who understood Marxism-Leninism from firsthand experience of over half a century. Kaisen thought that "the logic of history" was pushing the Soviet Union to readjust its economy, which would lead to a "reordering of its social structure." Since this was being endangered by left militants—that is, Chinese

Communists—"outside assistance in easing the transition could be decisive."

And so I tried an initiative of my own. I directed somewhat similar views in a long telegram to the secretary and under secretary of State with a copy for Ambassador Foy Kohler in Moscow. Kohler, however, was not encouraging. I signed off gracefully with the State Department and abandoned any further efforts along these lines. The Germans did not raise them again either.

On October 9 I participated in the commemoration of Berlin Week in Nuremberg, addressing my remarks to U.S. policy toward Berlin and dealing particularly with the question of West Berlin's relations with the FRG.

I recalled that the American commitment to West Berlin was reaffirmed as recently as late June by President Kennedy during his visit there. Americans understood and appreciated the desire of the Berlin authorities and the city's people to have more normal relations with their compatriots in the Federal Republic. At the same time, however, if we were to defend Berlin and to ensure the continuing freedom and prosperity of its citizens, we believed it essential to preserve a strong legal position in the city. We must strive to maintain the hopes of the people who had been shut off from contact with their fellow Germans by the brutal Wall and to ameliorate the human and physical hardships of East Germans caused by the Wall's construction.

We had heard the Communist defense of the Wall, I said. They pleaded a need to defend their "gains" from attack by the West. We all knew that this was false, that they really feared the magnetic appeal which freedom, as found in West Berlin, had. We were entitled to say to them: "If you are so confident of the virtue of your ideas, let the people make a free choice between the two systems." I challenged the Soviet leadership, which had ultimate responsibility for East Germany, to allow an improvement in the conditions of the people there. Let the Communists stop their untruthful propaganda barrage and allow their people to see and judge the situation in the West for themselves. If the people of the East were free to choose, the attraction of our system in the West was such that the ultimate victory would be ours.

John J. (Jack) McCloy, who had served as U.S. military governor and high commissioner to Germany from 1949 to 1952, visited Berlin and Bonn, October 11–18. Jack, who was immensely popular in Germany, took advantage of his visit to see everyone of importance, from Adenauer and Brandt on down. Although he usually saw people alone, he talked with me before his visits to obtain the embassy view of the current scene and reported the results of his discussions. Dealing with friends who respected him, Jack was effective in getting his point of view across to Germans, and I always welcomed his visits. (Memorandum of talks with German leaders during period of visit to Berlin and Bonn, Oct. 11–16, 1963, John J. McCloy files, Amemb Bonn; airgram, Amemb Bonn, A–476, Nov. 4, 1963.)

During his conversations with German leaders, McCloy stressed U.S. steadfastness in the defense of Berlin and in favor of reunification, our good record of consultation on the Test Ban Treaty, and our firmness against a nonaggression pact as a condition for the treaty. He deplored the trend toward negative thinking and the strong nationalist tendency he had found widespread in European government circles. This was, he thought, inadequate for the nuclear age and for standing up against strong Sino-Soviet pressure against the West.

McCloy considered the West to be in a critical period of the postwar era; there could be no equivocation. The only counter to Eastern pressure was a solid Western front, which required military, economic, and political unity between the United States and Europe. With Adenauer, McCloy went over the evidence to show that we had consulted fully with the Germans on the Test Ban Treaty and denied vigorously that we had aided the recognition of East Germany.

McCloy emphasized that we did not seek to impair French or European independence but that no European axis or Franco-German alliance could, alone, stand up against the pressure of the East or bring about German reunification. Unlike some European politicians, he considered the Soviets to be strong enough to "blot out" Europe with one blow. We should attempt to lessen tensions with the Soviets by finding areas of agreement. A balance of deterrents was a dangerous way to avoid nuclear war. McCloy advised that in his judgment our show of strength in Cuba during the missile crisis had created an atmosphere that might make possible a reduction in tensions.

McCloy pointed out to those he spoke to the importance of consultation before the Americans, the Germans, or the French took important steps affecting the others. He emphasized to Adenauer, and later to a large Bundestag luncheon group, that other great issues and forces in the world were not centered in Germany and that Germans should put these matters into perspective. He deplored what he considered to be an increasing polarization between Europe and the United States. Without a broad and united Western policy we would, in all probability, be unable to avoid a nuclear war and the destruction of Europe. McCloy's visit made an important contribution toward strengthening confidence in German leadership circles.

11

Erhard Takes Over
October 1963

On October 14, 1963, Ludwig Erhard finally had his day. After a long, embarrassing wait, attended by constant harassment from his aged and autocratic predecessor, Adenauer, the patient, modest man who more than any other individual was responsible for the postwar economic recovery of Germany, finally achieved his long-awaited goal of becoming chancellor. After the ceremonies, Erhard gave a two-hour speech before the Bundestag in which he set the policy and the tone of his administration (telegram, Amemb Bonn to Secstate, 1430, Oct. 18, 1963). He announced that he supported the Test Ban Treaty. He cautioned that expectations should be realistic but urged that every opportunity be seized for East-West talks, particularly direct U.S.-Soviet talks. He also reaffirmed that the will of the German people to restore their unity was a reality that the Soviets should not ignore. He urged the Western powers and the Soviet Union to exercise their joint responsibilities in carrying out their commitments to Germany as a whole.

Erhard also pledged continuing German support for NATO and increased political consultation and integration with the United States and Germany's European partners. He declared that an MLF could make a substantial contribution to German recovery and the development of its military forces. He further urged measures to secure better living conditions for the people of the GDR and proposed that these be linked to improved trade with Eastern Europe. He emphasized the need for continued political support from the Allies for West Berlin, adding that Bonn was prepared to increase its economic support for the city.

Erhard then pledged support for European integration, including steps toward further transfer of sovereign rights to European institutions and possibly even an elected European parliament. He expressed strong support both for the Franco-German treaty as a link in European unification and for eventual British entry into the Common Market. He also strongly supported the principle of free world trade and the Kennedy Round negotiations. I thought that Erhard had succeeded in giving his speech his own stamp, although more in style than policy (telegram, Amemb Bonn to Secstate, 1438, Oct. 19, 1963).

The first reaction of the opposition parties was that Erhard had aligned himself, although cautiously, with a more active "policy of movement." Although deprecatory in his comments, Adenauer showed understanding of the speech as an expression of continuity. The U.S. embassy saw in Erhard's words a recognition that East-West relations were in a state of flux, a fact that Germany could not change even though it must try to protect German interests involved. Erhard's emphasis on reunification and Berlin, although unattached to any specific advances, was well received by the Bundestag. His East-West pronouncements, however, did not go beyond Adenauer's position.

Overall, I thought Erhard had demonstrated restraint, perhaps in deference to the ongoing internal debate between the Gaullists and Atlanticists within his own party on economic and disarmament matters. He made no comment at all on direct relations between the Soviet Union and the Federal Republic. He did, however, make a clear break with Adenauer's strong pro-French stance. His support for the MLF and for further European political integration was also a significant departure from Adenauer's policy.

There appeared to be uncertainty in the Foreign Office as to how far to press Erhard's proposal for exercise of four-power responsibility for German reunification. Five weeks before his inauguration, Erhard himself had given me some insights into his views on current East-West negotiations (telegram, Amemb Bonn to Secstate, 883, Sept. 7, 1963). He believed that the observation posts that had recently been proposed as a warning against surprise attacks should not be limited to the two Germanies but should extend to corresponding areas on both sides of the Iron Curtain and as far as the Soviet border. He felt that we must know what was happening there. I responded that we agreed to this. The United States would be willing to have observation posts on its own territory, I added. At the same time, like Springer, Erhard favored some "new gesture" of "sacrifice" as a bargaining chip against political concessions. I observed that we had told the Foreign Office we did not believe the Soviets would be tempted by offers of generous financing of East-West trade.

Erhard expressed regret over the publicity given the German delay in signing the Test Ban Treaty. He thought it had given the world the impression that the Germans were "difficult" in dealing with East-West problems. In his judgment, a proper balance was necessary. In considering matters of a more or less technical nature, he believed Germany should be willing to negotiate on the merits of the case but must nonetheless continue to oppose arguments that represented a "substitute for reunification." There were people, not including himself, who believed the United States was seeking better East-West relations only in order to improve the status quo, he said. He warned us against giving the impression that we were not actively seeking reunification.

In closing, Erhard said that after the change in government he would like very much to talk with President Kennedy about these and other matters. Although he seemed reluctant to make formal arrangements before his inauguration, he authorized me to take this matter up during my forthcoming consultation in Washington. There was no opportunity to delve further into his thoughts, but Erhard's comments indicated his views on matters he had hitherto been reluctant to discuss. They reflected a certain caution, but also originality, and revealed his expected economic slant.

In October the East Germans twice detained U.S. military truck convoys traversing the Berlin Autobahn with equipment and personnel. These led to serious confrontations between U.S. commanders and the East German military officials who operated the checkpoints. The incidents originated with demands by the East German authorities that appeared new and unprecedented. In the process of checking the number of U.S. personnel in a military vehicle, the Germans now demanded that the tailgate of the vehicle be lowered and that, if there were over thirty in a truck, they must dismount to be counted. The U.S. officer in charge of the convoy refused, saying that past procedures had involved only a visual inspection of the interior of the truck from the outside, with the tailgate lowered only if it was too high to look over. We wanted to avoid setting new precedents that might serve to justify future delays and continuing harassment.

When the first convoy was stopped, the U.S. military mission in Berlin was informed, and we lodged a protest with the Soviet military authorities in Berlin. But they refused to interfere, saying it was an East

German responsibility. We then had a direct confrontation with the East Germans. Accepted procedure at this juncture was for the commander of our convoy to give an ultimatum to the East German officer in charge of the checkpoint. Either the barrier must be raised within a specified short period of time or the convoy would go through anyway. On this occasion, the barrier had not been raised within the specified time, so the driver of the lead truck dismounted and raised the barrier, and the convoy proceeded. The East Germans then brought out two armored personnel carriers, facing each other, blocking the road ahead, and pointed machine guns at the oncoming lead truck of the U.S. convoy. According to instructions, the U.S. truck proceeded as far as it could without ramming the personnel carriers and stopped. The incident was then referred to Washington to be taken up with the Soviets in Moscow. Eventually agreement was reached and the convoy was allowed to proceed.

This incident might have been dismissed as an accident or a mistake had there not been a second similar stoppage. All negotiations failed and the situation looked serious. We decided as a tactic to bring in other U.S. convoys, sympathetic convoys one might say, that would allow themselves to be stopped. Eventually the congestion of the Autobahn became so great that traffic was completely blocked and the East Germans were forced to give in. I recall no example in either main stoppage of our giving in on any important point of principle. A number of times, however, we feared that the East Germans would call our bluff, and there was a genuine threat that force would be used.

When Secretary of State Rusk visited Bonn in October he was asked by reporters why he thought the Autobahn incidents had occurred. Rusk believed that the first convoy had been stopped as an East German response to erroneous reports that the Allies were trying to change the existing convoy procedures and that Soviet military headquarters had backed the East Germans. But it was really the East Germans who were trying to change the accepted arrangements, he charged. To complicate things, neither side had ever clarified these procedures because the Allies refused to request Soviet approval for conduct in obtaining access to Berlin. Rusk said that he would have taken a different view if a third stoppage had occurred and emphasized that the problem had been resolved on the basis of Allied understanding of existing procedures. He did not believe the Soviets wanted to create a major confrontation over the incidents.

During a meeting in early November with George Ball and Llewellyn

(Tommy) Thompson, former U.S. ambassador to the Soviet Union and a recognized expert on Soviet behavior, Erhard asked Thompson why he thought the Soviets had blocked the U.S. convoys. Thompson answered that in his opinion the impulse had originated in the Soviet armed forces. It was clear to him that when Soviet Foreign Minister Andrey Gromyko called on President Kennedy in Washington shortly before the Autobahn confrontations, Gromyko was ignorant of what was to happen there. Thompson thought it unlikely that Khrushchev would have ordered an interruption at that moment and that if Khrushchev had wished one, he would have done it earlier or would have waited for Gromyko's return.

Erhard agreed that this might explain the first incident, but he asked how it bore on the second. Thompson explained that once the prestige of the Soviet military was engaged, Khrushchev had to support them. Naturally he desired to try to push us when he could readily do so, and he was not free to ignore the military.

The possibility that such incidents might start another world war was often in our minds. On such occasions, the embassy and our Berlin mission were in constant communication with the commandant in Berlin and with the State Department. During the Autobahn confrontations, I was also in direct telephone contact with the responsible officers at NATO headquarters in Paris. When President Kennedy heard about our ultimatum procedure, he forbade its future use without referral to Washington and his personal approval. I believe he was right. In November the East Germans, obviously on directions from the Soviets, stopped harassing U.S. convoys for good.

Apart from his views on the Autobahn incidents, Rusk's meetings with the press and German officials during his visit provided some interesting insights into his views of current U.S.-German relations. Rusk tactfully prodded the European allies to meet their NATO commitments, pointing out that thus far only the United States had done so (pamphlet, Chiefs of Mission Conference, Amemb Bonn, Oct. 24–26, 1963). He deplored the European tendency to apply a double standard on NATO force goals and trade with the East.

Rusk's talks with Chancellor Erhard and former chancellor Adenauer were perfunctory. Adenauer raised only the question of trade with the Soviet Union, on which he promised to send Rusk a memorandum for comment (memorandum for the record, Amemb Bonn, Oct. 25, 1963). The Soviets were short of food. When the Germans negotiated a new trade agreement with the Soviets in November, Adenauer thought they should take into account overall NATO policy in deciding whether to furnish tractors and farm equipment. Rusk agreed on the importance of trade with the Soviets and said he would welcome the question being taken up by NATO. He pointed out, however, that it was mainly a question for the European members, whose trade with the East was much greater than ours.

Rusk's meeting with Foreign Minister Gerhard Schröder was by far the most important of his visit (telegram, Amemb Bonn to Secstate, 1552, Oct. 27, 1963). Schröder disclaimed any concern that Deputy Secretary of Defense Roswell Gilpatric's speech on a new U.S. military "big lift" to Europe implied a change in U.S. defense policy. He reported to Rusk on the recent Western European Union meeting he had attended in The Hague. On a German initiative it had been agreed that these would be held every three months, with a fixed agenda to discuss any dangerous political or economic developments facing the union. Foreign Minister Maurice Couve de Murville of France had deprecated the value of any new move toward the Soviets, since in his view recent negotiations had achieved nothing.

The day after Rusk's departure, I asked for a meeting with Adenauer. United States relations with the former chancellor were still good, and I wanted to create a basis for continuing rapport and discussions with him largely for defensive reasons. Although some of his views were stereotyped, I thought his advice worth considering. I also sought to avoid the mischievous moves he was capable of making if he considered himself to have been neglected. In our talk, Adenauer insisted that he had no criticism of present American policy, that he had not joined in the recent dissents which had been expressed by some Germans. I did not point out that this was somewhat of an oversimplification of his position. He said that he would be glad to receive me again and that he looked forward to our continued comradeship.

After the last world war, Adenauer said, he had decided that the future of Europe would be determined by whether Germany sided with Russia or with the West. He claimed that when he visited Moscow in 1955 Khrushchev had attempted to get him to join him against China and the United States. Adenauer understood then, he told me, that not Germany but the United States was the objective of Russian policy. If Germany had sided with Russia, however, then France, Italy, and other Western European countries would have had no choice but to go along. The resulting power grouping would have been too formidable for the

United States to contend with. This was why he attached so much importance to the Franco-German treaty, Adenauer emphasized.

Adenauer recalled that he had visited Charles de Gaulle first in 1958. A representative of de Gaulle had on two previous occasions suggested such a visit, but he had declined since he did not consider it appropriate for the leader of a defeated country. In extending the second invitation, de Gaulle had attempted to influence him by pointing out that John Foster Dulles had visited him, but Adenauer had replied that Dulles was the representative of a victorious country. On the third invitation, however, he had met with de Gaulle at the general's estate for a day and a half. He said that he had been somewhat taken aback by the American opposition to the Franco-German treaty of cooperation. He did not understand why Americans wished Germany to choose between France and the United States.

I then went over the familiar ground of U.S. reaction to the treaty. We did not by any means wish to force Germany to choose between France and the United States. This would be like asking us to choose between Canada and the United Kingdom. We had an intimate relationship with Canada because of our long common border and our common interests, as is true for Germany and France. We welcomed a French-German rapprochement, which we considered basic to European peace and unity. Had it not been accomplished, it would be a prime objective of our present policy in Bonn and Paris.

The reaction in our country to the treaty, not so much in the government as on the part of the public and in the press, was due to three factors. I told Adenauer that he must recognize that France and the United States had many political differences, including our policies on Southeast Asia, the Congo, the United Nations, and assignment of forces to NATO, apart from British entry into the Common Market. If we appeared to be competing with the French, it was not just over Germany itself but also over our respective policies in other countries and on other subjects. In taking leave of Adenauer, I said that I hoped we could discuss the matter of East-West negotiations at our next meeting. He apparently thought the United States was willing to make unilateral concessions merely to induce a favorable attitude on the part of the Soviet Union and was concerned not over American policy but over Soviet misunderstanding of that policy.

Shortly after this meeting with Adenauer, I talked to Alfried Krupp, whom I had been interested in meeting since my arrival. Krupp was the last of his family to be associated with the great steel and munitions firm in Essen. The family fortunes can be traced to Arndt Krupp, who founded his firm in Essen in 1587. The family entered the munitions business in 1621 and became the exclusive armorer to Germany and the German arms supplier for the Franco-Prussian War and World Wars I and II.

Alfried's life involved a series of tragedies. An early marriage was rejected by the family as unacceptable. Alfried had taken title to the firm and the name Krupp only when Germany's defeat in World War II was seen as inevitable. He stood trial in 1946 for war crimes, including the use of slave labor and the confiscation of captive steel mills, and in 1948 was sentenced to twelve years in prison and had his property confiscated. But on February 3, 1951, he was released from prison and his property restored in a highly publicized amnesty decision by U.S. High Commissioner John McCloy.

On October 30, 1963, Beitz invited me to lunch with Alfried at Beitz's residence near Essen. Krupp's only son, Arndt, then in his early twenties, was also present (telegram, Amemb Bonn to Secstate, 1648, Nov. 1, 1963). Alfried, a handsome man with a sober, gaunt appearance, still showed some effects of a recent illness, and he let Beitz do most of the talking. Like Beitz, Krupp took the line that Western action to raise the standard of living in the Soviet satellites would ultimately pay dividends by reducing the risk of East-West confrontations. The Soviets were in trouble, he said, and the Eastern bloc as a whole was "in a sorry state" because of mistakes in economic planning. He believed that the situation offered useful opportunities for Western leverage. In the end, I commented that both "we and the Federal Republic would find it difficult to extend long-term credit to the Bloc in the absence of concrete political concessions by the Soviets." Krupp conducted himself at all times in a manner of quiet dignity, usually looking down at the table, and we did not discuss his personal problems. On parting, however, he confided that he would like to meet with me privately in Bonn. I told him I would be pleased to receive him.

On December 13 we lunched alone. We engaged in a desultory discussion of the state of the German steel industry, and Krupp told me that German industrialists did not have a high regard for Erhard in business and economic matters. They thought he talked like a professor and had never felt close to him. I then raised the question of his problems in obtaining a visa for the United States, which I knew was the purpose of his visit. He grumbled a bit that it was Beitz who had raised the problem and added that he had no present intention of going to the United States. But if he wanted to go, he asked, why could he not have a normal visa rather than one that required waiver of his war criminal status? I attempted to reassure him that, while a waiver was necessary under U.S. law, this could be done quietly. The notation on the visa would be incomprehensible to nonofficials.

Understandably, Krupp felt uneasy about a visit to the United States, fearing the attendant publicity and possible public confrontations. I attempted to minimize this danger, pointing out that he would be free to travel by private plane and that he could visit many places, including Washington, where he would find less latent antagonism than he might in New York City. In the end he decided not to go, but further disasters were to befall him. Because of the huge debts Beitz had incurred in rebuilding the firm, Krupp was converted to a public company. Alfried himself died shortly thereafter under suspicious circumstances. His son, Arndt, renounced any interest in the firm and became one of Germany's leading playboys.

One could scarcely grasp the enormity of the loss and grief that had been incurred by one family and by one man who was destined to bear the brunt. The retribution to the Krupps for having produced to their great profit such a multitude of weapons of mass destruction over so many centuries was slow but complete.

Ambassador McGhee at his desk in Bonn

"Ich bin ein Berliner" speech, Berlin, June 26, 1963; *left to right*: military aides, President Kennedy, Ambassador McGhee, Gen. Lucius Clay, and Gen. James Polk

Ambassador McGhee and President Johnson

Chancellor Erhard and President Johnson stand at attention during welcoming ceremonies for Erhard at Bergstrom Air Force Base, Austin, Texas, December 28, 1964; behind them are, *left to right:* Amb. Heinrich Knappstein, Ambassador McGhee, Gov. John B. Connally of Texas, and Secretary of State Dean Rusk

Chancellor Kurt Kiesinger

Farewell call at the White House, May 14, 1963

Chancellor Konrad Adenauer

Chancellor Ludwig Erhard

Ambassador McGhee being greeted by Mayor Willy Brandt, Berlin, 1963

Ambassador McGhee inspects the Wall, Berlin, 1963

Ambassador McGhee and Gen. James Polk at U.S. Army exercises

Left to right: Former Chancellor Adenauer, Ambassador McGhee, Mrs. McGhee, aide, Vice Chancellor Eric Mende

Ambassador McGhee and President Heinrich Lübke hunting

1964

February 16	SPD elects Willy Brandt chairman
March 6	German-Bulgarian trade agreement concluded
May 4	Kennedy Round of tariff negotiations under GATT open
June 5	Bundestag approves the Nuclear Test Ban Treaty
June 12	Treaty on friendship, mutual assistance, and cooperation between the GDR and the Soviet Union concluded
July 1	Heinrich Lübke reelected federal president
August 7	U.S. Congress passes Tonkin Gulf Resolution, broadening U.S. intervention in Vietnam
September 3	FRG announces Khrushchev's visit to Bonn
October 14–15	Khrushchev is overthrown and replaced by a collective leadership
October 16	People's Republic of China detonates its first atomic bomb
November 28	Right-wing National Democratic party (NPD) is founded
December 15	European Economic Community agrees on a common grain market

12

Johnson Succeeds Kennedy November 22, 1963– February 1964

Kennedy's assassination on November 22, 1963, will always stand out as a landmark in history. It brought Lyndon Johnson, an entirely different type of man, to the presidency. Johnson was only nine years Kennedy's senior, but Kennedy, a product of the postwar era, represented a new generation. Johnson's regional, social, and educational background as well as personality were completely different. The two men had, of course, much in common. Both were Democrats of a middle-of-the-road stripe who had served in the House and Senate. Both were highly intelligent, gregarious individuals with a strong reformist, idealistic, and populist streak. But beyond this they were quite different men with widely varying styles. This inevitably created changes when Johnson succeeded to the office, changes that could be felt abroad by an important ally like West Germany.

John Fitzgerald Kennedy, who was forty-six when he died, came from a background of wealthy, prestigious, and politically minded ancestors. In American terms he was considered aristocratic, except by Boston Back Bay Brahmins. His father, a tough, self-made Wall Street businessman, had early in life amassed a fortune that provided for young John Kennedy every advantage and opportunity. This included a Harvard education and life in the U.S. embassy in London, where his father served as ambassador. Highly intelligent, alert, with a winning smile that was a part of his great charm, plus an overwhelming ambition, Jack Kennedy could have been spotted early as destined for great things— even the presidency. While not himself an intellectual, he sought their ideas and knew how to use them. He exuded an aura of complete confidence and self-assurance.

Hedley Donovan (1985, 84–85), in a recent excellent appraisal of presidents, has called Kennedy a fiscal conservative but a political pragmatist, not given to philosophizing or to listening to others do so. Donovan cites Kennedy's masterful handling of the Cuban missile crisis and the Test Ban Treaty as his greatest achievements. On the negative side, Donovan has cited Kennedy's increase in the number of American "advisers" in Vietnam to 16,500, of whom 109 were killed. This, together with the U.S. association with the Diem assassination, still arouses controversy as to the wisdom of Kennedy's policies, which got the United States involved inextricably in the Vietnam War. Donovan doubts that Kennedy, had he lived, would have become a great president. On balance, I think he could have.

History appears to have vindicated Kennedy. A Harris poll taken in 1983 gave Kennedy 40 percent in public support as the president who "most inspired confidence in the White House," despite publicity of his extramarital peccadilloes. Franklin D. Roosevelt polled 23 percent, Dwight D. Eisenhower and Harry S Truman only 8 percent each.

Lyndon Baines Johnson was born near Stonewall, Texas, of good country stock. His family was hard pressed by the Great Depression, which took a particularly heavy toll in the rural areas of southwest Texas. Educated as a teacher at Southwest Texas State College in San Marcos, Johnson fought his way up the hard ladder of Texas politics to the highest office in the country. Johnson was a friendly man with a powerful personality and a sharp political sense. He was a shrewd judge of men, had tremendous ambition, and displayed a keen sense of how to concentrate his efforts in his long struggle for electoral success and political power. He owed much to the political education and support given by his close Texas friend the great Speaker of the House Sam Rayburn. And yet, despite his valuable personal assets and accomplishments, underneath Johnson had a basic insecurity that undoubtedly contributed to his political fall.

I had known Kennedy well, having had personal contacts with him while serving in the State Department under Dean Rusk. On several occasions I did trouble-shooting jobs for Kennedy on direct assignment, and he appointed me to my highest positions in government, head of policy planning and under secretary for political affairs, the latter representing a double promotion. Germany, to which he appointed me as ambassador, I considered one of our two or three most important foreign posts.

By chance, I knew Johnson well from our days in early wartime Washington when he was a member of Congress and I was serving on the War Production Board. I had often been able to help Lady Bird Johnson with wartime problems in her husband's constituency. My wife and I were fond of Lady Bird Johnson and the Johnsons' daughters, and we were often together in Texas conclaves and occasionally in one another's homes. I had followed Johnson's political career with interest, particularly when he stepped down as a candidate for the presidency in favor of Kennedy at the Los Angeles convention in 1960. I respected his political acumen and was pleased to have a fellow Texan in the White House. This meant that I would have readier access to the White House in carrying out ambassadorial duties.

The change in presidents had little immediate impact on the conduct of U.S. foreign policy. Johnson did not claim to be an expert in foreign affairs, although he had naturally learned a great deal as a U.S. senator and as vice president. When I had been with him in National Security Council and other meetings, he listened attentively but deferred to Kennedy, who had a flair for foreign policy and wanted, in effect, to be his own secretary of state. This tendency at times created difficulties for Dean Rusk and the remaining State Department hierarchy, for George Ball as under secretary and, before I went to Germany, for myself as under secretary for political affairs.

Johnson placed great confidence in Rusk, and, since his principal concern was the package of social legislation associated with his concept of the Great Society, he allowed Rusk to run the State Department without much interference. This gave Rusk a stronger hand than he had had under Kennedy. Rusk and Kennedy had seen eye to eye on most issues, so this meant that their joint policies continued for the most part under Johnson. The exception was the burgeoning U.S. involvement in Vietnam, which absorbed increasing amounts of Johnson's attention and over which Johnson, aided by his strong secretary of defense, Robert McNamara, assumed personal control.

President Kennedy's death had disrupted plans for a visit to the United States by Chancellor Erhard. Nonetheless, the Bonn Foreign Office urged that the chancellor's visit keep "its place in line" when President Johnson reinstated state visits. Having completed the rounds of Western European capitals after taking office, Erhard attached the highest importance to establishing personal contact with Johnson as soon as possible. I recommended this strongly to the president, and the visit was announced on December 1 in the form of an invitation to visit the Johnson ranch in Texas over the Christmas holidays.

I met with Erhard the next day, and he expressed appreciation for the early date set and the favorable circumstances. He considered the invitation to visit Johnson's farm a compliment to himself and an affirmation of the close relations between the two countries (telegram, Amemb Bonn to Secstate, 1981, Dec. 3, 1963). He planned to take only a small party and would be happy to maintain the same agenda that had been planned for the meeting with President Kennedy in November. He also said that he had been favorably impressed by Johnson at the Kennedy funeral and that he felt sure there would be no letdown in U.S.-German relations.

Erhard then proceeded to tell me about his recent visit with Charles de Gaulle in Paris. He sensed that de Gaulle wished to change his general stance toward his allies, but he could not be specific as to how this would affect de Gaulle's attitude on particular issues. He offered his own assumption of the chancellorship as one explanation for de Gaulle's change of position. With Adenauer's backing, de Gaulle knew that France was much more certain of playing an important European role. But although Erhard intended to be honest with him and loyal to the Franco-German treaty, de Gaulle knew he could not take Erhard for granted. Erhard thought this might explain de Gaulle's apparent desire to reestablish ties with his other allies, which he had allowed to deteriorate.

Perhaps because he had not yet formed a core of political opposition to Gaullism, Erhard appeared to focus less on de Gaulle as a potential threat than on the positive opportunities that might arise from a change in de Gaulle's positions. He seemed to have considerable confidence that the strong German position in the Common Market would provide him enough leverage to assure French cooperation in trade negotiations. In reporting the conversation to Washington, I gave Erhard full marks for his cooperation in meeting German defense obligations and recommended that we press him to reinstate, in his forthcoming budget, defense cuts he had announced but not effected. I argued that his rigid views on budget ceilings probably reflected a need to defend himself against accusations that he was a "rubber lion," as those skeptical of his qualifications to be chancellor sometimes called him.

I also recommended that when Johnson received Erhard he indicate disappointment over the announced 25 percent reduction in German foreign economic aid loans and urge Erhard to put greater pressure on de Gaulle to liberalize trade. I emphasized Erhard's devotion to the concept of Atlantic partnership, which corresponded more closely to our view than that of any other European head of state. I also reported that Erhard expected Johnson to continue Kennedy's plans to build the Atlantic alliance, defend Berlin, and work toward German reunification.

On December 7, I returned to Berlin and met with Brandt to discuss the perennially frustrating problem of arranging Christmas passes for West Berliners to visit relatives and friends in East Berlin (telegram, Amemb Bonn to Secstate, 2066, Dec. 9, 1963). This was an annual emotional issue that was difficult to resolve without having the Berlin Senate deal directly with the East Germans, something all wanted to avoid. Given a free hand by Erhard, however, Brandt was able to work out an arrangement that allowed for 1.2 million visits by West Berliners to East Berlin during an eighteen-day period over Christmas 1963. This was followed by four separate fortnightly visit periods by West Berliners during 1964.

Brandt, who had been giving serious thought to East-West relations since he first became mayor of West Berlin in 1958, had concluded in 1961 that any Ostpolitik, as the normalization of relations between West Germany and Eastern Europe came to be called, must start with the acceptance of the status quo. The Christmas visits were, indeed, a great coup for him, the beginning of a larger foreign policy concept that reached full bloom during his period as chancellor after 1969. Negotiation of the Christmas visits was a "small step" of the kind Brandt had been advocating as part of a "policy of small steps" and addressed a humanitarian purpose no one could object to.

I was pleased with this result. I believed that we should support Brandt and told him so. Particularly at Christmas, I did not consider it necessary to wait for the big problem of Germany's unification to be settled before relieving the buildup of tension arising out of the arbitrary separation of families and friends.

Brandt expressed disappointment with the present state of the movement toward European union and Atlantic partnership. He said that the SPD intended to play a positive role in stimulating progress and would be cooperating closely with Jean Monnet's Action Committee. I gave Brandt a general rundown on my first discussion with Abrasimov, observing that the Soviet official apparently wished to establish good personal relations by making a few minor concessions. In terms of Soviet intentions toward Berlin, I told Brandt that I did not anticipate any increase in Soviet harassment for the immediate future. I believed the Soviets would observe a waiting period following Kennedy's death to give Johnson an opportunity to establish his administration before making any move.

Before my return to Bonn, Abrasimov paid me a return call at the Berlin residence (telegram, Amemb Bonn to Secstate, 667, Dec. 5, 1963). Since we had broken the ice in our first meeting, the conversation flowed easily. Abrasimov expressed condolences over the death of President Kennedy, and I assured him that U.S.-Soviet relations would continue to develop in a positive way under President Johnson. Just as Johnson would meet the Soviets halfway in efforts to reduce tensions and find areas of agreement, I reiterated my hopes that he and I could contribute by lessening tensions in Berlin.

In the discussion that followed, Abrasimov showed his capacity to make decisions on a number of problems, including some that the Soviet military would normally have dealt with. This affirmed my impression of Abrasimov's influence in Moscow. We amicably discussed a variety of practical problems, including the recent convoy incidents on the Autobahn and alleged incidents caused by U.S. military traffic in East Berlin. Abrasimov acceded to my earlier request to arrange with the East Germans for a smooth visit to East Berlin by General Polk, the U.S. military commandant.

Before leaving, Abrasimov invited my wife and me to attend a West Berlin performance by the Soviet pianist Sviatoslav Richter. "It would create a good impression on West Berliners if the Soviet and U.S. ambassadors were to appear together at a concert," he said, also asking for my assistance in removing any difficulties in completing the arrangements for the concert. I said that we would not stand in the way of Richter's appearance, but I deliberately did not respond to the ambassador's suggestion that we attend it together. Although I had no objection to exchanging official visits with Abrasimov, which were always highlighted in the local press, I was concerned about the German reaction to being seen with him publicly on an unofficial social basis. Unperturbed, Abrasimov presented me a book of photographs on the Russian ballet in Moscow. The U.S. mission in Berlin concluded that Abrasimov's discussion with me of matters that the East German regime considered its own domain represented a setback for Walter Ulbricht, the East German leader, and a return of decision-making to the Soviet political level.

The questions of East-West relations and German reunification are inseparable. It is difficult to say which is cause and which is effect— as Ferenc A. Vali pointed out in *The Quest for a United Germany*— whether the division of Germany created the tensions existing in East-West relations or whether these tensions continue to justify the division of Germany (1967, 286). In either event it is clear that Germany, granted the opportunity, can only be reunited if the people in both parts so choose.

Germany is divided as a result of its defeat in the most disastrous war of modern history. The victorious Allies, although all originally committed to a united Germany, later, in deciding on the ultimate form the German state of the future should take, were guided by different considerations. Before the Yalta Conference both Roosevelt and Churchill were inclined to dismember Germany but remained undecided, whereas Stalin wanted Germany divided, if necessary by force. By Yalta the military situation had changed, and Roosevelt and Churchill, fearing that a fragmented Germany would play into Soviet hands, insisted on a delay in the decision on dismemberment.

Since 1945 there had been a virtual stalemate among the powers on the "German question." At the 1959 foreign ministers' conference in Geneva, the Soviets rejected Christian Herter's "package-plan" for Berlin and reunification, which called for a step-by-step merger. The failure of subsequent efforts by the United States and Germany and the disaster of the Berlin Wall led in part to Adenauer's decline in strength in the 1961 elections and his forced resignation in 1963. But Erhard's position on unity in his opening policy statement differed little from existing policy, merely opposing any agreements between the Western powers and the Soviets "at the expense of Germany's vital interests."

German opinion polls on this question are revealing. During the 1950s, polls showed a preference for German reunification over European unification of 55 percent versus 27 percent in 1951, increasing to 70 percent versus 23 percent in 1959. By 1976, however, although reunification still remained the goal, only 13 percent of Germans, down from 29 percent in 1966, thought they would live to see it attained. Nonetheless, 72 percent of Germans responding to a poll taken in 1980 opposed deleting the following sentence from the preamble to the basic law: "The entire German people are called upon to achieve in self-determination the unity and freedom of Germany."

It has become evident, no matter what original expectations or intentions were, that the USSR long ago decided that its interests are best served by the continued division of Germany. The possibility of a united Germany they could control, or even a neutral Germany, must now seem remote to the Soviets. There is no evidence that such a position, even as a price to be paid for reunification, would be acceptable to the West Germans. The reason, of course, lies deep in the historic enmity between the Russian and Teutonic peoples, which has frequently dominated the course of events in Eastern Europe. During two world wars Germans have penetrated into the USSR and have inflicted tremendous casualties. Since its emergence from the ruins of World War II, the Soviet Communist state appears to have adopted as its basic premise the need to keep Germany divided and weak and the Eastern European countries Communist and under their military control.

The Soviets still seem to consider this necessary to prevent some future German leader from attempting to march again across the flat north European plain that separates Germany from Moscow and provides no natural line of defense. This view is reflected to a lesser and varying extent by the other European countries invaded by Nazi Germany, all of whom underwent suffering and destruction that are not easily forgotten. Although they do not say so bluntly, all share some fear of a united Germany. Having done well in the postwar period and having made great progress in gaining acceptance by their former enemies, the Germans now appear not to want to press their luck. They could risk bringing the unspoken into the open. The Germans have a long view of history and are willing to bide their time.

In his memoirs, Charles Bohlen (1973, 514–15) reports that when he was ambassador to France in the late 1960s de Gaulle confided to him that he secretly favored the division of Germany. "Why are you Americans so interested in the unification of Germany?" he asked. When Bohlen gave him the standard U.S. reply that the continued division of Germany would "cause trouble and would be dangerous to the peace of the world," de Gaulle shot back, "So would a united Germany." Bohlen attributed to de Gaulle the "Frenchman's instinctive fear of Germany." He respected but distrusted Germany.

Americans, particularly American Jews who remember most vividly the atrocities of the concentration camps, share this apprehension. But we are far away and came late into the war with Germany. The Germans did not invade us. Most Americans have largely forgiven the Germans as we have the Japanese, and the U.S. government has built alliances with both. As a result, we have had a clear policy on German reunification ever since it was proposed in the Byrnes Stuttgart speech in September 1946. Any remaining reservations go unspoken. When I went to Germany in 1963, I made it clear that, if this was the express wish of the German people, the United States supported their right, in exercising self-determination, to reunite.

The Germans did not in 1946, and do not now, expect the United States to take the initiative in making this happen. I used to say that there was no reason for us to be "more German than the Germans." If, taking into account the realities of their situation, they were willing to wait, why should we urge them to take risks for which, if ill-timed, they would have to pay a serious price? I encountered no criticism of official U.S. policy while in Germany, even though I spoke frequently on the question as realistically as I could. The only negative reactions we ever received resulted from the occasional careless expression of U.S. policy by an American official, which I was usually able to explain away.

But the situation regarding German reunification has changed since 1963. Since its realization has been so long delayed, its absence is more comfortable to deal with. Pain over the division of Germany has been relieved by arrangements for West German subsidies to improve the lot of East Germans, by visits of elderly relatives, and by easy communications between the two Germanies. Even though the freedom of individuals and the living standards in the two Germanies still differ markedly, conditions in the East have improved. Many East Germans have acquired a vested interest in the division, a sense of pride in their own meager accomplishments. There is a tendency in the East, and even in the West, to make a virtue of the necessity of division.

Other factors arising from the changes over time make reunification less attractive to West Germans. Since the CDU and CSU together have not since 1957–61 had a popular majority, a united Germany would almost certainly be socialist. The problem of socializing the West would be enormous, the loss in productivity, wages, and living standards great. A united Germany, it is generally accepted, would have to be a neutral Germany. No longer would there be U.S. or other Allied troops or a NATO guarantee of mutual defense.

If the Germans miscalculated, and the Soviets, after rendering them defenseless, returned to conquer or dominate them, it would be too late to return to the West. Unless the unity of Germany was attended by the unity of Europe, Germany would end up a part of Eastern rather than Western Europe. Although they have always had a fascination for the East and a feeling that they have a role to play there and a profit to make, the Germans have never envisioned turning their backs on the West. The hope, vaguely articulated, will always be there, but most Germans realize that reunification will be possible only if basic changes occur in either the nature of the Soviet Union or the organization of Europe, neither of which seems likely in the near future.

And if the Germans, in facing these realities, have been forced to lower their expectations for reunification, so must their European allies and the United States. Even though the term *cold war* is seldom used, many still consider *détente* a "dirty word." Starting with their deterioration following the Soviet invasion of Afghanistan, U.S.-Soviet relations reached their lowest point in a decade. If the prospects for German reunification hinge on a significant bettering of relations between the East and West, they would seem to be slight.

The attitude of West Germans toward their country's relations with East Germany has changed since the founding of the Federal Republic. The duality of German policy in seeking a balance between East and West, which had been present under Bismarck, the Weimar Republic, and Hitler, was changed decisively by Adenauer when, in one of his first acts as chancellor, he anchored German policy firmly to the West. Since then, integration of Germany with Europe and the United States has taken precedence over reunification. In October 1957 the FRG broke relations with Yugoslavia on the basis of what became known as the Hallstein Doctrine. The doctrine established that recognition of the GDR by any state would be considered an unfriendly act, that the FRG would break relations with any state that did so, and that the FRG would not recognize any state (except the USSR) that had already recognized the GDR.

The Soviet Union had offered a plan for German reunification in 1952, the conditions of which were unacceptable to West Germany. Frank Roberts, who as a member of the British Foreign Office had participated in answering these proposals, believes that they constituted only a Soviet tactical delaying move. He points out that West Germany was then being offered its sovereignty under the 1952 Bonn Agreements, which were linked to the ongoing negotiations for German membership in the European Defense Community. By 1959 the Soviet Union was proposing a peace treaty between the two Germanies. By

1963 there was a rising feeling among Germans that their orientation toward the West, successful though it had been in ensuring Germany's security and facilitating its remarkable economic recovery, was too inflexible. In particular, no progress had been made toward reunification. The German summit of 1955 and the foreign ministers' meeting following it had produced no progress on Germany unless certain (unspecified) fundamental conditions regarding the peace of Europe were met. The last Western proposal for reunification was rejected by the Soviets.

Adenauer had done little about Ostpolitik because he considered this could be successful only after Germany had created for itself a position of strength through integration with the West. Both he and the allies rejected Soviet offers made between 1952 and 1954 for reunification at the price of neutralization. This accorded with prevailing popular sentiment, as expressed in Germany's 1957 elections. Germany and the other Western powers tacitly accepted the status quo.

In 1961 Kennedy had made overtures to the Soviets to improve East-West relations. Although Adenauer himself had until then taken no such initiatives, German trade with the USSR and Eastern Europe had increased steadily up to 1962, when it dropped sharply due in large part to lack of German credits. Under the leadership of Schröder, Germany made overtures to the USSR in April 1962 in what was later called a "policy of movement." Schröder linked this move to the East with an effort to strengthen U.S.-German relations, which had deteriorated under Adenauer because of the Berlin Wall crisis and the generation gap between Adenauer and Kennedy. Schröder's turn to the United States angered the Gaullists. In June 1963 the FRG had, pursuant to Schröder's policy, proposed reestablishing official contact with the Eastern European states, as had already been done with Poland, to ease the atmosphere and to create a basis for better understanding.

Soon after his inauguration as chancellor in October, Erhard proposed increased trade with the Eastern states. In April 1964 Schröder made it clear that the FRG considered increased trade a step in reestablishing political contacts. An official German trade mission was established in Warsaw in 1963, and similar missions were opened in Budapest, Bucharest, and Sofia in 1964. Schröder's efforts, however, were limited by the realities of Germany's inability to recognize the Oder-Neisse line, to establish diplomatic relations with the GDR, or to abandon the Hallstein Doctrine. In January 1964 relations with Cuba were broken off when Fidel Castro recognized the GDR.

Within the SPD, Egon Bahr, who was Willy Brandt's closest adviser, introduced in 1963 the phrase "change through rapprochement" to describe his idea of a possible means of bringing East and West Germany closer. In January 1965 Fritz Erler, SPD foreign affairs spokesman, went so far as to propose that Germany recognize the Oder-Neisse frontier and normalize relations with Poland. In May 1965 Schröder advised the Bundestag that "abstract conceptions" would not be allowed to block the establishment of diplomatic relations with Eastern Europe. From then on countries that had recognized the GDR from the beginning were not subject to the Hallstein Doctrine.

On June 10, 1963, at American University in Washington, D.C., President Kennedy opened his dramatic broadside for détente in a speech in search of world peace (Kennedy 1964, 53–57). He called freedom "a process, a way of solving problems." World peace, he said, "does not require that each man love his neighbor; it requires only that they live together in mutual tolerance, submitting their disputes to a just and peaceful settlement. . . . We must, therefore, persevere in the search for peace in the hope that constructive changes in the Communist bloc might bring within reach solutions which now seem beyond us. . . . Our diplomats are instructed to avoid unnecessary irritants and purely rhetorical hostility." The young president had set a bold and idealistic course for the world to follow. The era of détente was underway.

What is détente, the concept so often spoken of in connection with East-West relations? Why did this obscure French word engage the world so long and give it hope? Ernst Majonica, a leading CDU theoretician, analyzed détente as

> methods of political conduct. The East-West conflict is to be contained through the search for cooperation between East and West until it dies down because of a lack of fuel. Thus one would begin by dealing with relatively simple problems until finally, after a long-drawn-out process, the hard-core problems could be tackled. The other side would be able to protect its vital interests and not be brought into a situation where the only choice open to it is either abject capitulation or atomic war, which would automatically put an end to all détente efforts. (1965, 38)

Majonica did not consider the search for détente the only road open— or even the most promising approach. It did not mean ignoring the justified demands of nations. He disagreed, though, with those who said that "the greatest loosening in the Eastern bloc took place in times of greatest tension."

In support of his thesis, Majonica quoted from an address I had given on East-West relations on February 18, 1964, before the Deutsche Gesellschaft für Auswartige Politik (German Foreign Policy Association), to the effect that the method of détente was "the patient search for possible areas of agreement, however small, as a contribution toward the eventual resolution of greater differences" (ibid., 38—39). I rejected the view that the avoidance of negotiations was justified as a means of creating tension to put pressure on the East for major concessions. Although I did not advocate concessions merely to create a favorable attitude on the part of the Soviets, but only to achieve concrete results, the attempt to negotiate was better than "drawing back from meaningful contact in mutual suspicion—to hurl recriminations at each other."

Long after this speech was delivered, the debate over détente, unfortunately obscured by emotions and semantics, continues. Revived by Kennedy, and later by Nixon and Kissinger, it has fallen again into disrepute. In the meantime, whatever of value détente might realize appears to become increasingly difficult to achieve.

13

Erhard at His Peak
December 1964–
June 1965

While tens of thousands of West Berliners visited relatives and friends in East Berlin for the first time since the Wall, Ludwig Erhard and I were visiting Lyndon Johnson at his Texas ranch. Johnson's early life had been spent in that part of southwest Texas which had, in the latter part of the nineteenth century, drawn many German settlers seeking land and political and religious freedom. Johnson was proud that he had been raised among Germans.

As vice president, Johnson had taken the initiative in offering to entertain Adenauer at his ranch near Johnson City. The same instinct led him to ask Erhard to meet him there during the new chancellor's first official visit. Johnson wanted to show off the German chancellors to his German neighbors, and vice versa. Both chancellors addressed local groups of German origin in German to the gratification of both sides. A few German commentators tried to interpret the Erhard invitation as second-class treatment, but Erhard, a homey, unpretentious man, considered it a compliment, as Johnson had intended.

Having preceded Erhard to the United States for preparatory briefings in Washington, I was there to help receive him when his Lufthansa plane landed at Austin on December 27, 1963. President and Mrs. Johnson, Gov. and Mrs. John Connally of Texas, and Secretary of State Dean Rusk, were also there. As announced, Erhard had with him only a small group, headed by Schröder. The warmth of the reception at the Johnson ranch, where a large *Willkommen* sign hung over the porch, presaged a congenial meeting. Erhard took readily to the big Texas hat Johnson gave him and made a statement to the many journalists there for the occasion. With only Rusk accompanying them, Johnson then took Erhard for a drive around the ranch, spotting almost one hundred deer. Later, alone with their interpreters, the two had ample opportunities for quiet talks sitting in rocking chairs on the shady ranch porches.

An important subject of conversation between the two chief executives was their common recognition of the need to ease the cold war. Both agreed that Germany should follow a more conciliatory policy toward the Soviet Union than it had under Adenauer. Both also agreed that there was little prospect for a reduction of tensions in Berlin or a successful nonaggression pact. The two leaders reaffirmed their commitment to eventual German reunification, with Johnson insisting that the Federal Republic, not the United States, should take whatever initiative seemed appropriate.

German fulfillment of the offset agreement was also a priority. Erhard was fully aware of the importance Johnson attached to this, given the continuing U.S. balance of payments deficit, and wanted very much to please him. He agreed not only to meet the offset but to make the necessary increases in the German defense budget.

Between relaxed, ranch-style meals, there were more detailed discussions between Rusk, Schröder, Carstens, Assistant Secretary of State Bill Tyler, National Security Adviser McGeorge Bundy, West German Ambassador Heinrich Knappstein, and myself (from State, unnumbered, U.S.-FRG Minutes, Dec. 29, 1963; State circular 1160, U.S.-FRG Economic Issues, Dec. 30, 1963; State circular 117, Erhard-LBJ Economic Subjects, Dec. 31, 1963). These included the Christmas pass problem, which was still deadlocked on the question of whether the Berlin Senate should be a direct signatory to the agreement. Schröder feared that the world public, seeing contacts between the two Germanies increased by this humane effort, might conclude that permanent agreement might be possible without basic institutional changes.

Rusk responded that although we had a cautious view on recognizing East Germany, "we were impressed with the longing of the East Germans to join their brothers in the West." He saw important implications with respect to wider East-West problems. Things were "moving in Eastern Europe," he declared. If the Eastern countries could "lose their fears" of Germany and a reunified Germany, some obstacles to reunification might be removed.

Schröder agreed but pointed out that Soviet and East European pressure was to change East German tactics for the benefit of the Soviet Union, and not the Federal Republic. The power of totalitarian rule should not be underestimated, he warned. Schröder felt that real progress could come only after basic changes in the world power structure or through armed intervention. He excluded the latter as a practical or desirable alternative. He was unconvinced that amelioration of their situation could change the nature of Communist regimes, Schröder said.

When the subject turned to economics, Erhard, who with Johnson had joined the group, reaffirmed West Germany's commitment to a successful Kennedy Round. Erhard had convinced de Gaulle that he meant business, Schröder added, thus contributing to the "reasonable compromises" that had already been achieved. Johnson emphasized his personal interest in the Kennedy Round because U.S. farmers were "adamant" in demanding access to foreign markets. Schröder replied that the problem was negotiable. The meeting ended in a warm renewal of close U.S.-German relations as they had developed during the postwar period. All considered the visit to have been a resounding success. At its close on December 29 Johnson and Erhard issued a joint communiqué whose principal points and language are of interest (*Department of State Bulletin*, Jan. 6, 1964).

The president and the chancellor agreed to oppose any arrangement that would help perpetuate a divided Germany and that they should explore all opportunities to improve East-West relations and ease tensions. They agreed that the West must strengthen the emerging Atlantic partnership, for which an increasingly unified Europe was vital. Johnson and Erhard concurred that the forthcoming trade negotiations should without delay seek to improve international trade and European economic integration, including agricultural as well as industrial products.

Johnson reviewed measures being taken to stabilize the U.S. international payments position, for which Erhard reaffirmed his support. Both emphasized the importance of aid to the developing nations. The two leaders reaffirmed their commitment to the peaceful reunification of the German people by self-determination in freedom. The chancellor promised to examine all paths that might lead to this goal and to improve West German relations with Eastern Europe. The president renewed the U.S. commitment to maintain the present six-division combat force in Germany for as long as it might be needed and to continue to fulfill U.S. commitments in Berlin. They also agreed that dollar expenditures for American forces in Germany would continue to be offset by German purchases of U.S. military equipment and that the MLF would strengthen Western defense.

Two minor occurrences during the Erhard visit provided me with a

new insight into Lyndon Johnson himself. On one occasion, while Erhard was resting, I was chatting with Johnson in his ranch living room
when the members of the Cabinet, who had flown down from Washington for this purpose, came in to take up their current problems with
the president. I stood up to leave, but Johnson waved me to sit down.
"Listen to this," he said. As I sat quietly, each separately reported
important developments in his respective field and sought Johnson's
decision on a variety of matters. After they left, Johnson turned to me
and said, "You probably don't think I'm a very good executive, do
you?" obviously expecting me to argue the contrary. Actually, I thought
he had done well and told him so. But I never forgot the insecurity
implicit in the question.

The other insight came from a discussion that began while we were
still at the ranch. I had urged that the president consider an early "get-
acquainted" trip to Europe. Johnson had visited there as vice president,
including a visit to Berlin after the erection of the Wall. But his contacts
with heads of government had been limited. After only a little more
than a month in the White House, he could not be expected to have
formulated any important new proposals. I argued, however, that it
would get him off to a better start as president if he visited the principal
West European heads of state, got to know them better and they him,
and obtained their views on key issues. This would show his interest
in Europe and would emphasize the continuity of American policy. He
could rely on Rusk to steer him to the right questions and keep him
out of trouble, whereas, if he put the visit off, he would be expected
to give his own opinion on the issues.

Johnson replied that his immediate advisers had urged him to wait
until the stage could be set for an important agreement. I pointed out
that such opportunities were rare and that questions might be raised if
he delayed too long. I declared that the good publicity and aura under
which he had undertaken his new responsibilities, combined with the
natural inquisitiveness of Europeans about a new American president,
would assure him a warm welcome, even though he might not have
much to say that was new.

Johnson was noncommittal, replying only that he would think about
the matter. I heard nothing more until I was about to depart from New
York to Bonn. The ingenious White House telephone operators caught
me at the TWA check-in desk at the newly renamed Kennedy Airport
in New York. While hundreds of passengers streamed by to check in
for their flights, Johnson and I must have discussed the question of an

early visit to Europe for twenty minutes. One of the problems that troubled the president was the propriety of his leaving Washington while the Vietnam War was in progress. This may have been a valid point. In something of an understatement under the circumstances, I pointed out that the war might last a long time and that the Europeans would resent his concentration on Vietnam to the exclusion of Europe. Before we hung up, Johnson asked me to get in touch with the U.S. ambassadors in the other key Western European countries and ask them their views when I got back to Bonn the next day.

After talking to my colleagues, I sent the president a summary of their opinions. Their reactions were admittedly mixed, but the majority favored an early visit, and no one foresaw a disaster. In the end, Johnson nonetheless decided not to come. I think this was a mistake, since the result was that he never made a proper official visit to Europe as president. His only visit was a brief trip in late April 1967, to attend Adenauer's funeral, where he had little opportunity for discussions. I believe his reluctance stemmed from the insecurity I have cited. He feared that he would not be able to make the impression or receive the recognition or press that Kennedy, who had graduated from Harvard instead of San Marcos Normal, had received so enthusiastically.

Everyone knows that after a brilliant start—the success of his Great Society program and polling the highest popular vote up to that time against Barry Goldwater in 1964—Johnson went into a decline. His popularity rating dropped from 70 percent in 1964 to 48 percent in 1966. The Tet Offensive of 1968, which demonstrated so dramatically the U.S. failure in Vietnam, the highly publicized "credibility gap" he had created, and his increasingly criticized personal behavior and style, left him no choice (as one of his intimates assured me at the time) but to stand down for reelection.

Shortly after his visit to the United States, Erhard reviewed developments in an hour-long statement before the Bundestag on January 9. He began with a ringing reaffirmation of the need for reconciliation with France. Erhard said that he had been asked on his U.S. visit how Germany's close relations with the United States could be squared with its friendship treaty with France. The Germans, he emphasized, would not fall between two stools. De Gaulle realized the importance of West Germany's defense relationship with the United States. Johnson had told him how important it was for Germany to have good relations with France.

Erhard said that his visit was characterized by a warm spirit, adding, amid laughter from the floor, that "a ranch is no Elysée Palace." He thought that the United States was pleased with its relations with the Federal Republic. The president had said that Germany was a strong European ally of the United States, not only because of the common endeavors of the two countries but also because Germany had come closest to accepting the concept of Atlantic partnership.

The United States, he noted, had welcomed West German trade agreements with the Eastern bloc countries. America stood firm in the defense of freedom but was also trying to reduce the dangers in the world. The Germans would try to make a similar contribution, he added. His government had taken a positive position on the MLF, but he had also reminded Johnson that other European partners were needed. The two had agreed to oppose long-term credits to the Eastern bloc. This would take away Khrushchev's incentive to arrive at acceptable agreements.

It was clear that Erhard regarded his statement to the Bundestag as an interim report to the nation on his stewardship as chancellor. Since he spoke from notes it was blunter and more effective than a prepared speech. Overall, reaction varied from "excellent" to "good." Adenauer approved Erhard's remarks on German-French relations. The FDP was less enthusiastic, viewing Erhard's statements on East-West relations as acceptance of the "status quo."

Taking our cue from Erhard's call for renewed activity in pursuit of European political unity, we reported to Washington on the need to reassess this possibility and to think anew about what stance the United States should assume in the light of various eventualities (telegram, Amemb Bonn to Secstate, 2451, Jan. 13, 1964).

The key substantive issue involved, I suggested, would probably be the extent to which a European consensus could be developed despite expected French resistance to any supranational arrangements. The German Foreign Office was skeptical that de Gaulle's stated desire for progress represented willingness to compromise. They assumed that the French would accept only some variant of a loose, consultative Europe des Patries, an agreement to reexamine the question of European federalism at a later date, but without commitment now. The French would prefer to expand the Franco-German treaty to include the other Common Market nations but would not soon accept the British in unification talks.

The Germans, I reasoned, believed that European political unity needed a stimulus, progress within the limits of the possible and acceptance of any reasonable proposals put forward, despite French limitations. From a tactical standpoint, however, the German Foreign Office preferred delay while moving French cooperation in the Kennedy Round and avoiding the thorny issue of British participation in the talks.

The United States should, I said, welcome an impetus toward European political unity, even though initially it might not go far. Indefinitely postponing could reduce interest and favor alternative national arrangements. I agreed with the State Department that we should keep an open mind on the form of initial steps. Experience had demonstrated that the self-interest of the other five members protected basic European political and security interests. It would be hard for de Gaulle to exploit any new political mechanism that might be created; rather, he could be forced to pay the price of concessions to the other five.

I suggested that Erhard might welcome a move on European political unification to mitigate the uncomfortable German relationship with France created by Adenauer. I reminded Washington that an important objective of European unity was to link Germany permanently to the West before it was subjected to temptation from the East.

Regarding U.S. tactics, I suggested that we assert our views early but, if basic U.S. interests were not involved, that we not inject ourselves into the intra-European debate. Any new European political forms should bear the label "made in Europe," including the solution of British participation. Conversely, we must not let it appear that any other country was our agent in European unity matters. I also suggested we leave timing to the chancellor.

I urged that we display sympathy toward unity initiatives that seem possible; make clear our view that this could lead toward an Atlantic partnership; indicate privately our hope that initiatives not detract from but strengthen the Kennedy Round; and espouse the ultimate adherence of the United Kingdom and other European powers to whatever mechanism would be created.

Not having had a recent opportunity for an extended discussion with Adenauer, I invited him to lunch on February 12 (memcon, Amemb Bonn, 1418, Feb. 12, 1965). Adenauer, who had recently celebrated his eighty-eighth birthday, was in fine physical and mental fettle, and had apparently escaped the nagging winter cold from which he often suffered. He restated many old theses and brought up a few new ones. In general, while stressing the importance of a continuing U.S. leadership role, he was critical of many specific U.S. policies and generally found reasons to justify current French policies.

Adenauer maintained that the Soviets remained the most dangerous opponent of the free world and that the West should make every effort to obtain advantages from the developing struggle between Russia and China. I noted that the hard-line policy on credits to the Soviet Union that he had been advocating had been supported by the United States and that, with the possible exception of the British, there seemed to be good prospects of holding the line against any extension of long-term credits. We were trying to limit loans to the Berne Union rules, which did not permit credit, and were urging other countries to do likewise.

Regarding NATO, Adenauer emphasized the need for an early look at required organizational modifications. He noted that the treaty would run out in 1969 and urged that the United States think now about required changes and discuss them within the alliance lest time run out. He had no changes to suggest, except that we might have to give up the unanimity rule. I attempted to disabuse him of his fear that our 1968 election would make it more difficult to reach a decision on any proposed changes.

Adenauer expressed pessimism regarding the possibility of progress on political integration. Here the British came in for considerable criticism. He argued essentially along the French lines that it was unreasonable to permit the British to participate in integration discussions on an equal basis when they were neither members of the Common Market organization nor committed to seeking membership.

He did finally agree, however, that the British should be given a chance to enter any political arrangement that might be made. He said that the best way to achieve this would be to avoid formal conferences and begin by taking informal soundings among the six nations as to the conditions under which unification might take place. If the six achieved some common ground, further informal discussions could be held with the British to see whether they were acceptable. In response to my query, Adenauer said that he did not believe de Gaulle could block British entry if the other five and the British were in agreement on terms.

Our conversation concluded with Adenauer's somewhat somber analysis of the internal German political situation, particularly the dying out of the old leadership and the uncertain quality of the new. Adenauer noted that the reason why he had agreed to remain on as party chairman was that Heinrich von Brentano's illness had removed him as the only likely replacement.

I later commented to the State Department that during this conversation Adenauer took positions that very probably resembled his stance within party councils. He professed a friendship for the United States that I believed was genuine. Criticism of specific U.S. policies, including the failure to exercise proper leadership, appeared, however, to have become a dominant strain in his thinking. He did not appear to have thought through what such U.S. leadership would really mean in relation to French policies that he defended. It seemed clear to me that Adenauer was far from ready to retire from the political scene and that if his choice was between devoting time to his memoirs (to which he referred on several occasions) or to politics, the former would suffer every time.

Before leaving for Paris on February 13, Erhard asked me to call on him for a general review of current problems (telegrams, Amemb Bonn to Secstate, 2881, 2882, 2883, and 2885, Feb. 13, 1963). We talked for an hour and a half about his forthcoming visit with President de Gaulle, about French recognition of Communist China, and about the status of the MLF. Erhard wanted us to regard his visit to Paris as one of the regular meetings agreed to under the Franco-German treaty "to maintain contacts." He assured me that no change of policy was involved on the part of the Federal Republic, an allusion to the then-taboo subject of recognizing mainland China, or in the loyalty and friendship of the German government toward the United States. I was not to believe everything the press was saying with regard to his visit, Erhard told me. He assured me that he would much prefer to be going to the United States.

Germans nonetheless agreed with de Gaulle on the question of friendship between France and Germany, he said, and in his view of German-German and Berlin matters. He expected de Gaulle to tell him that he sought a Europe independent of the United States. Erhard expected to tell de Gaulle that he felt that Germany was not controlled, but rather protected, by the American alliance. Referring to de Gaulle's recent press conference of January 31, Erhard said he had been shocked at the harshness of de Gaulle's attacks against Britain and the United States.

I asked Erhard whether we could hold the line against long-term credits to the Soviets, even if the British extended such credits. He seemed to think we could. But he felt it depended entirely on the French. The Italians, in his opinion, could not be counted on. Referring to de Gaulle's effect on European integration, Erhard said that progress was impossible there too as long as de Gaulle kept on "going it alone." Erhard thought it best to delay any discussions of British Common Market entry until after the impending British elections, during which time opinion in Europe might develop along lines favorable to the British. But even if political unity discussions were thus delayed, he was convinced that de Gaulle would still oppose British inclusion. "We are doing our best to keep the Common Market going," he said, "but it is indeed a difficult task."

Erhard said that he was also "afraid for the Kennedy Round." Inflationary conditions in Italy and France made it difficult for those countries to make drastic tariff cuts without currency manipulation, which would involve a loss of prestige. I replied that we were also much concerned and hoped that he could make it clear to de Gaulle that he considered France, during talks in Brussels the year before, to have committed itself to participating wholeheartedly in these negotiations.

In light of the great interest Johnson expressed to Erhard in Texas regarding German aid to developing countries, I told Erhard that we had been gratified to hear that consideration was being given to raising the requests for development aid in the current budget from DM 750 million to DM 1 billion. Erhard seemed somewhat skeptical about this, pointing out that there was a large overhang of undisbursed funds already appropriated. Granting this, I said that it was still important not to decrease the amount currently available for "new starts," which would result in a deficiency of funds available for disbursement in subsequent years.

While Erhard worried about de Gaulle, the U.S. government made another effort to focus attention on the beleaguered MLF (State Department to all NATO capitals, Feb. 17, 1964). The prognosis was circumspect but bleakly hopeful. After a thorough review of the State Department's position, I replied that the arguments presented in favor of the MLF were indeed formidable but that its chances of success still depended on the Europeans. France was out. If Britain opted out, too, taking Belgium and Holland along, the remaining countries—Italy, Greece, and Turkey—seemed meager. I was concerned for the future of MLF and what would happen if it failed.

On April 16 Ambassador Thomas Finletter, the U.S. permanent representative to NATO, visited Bonn, largely to talk about the MLF. President Johnson, he reported, was fully cognizant of the need to move ahead. The study period was now over and the action phase must begin, Johnson had agreed. This would require close German cooperation. Finletter believed that the overall MLF situation was favorable and that the United Kingdom would eventually come in.

Erhard assured Finletter that the Germans were still on board and wished to avoid any suspicion that they wanted a part of the French force de frappe. A major point favoring the MLF in German eyes, Erhard added, was that it would tie the United States and Germany together in Europe. The SPD supported the government on MLF despite some opposition, and Erhard doubted that there would be any trouble getting it through the Bundestag. Having always been lukewarm on this issue, I personally thought that both men were engaged in wishful thinking as a result of their strong personal commitments.

Yet even in early June, Fritz Erler told me that European participation in the MLF could be a useful means to familiarize military leaders with what he called the "awesome potential of nuclear weapons" and that it could correct some of the "naive strategic concepts" currently being considered in Europe (telegram, Amemb Bonn to Secstate, 4540, June 8, 1964). In particular, Erler thought it would restrain the impulse to respond immediately with nuclear weapons to any limited attack from the East. He also thought that the MLF might provide leverage for ultimate German reunification, either by constituting a bargaining chip to be yielded for political concessions or as proof that a reunited Germany would "not strike out on its own" in the nuclear field.

During a meeting with Schröder on March 11, Schröder had told me about meetings of the CDU steering group held over the past several days, which had dealt principally with the question of East-West negotiations (letter, McGhee to Thomas M. Finletter, files of Amemb Bonn, Aug. 14, 1964). No one had taken a die-hard line against negotiations, not even Baron Gutenberg. Majonica had also been quite reasonable. The discussion had included the question of which position would have a greater tendency to freeze the status quo. Schröder believed a refusal to negotiate at all would be most likely to have this effect. He did not say how strong a position he had taken but commented to me as an aside that he was not, in fact, the inventor of the "policy of movement" toward the East generally attributed to him; he had inherited it.

Bundestag member Kurt Birrenbach, who was at the meeting, later advised me that Schröder had not taken a strong line and had only spoken briefly after a consensus had emerged. This, according to Birrenbach, represented a victory for the seeking of limited agreements with the Soviets. Birrenbach said that my recent well-publicized speech on East-West relations before the German Foreign Policy Association had been quoted in the debate in a helpful way.

1965

February 13	President Johnson authorizes bombing in North Vietnam
March 25	The Bundestag approves an extension for the prosecution of National Socialist crimes
April 28	The U.S. military intervenes in the Dominican Republic
May 23	Diplomatic relations between Israel and the FRG announced; Arab states, Libya, Morocco, and Tunisia break off relations with the FRG
May 18–28	Queen Elizabeth II visits the FRG
August 19	Verdict is given in the Auschwitz trial
September 19	Elections are held for the Fifth German Bundestag
December 5	German Catholic bishops send a letter to the bishops of Poland

14

Clouds on
the Horizon
May 1964–May 1965

O n May 11, 1964, Secretary of Defense Robert McNamara returned to Bonn for his first visit with Erhard as chancellor (telegram, Amemb Bonn to Sec State, 1511, May 11, 1964). The meeting provided an opportunity for a hard-hitting appeal for German support of the United States's increasingly difficult situation in Vietnam. After noting the continuing high level of expenditures in our defense budget and our determination to meet our worldwise security obligations, McNamara stated that he hoped that the Federal Republic would be able to support us in our efforts to defend the free world in areas outside Europe. In particular, McNamara hoped for a strong statement in favor of the South Vietnamese effort to defeat the Viet Cong, for public support of U.S. assistance to the South Vietnamese, and for a direct contribution to the war effort, for example, a German military medical unit.

Erhard agreed. He said that he had discussed in Texas with President Johnson the need for all members of the alliance to help defend the Free World against communism wherever necessary. The FRG fully supported U.S. efforts to bring about a relaxation of East-West tensions in its relations with the Soviets and with Eastern Europe. They had not objected when the United States had taken actions calculated to relieve tensions—such as the reduction of the production of fissionable material.

McNamara was grateful to Erhard for his commitment to fulfilling the offset agreement. Erhard replied that he supported this arrangement in principle, but not as a merchant "looking at his books to see who needs paying." He thought it understandable that as more military

143

equipment could be made in Germany there would be less need to buy it in the United States. Given Germany's favorable export position, McNamara thought that the Federal Republic should continue to manufacture for export rather than shift to manufacture of military equipment. Erhard replied that the issue was not the balance of payments but the budget itself. McNamara pointed out that the German defense budget was being altered to face rising troop costs, reducing the amount available for equipment purchases. Erhard replied by pointing to the importance of German economic stability to Europe as a whole. If Germany slipped, the prospects for Europe's further economic progress would be greatly diminished. McNamara said he fully recognized the immense influence Erhard's accomplishments in rebuilding the German economy had exercised on the stability of Europe. But he emphasized that the United States simply could not continue to maintain forces in Germany without full offset payments.

Changing the subject Erhard said that Germany pursued its policy toward NATO for political reasons. As he promised President Johnson in Texas, he wanted Germany to help decrease East-West tensions. It greatly assisted Germany in carrying out its Eastern European policy and bettering its bilateral relations with the Soviets, if all German forces were assigned to NATO, Erhard pointed out. Under such circumstances, the Soviets knew Germany would be unable to use force independently. In any event, he added with a smile, the Americans would not permit this.

The meeting showed the trend in U.S.-German relations caused by several unresolved problems between the two countries. More than ever, McNamara wanted an increased German contribution in Vietnam. While promising continued support in principle and at existing civil aid levels, Erhard was noncommittal. He expressed concern that a more conspicuous German posture would have adverse reactions to Germany's relations with the Eastern bloc and to reunification.

Both leaders expressed apprehension about de Gaulle's future intentions toward NATO. I thought it was significant that Erhard hedged in his response to McNamara's pitch for a full German offset payment, and I was struck by how Erhard pointed out the possible effect on the German economy, which was so important to the future stability of Europe. McNamara's response startled me. Although I realized that it was largely tactical, reflecting McNamara's well-known ability to apply pressure, I thought the threat to remove U.S. forces had gone too far and would not be credible to Erhard. The pressure on Germany, however, was to continue and increase.

As a follow-up to Erhard's visit to the ranch in December, arrangements were being made for Erhard to meet with President Johnson in Washington on June 12. Both the embassy and the State Department anticipated that German reunification would be the subject that Erhard and Schröder would be most anxious to discuss.

In a meeting on May 8, Erhard had asked me to convey to President Johnson his views on the German reunification proposal now before the Ambassadorial Group, a proposal based on the same principles that Erhard and Johnson had discussed during their December meeting (telegram, Amemb Bonn to Secstate, 4100, May 8, 1964). Erhard had gained the impression that the German proposal had not been well received by the other three members of the group, which would provoke an acute German internal political problem. Suspicion that the United States had been responsible would play into the hands of the small but powerful pro-French group in Germany, Erhard told me.

Erhard favored the policy, which he and President Johnson had agreed upon, of seeking limited understandings with the Soviets, even if the chances of reaching a major agreement were slight. Erhard considered it important to demonstrate to the German people that reunification had not been forgotten. I replied that the main problem about the FRG proposal was not whether it was negotiable but whether a credible Western position could be developed, one that was realistic but did not represent a retrogression.

It was obvious that Erhard, who had been criticized domestically for lack of progress toward reunification, was under great pressure from the Adenauer wing of the CDU to produce results. Although the precise form such a proposal would take was not clear, Erhard badly needed four-power agreement to a concerted move that would indicate support for the idea of German reunification. It was hoped that this would include substantive terms, in addition to the perennial proposal for a standing four-power commission on Berlin and Eastern problems, which was a possible fallback position.

Another issue sure to be on the agenda during the second Erhard-Johnson talks was German assistance to the U.S. war effort in Vietnam. The increased tempo of the war had led to a rising requirement for U.S. military assistance, including equipment and both advisers and training personnel, who numbered sixteen thousand. The cost of the war was escalating. Questions were being raised both in the United States and abroad about U.S. objectives in Vietnam and where they would lead. So far U.S. military involvement—and casualties—had been slight. As the pressure on the United States increased, President Johnson stepped up pressure on our allies both for support for our policies and token nonmilitary assistance to the South Vietnamese.

During my call on Erhard on May 8, I also made a general plea for FRG support in helping the South Vietnamese defend their freedom (telegram, Amemb Bonn to Secstate, 4100, May 8, 1964). I pointed out that up to this point the United States had borne the entire burden of outside support, which we believed should be shared by the other nations of the free world. So far the response had been disappointing. We had submitted a list of personnel requested by the South Vietnamese. We hoped the German government would respond in terms of many hundreds of men, not just a handful.

I indicated to Erhard that it had been rumored in the international press that the German government was only lukewarm in its support of U.S. policy in South Vietnam; we believed this should be set straight. We sought support from other free world nations at what we considered to be a critical time in South Vietnam. The secretary of state planned to talk with Foreign Minister Schröder about this in The Hague on May 11. Erhard indicated that he fully understood the issue but gave no indication as to what, if anything, the German government would do.

On May 29 the embassy sent an aide-memoire to the Foreign Office urging the Germans to contribute surgical teams or a hospital ship to Vietnam. The pressure from Washington was mounting. Last minute instructions from the State Department for the meeting were directed at pressuring Erhard to increase German aid to developing countries to match the level of percentage of GNP spent by the United States and to avoid direct U.S. involvement in the strategy and tactics for European unification. Both approaches gave me trouble, as I pointed out to the State Department in a response. Final word from the Foreign Office advised that Erhard's particular concern was to get an agreement from President Johnson on a new impetus toward European unification efforts.

For background, I informed the State Department of where I thought Erhard stood politically in Germany (telegram, Amemb Bonn to Secstate, 4541, June 8, 1964). Erhard was riding a crest of popularity. Polls showed him leading his own party by 52 percent to 33 percent, and he was given a large part of the credit for the CDU's sweeping gains in the recent state elections in Baden-Württemberg. He was also regarded as the leader in the defense of the deutsche mark and a major promoter of European unity. According to Gallup, 71 percent approved the way he handled his job, whereas only 23 percent believed that Brandt, as leader of the opposition, could do better. There was no unemployment; indeed 850,000 jobs were unfilled. Wages were up 8.5 percent compared with a 2.5 percent rise in the cost of living. Overall production was also up 8.5 percent.

There were nonetheless critics, particularly among the press and the intellectuals, who belittled Erhard's policies and style and pointed to his tendency to follow rather than to lead current trends. We concluded that Erhard's support was wide but not unlimited and that there was a basis for what one commentator called "doubts as to the Chancellor's decisiveness and strength of character."

The continuing hostility of Adenauer, Strauss, and other CDU Gaullists obviously worked to Erhard's disadvantage. Adenauer was no longer on speaking terms with him. Erhard was baffled by his adversaries' slavish support of de Gaulle in the face of French views on Eastern policy, détente, and European nuclear policy that differed sharply from traditional German positions. Gaullist support for union with France as a first step toward political unification of Europe also ran counter to the views of other Common Market countries.

What Washington needed to be aware of was Erhard's determination to hold the line on his overall budget. Our interest in increased German aid to developing countries would accordingly depend on how strong a pitch President Johnson would make. The Germans, meanwhile, were preparing a reduction in aid. As a conciliatory gesture, I urged that we express approval of Erhard's interest in Europe-building, even though we did not wish to take a stand on any particular tactic. I thought we should urge a German military budget level adequate to meet NATO force goals and German offset obligations to us and that the president should emphasize strong support for a successful Kennedy Round while remaining ambiguous on the difficult question of grain price.

I thought there was little chance for even indirect military support for the war in Vietnam, given the unpopularity in Germany of aid to Vietnam. But in anticipation of the Washington talks, the Foreign Office advised us that the German Cabinet had approved more aid to South Vietnam for economic development (telegram, Amemb Bonn to Secstate, 4566, June 9, 1964). The projects were to be handled as normal economic aid, and a hospital ship, staffed by Red Cross personnel, was also under consideration.

We considered that the domestic success of Erhard's visit would be largely judged by the extent to which he could persuade Johnson of the need for a new initiative toward German reunification. Erhard would also be judged by public perception of his forcefulness in presenting the German position on other outstanding issues. But in June 1964 German reunification was hardly among the high-priority items on the White House agenda. Although the United States had always given lip service to the goal of reunification, attainment of it had grown increasingly unlikely. Particularly after the Cuban missile crisis, the priorities of U.S. policy had shifted toward a search for détente with the Soviets.

At their meetings in Washington, Johnson told Erhard that he considered this the best approach both to reunification and to progress on other issues pending with the Soviets. Although Erhard and Schröder were encouraged to continue on their own, they could expect no initiatives on the part of the United States (memcon, President and Erhard, Department of State, June 10, 1964). The final communiqué declared only that "there can be no stability in Europe as long as Germany is divided." From a German viewpoint, this was not much. The communiqué also said: "The Chancellor stated that his government would increase assistance to South Vietnam in the political and economic fields."

Pursuant to this, Erhard pledged economic aid in the value of approximately $15 million, the largest contribution of any nation but the United States. He knew he had to, and he was prepared to do it, but he knew he would face difficulties at home. McNamara and Johnson's pressure had achieved a modest result. From a political viewpoint, however, even the limited German contribution was of considerable importance to Johnson.

But this was not the end of the story. On July 2, 1964, I received ex officio, to the ambassador from the president, a telegram stepping up further the pressure on our Western allies to make a contribution to the war in Vietnam (circular telegram, for the Ambassador from the President, 14, July 2, 1964). This telegram was not, of course, sent just to Germany. It said in part:

> Gravely disappointed by the inadequacy of our friends and allies in response to our request that they share the burden of free world

responsibility in Vietnam. Although they indicate sympathy, their actual performance does not show that they recognize their share of this responsibility. . . . I am charging you personally to see that governments understand how seriously we view the challenge. Must think in terms of many hundreds. I will review your progress. Hope to see every success in near future.

In early July, Charles de Gaulle came to Bonn, and Adenauer did his best to embarrass Erhard, who hosted the visit. The former chancellor had invited de Gaulle to visit his office first, thus making him half an hour late for his meeting with Erhard. Adenauer criticized the way de Gaulle had been received by Erhard's government. Reports I received from the Foreign Office on July 10 indicated that the meeting had not gone well (telegram, Amemb Bonn to Secstate, 107, July 10, 1964). "Why does Germany want to join the MLF?" de Gaulle asked Erhard. "It is not a European effort." He did not, however, offer Germany an alternative.

When de Gaulle asked Erhard why he supported U.S. policy in Southeast Asia, Erhard pleaded loyalty to the United States as an ally while admitting that Germans knew little about Southeast Asia and lacked strong feelings on the question. According to Carstens, de Gaulle chided Erhard for this reply, whereupon Erhard reminded de Gaulle that de Gaulle had not consulted him when he recognized the People's Republic of China.

Erhard told de Gaulle that he was quite willing to continue cooperating with him, but not at the expense of breaking with the United States and the other Western allies. Germany needed U.S. support for reunification and for its security. When Erhard described his goal as a Europe larger than West Germany and France, de Gaulle assured him the other Europeans would follow a German-French initiative. Erhard expressed doubts about this, suggesting instead that, fearing Franco-German domination, the others would look to Britain and the United States.

On July 12 Erhard spoke at his party's convention in Munich, moving decisively to assert his leadership and to put the Gaullists in their place. He challenged his opponents to attempt a vote of no confidence, knowing they would dare nothing of the sort. Erhard laid out these points as the basic elements of his policy: the indispensability of NATO for Germany and Germany's support for the MLF; the need to complete the economic integration of Europe with new political starting points toward European political unity, on the basis of the six members of the EEC rather than a smaller forum; the value of the Franco-German treaty, but not as an end in itself; the impossibility of moving forward in Europe without giving full trust to the United States in view of the degree to which Germany, Europe, and the United States were bound together; the necessity for a successful conclusion to the Kennedy Round, without letting it be "reduced to the single question of the grain price"; and, finally, patience and firmness in East-West relations, since real changes could occur only through deeds, not words.

After commenting that a Europe built on the basis of France and Germany alone would be a contradiction in itself, Erhard mentioned that he would later come forward with new proposals on European unity. He added that the period after the U.S. and U.K. elections would appear to be a favorable time for the NATO governing heads to come to agreement on NATO problems. Erhard showed himself stronger on this occasion than at any time I can recall, and it appeared that popular reaction would be overwhelmingly in his favor.

The next day I had Adenauer to lunch to ask him his views of the last ten days (telegram, Amemb Bonn to Secstate, 136, July 13, 1964). He replied that Erhard's speech was "not very good," made several derogatory remarks about Erhard's lack of firmness, and implied that there would be little follow-up. Adenauer also made his usual spirited defense of de Gaulle and his policies, emphasizing the sad state France would now be in had de Gaulle not returned to power. But he was obviously interested in playing down the uproar of recent days and could probably be counted on to breathe reconciliation and party harmony in public while continuing to make snide remarks about Erhard in private. His preeminent concern for electoral victory in 1965 and his recognition that internal squabbling could only run counter to its achievement put him on the side of those counseling restraint to the firebrands on the right.

At eighty-nine, the former chancellor seemed to have tapped a rejuvenescent spring. He saw nothing incongruous in his expressions of concern for the survival of the comparatively youthful, seventy-three-year-old de Gaulle and, in fact, outlived him. Adenauer's underlying assumption seemed to be that he himself would be around for a long time to come. It nevertheless appeared that Erhard had won this round.

On August 6 Schröder asked me to visit him at his vacation home on the Friesian island of Sylt (telegram, Amemb Bonn to Secstate, 166, Aug. 7, 1964). He wanted me to brief him on the alarming developments in North Vietnam of the previous few days. I enjoyed my day with Schröder and his wife at their simple but attractive cottage on this delightful sandy spot so popular among top-level Germans. We reviewed in considerable detail the implications of what appeared to be North Vietnamese naval attacks against American destroyers in the Tonkin Gulf. After obtaining congressional support, Johnson had ordered a counterattack. In a speech at Syracuse University on August 5 he had also made it clear that the United States would retaliate against any other nation seeking to widen the hostilities.

I advised Schröder of the reactions of our other allies and the communist states concerned. Schröder expressed approval of President Johnson's actions and sympathy with the new situation faced by the United States. But since Germany was not a member of the United Nations and was not a Southeast Asian power, it was not in a position to do anything to support us. He therefore believed Germany should be relatively restrained in its public statements.

In the course of a long afternoon in the intimacy of his summer cottage, Schröder also gave me some insight into his personal situation. He had been under constant attack from his Gaullist colleagues since de Gaulle's visit in July, and only in the past week, he believed, had he made his peace with Adenauer. Indeed, he was now on better terms with Adenauer than with Erhard, whom Adenauer never ceased to disparage and undercut. Schröder showed no particular concern about his relations with Erhard, although it was clear that there was not much coordination, and perhaps not even much rapport, between the two.

He believed that the French, supported by the German Gaullists, would make an increasing effort to block the MLF as the date for its implementation drew near. The French argued that Europe should rely on the force de frappe, since France was part of Europe and would share its fate, while the Americans were distant and could not be relied on to risk their own people in order to save European lives "when the chips are down." When challenged about the modest size of their nuclear force, Schröder said, the French described it as a lever to force the involvement of American nuclear power. Schröder would reply that, in such a case, the United States needed but to advise the Russians of their intent to keep their distance. The Russians could hardly be expected to take seriously a deterrent that invited France's own destruction. But to this the French would say only that the Soviets could not count on them acting rationally.

In reply I expressed to Schröder the U.S. belief that the defense of

Europe and North America was indivisible and that Europe could count on U.S. nuclear power to be available both as a deterrent and a response to a Soviet "breakthrough." I pointed to the large number of Americans in Germany and repeated Rusk's argument that we could not afford to have our atomic weapons in Europe captured. Given the vulnerability and small size of the force de frappe, we did not believe either that the Soviets would view it as a credible deterrent. Schröder agreed but added that we could help him by providing a good answer to every argument the French could make in favor of their force.

When I visited Berlin shortly afterward, its economy was again a problem. In a previous meeting with him, on April 24, Willy Brandt had assured me that the political and economic situation in Berlin was stable. The rate of economic growth was satisfactory and the federal financial subvention for fiscal year 1964 was expected to be adequate. On August 12 the Berlin Senat, on the initiative of Mayor Albertz, who ranked just below Brandt, gave me a somewhat different picture. He and other leading members of the Senat provided me a detailed briefing on the economic, demographic, and cultural aspects of West Berlin. Of particular interest was the large difference between Bonn and Berlin on the 1965 federal contribution to the Berlin budget. By its nature, West Berlin was and remains a heavily subsidized city. During the fiscal years 1961–65, expenditures funded by local taxes had declined from 45.4 percent to 33.7 percent, whereas those funded from Bonn increased from 39.4 percent to 47.4 percent. Now there seemed to be a DM 385 million difference of opinion regarding the size of Bonn's contribution. This difference exceeded the 5 percent Bonn had set on budget increases for the coming year. If the subsidy were cut, the result would be a decline in planned construction projects, which would adversely affect Berlin's economic development. Brandt might then ask the allied embassies in Bonn to intercede in Berlin's behalf.

West Berlin, I was reminded, was a part of the social order of West Germany, where 68 percent of the city's industrial production was sold. The political objective of the Berlin government was enough economic expansion to make the city a modern industrial center. The idea was not only to solve internal Berlin problems but to prove to the world the superiority of the democratic free enterprise system over the Communist regime in East Berlin and East Germany. But its success in achieving this had been decreasing. Growth had declined from 5.2 percent in 1962 to 2.6 percent in 1963, and, whereas savings had doubled between 1958 and 1964, productivity increases over the preceding year had declined from 10.5 percent to 7.7 percent. The rate of increase in industrial orders was only about half the increase in West Germany. Although the Senat considered the overall picture gratifying, it also wanted to add to the 172 outside firms that had settled in Berlin since the Wall was built.

Contrary to the Soviet assumption that West Berlin would wither, the population of the city had actually increased in 1963 by 13,170, reaching a total 2,192,700. This contrasted with a net population decrease during the preceding five years averaging 10,000 a year. The inflow had resulted from government income supplements, subsidies for new households, favorable career opportunities, and help in education. But it was believed that it also derived from the willingness of young West Germans to commit themselves politically by a stay in Berlin. The age structure, however, was unfavorable. The 15–45 age cohort, who should have outnumbered the 45–65 age cohort by half, were only equal to it.

As a result of efforts to reunite families, 13,000 people had moved to Berlin from the East since the erection of the Wall, 92 percent over 60. While employment remained level in 1964 at 895,000, the number of unemployed had also decreased to 8,727, in contrast to 22,500 open jobs. The principal limitation in attracting outside labor was housing, five thousand new units being needed over the next two years.

The Senat hoped to make up for the loss since 1961 of Berlin's function as an East-West bridge by making the city more culturally and educationally interesting. With assistance from U.S. private sources, an academy of arts as well as other schools and institutes had been established. Museums, theaters, concerts, and motion pictures were subsidized to attract visitors from the West. An effort had been made to recreate in West Berlin the equivalent of a cultural capital of Germany. Berlin had already been reestablished as the museum center of Germany, and the Free University, founded in 1948 with U.S. help, was so full that it had to reject six thousand applications a year. The great effort that had been made with U.S. help, including that by the Ford Foundation, was bearing fruit. But age group distribution, the housing shortage, and West Berlin's increasing dependence on Bonn were portents of trouble ahead.

I was not discouraged about the future of Berlin, in spite of some grave problems revealed by the Senat briefing. Berlin still had a great deal going for it: the strong budgetary and other support of the Federal

Republic, the token military support of the allies, guaranteeing their full involvement in the event of an aggressive Soviet move; but even more important the magnificent spirit of the Berliners themselves. They willingly accepted hardships and risks not present in the rest of West Germany, in their determination to "stick it out in Berlin." And time has still not greatly eroded that spirit.

Another threat to world peace was also arising in distant Vietnam, even though the war to this point had involved few U.S. casualties and not great dollar costs. But as the situation worsened, the United States became increasingly concerned about the support of its allies, and Henry Cabot Lodge, who was later to succeed me in Bonn but was then U.S. ambassador to Saigon, was dispatched to Europe to plead our cause.

On August 25, Lodge called on Chancellor Erhard at his villa on the Tegernsee to acquaint him with our innermost thoughts and aims on Southeast Asia (airgram, Amemb Bonn to Department of State, A-463, Sept. 8, 1964). We were grateful for what the West Germans were doing to help us but were interested in obtaining their understanding of and agreement with our policies. Lodge declared that Vietnam was a world-wide and not just a regional problem and that a Communist victory would have repercussions everywhere. He pointed, for example, to the possible revival of a "fortress America" mentality in the United States. Erhard agreed and said that the free world could not be grateful enough for the American effort in Vietnam, though the solution might be uncertain.

Lodge stressed that the war was essentially with guerrillas and ter-rorists. When the terrorists could no longer go into the average citizen's home for help, the war would be over. When de Gaulle said that Amer-ica wants only a military solution, he was wrong. All Americans, in-cluding the military, knew that a solution must also be found in the social, psychological, political, economic, and technical areas, Lodge continued. Although military action was essential to provide basic se-curity, the United States could not win this fight simply by killing the Viet Cong. This was why he considered it so important to get young Germans to Vietnam to engage in noncombat work alongside the one thousand Americans in trade, agriculture, and medicine. Young Ger-man doctors would be particularly valuable in a country like Vietnam, he emphasized. Lodge thought their involvement would make a favor-able impression both in Vietnam and in the United States.

Erhard replied that Vietnam had of course been a major source of difference between Germany and France. De Gaulle had gone so far as to claim during his June meeting with Erhard that German financial and moral support for South Vietnam was against the content and the spirit of the Franco-German treaty. This difference was a serious problem, Erhard continued, but it would not change the German position on Vietnam. The Germans knew that freedom must be defended everywhere in the world, not merely in Berlin and Germany.

Lodge responded that the war now was essentially in low gear and that the Chinese, despite their verbal violence, were cautious. The United States hoped to win the struggle by having the South Vietnamese make the main effort. A totally different situation would arise if the nature and scope of the conflict were to change. The cost of the war to the United States was only $1.1 million per day, less per year than the cost of an aircraft carrier. We had lost just two hundred men in the past two and a half years. In response to Erhard's query, Lodge reported that the Belgians were now sending an ambassador to Saigon, the Dutch had agreed to send a technical mission and to place Vietnamese students in the Netherlands, and, although hampered by forthcoming elections, the Danes had promised to do something.

Erhard asked whether Vietnam was a partisan issue in the United States. Lodge observed that it would be political suicide for any American politician to advocate U.S. withdrawal. What we were trying to do, he explained, was to pull Vietnam into the twentieth century. He stressed that there was little national patriotism as we know it in Vietnam, but only a sort of perversion of Confucianism that emphasized looking after one's own family and oneself. Politically uninterested peasants comprised 85 percent of the population.

Lodge was unusually frank in his analysis. He displayed complete candor in describing to Erhard the reasons for, and degree of, U.S. involvement and the dangers that lay ahead. Although admitting the possibility that the United States might have to play a military role, which up to that time had been minimal, he in no way anticipated later massive U.S. involvement with ground forces.

Erhard's reaction to Lodge's presentation was influenced by the fact that Germany had never had direct interests in Southeast Asia and was reluctant to undertake responsibilities there. German budgetary limitations also made it difficult to offer much financial assistance. It was still too soon after World War II for Germans to engage in foreign military enterprises. Anyway, Germans tended to see Vietnam less as a test of U.S. will than of U.S. wisdom in making such a large commitment. They did not want us to get so involved there that we might be forced to reduce our forces in Germany or our commitment to Western Europe, which they considered the most vital common interest.

Erhard's questions were remarkably astute, particularly in retrospect. He addressed all the most disagreeable possibilities that we might face in Vietnam. But while Lodge answered as honestly as he could, he could not have predicted the disaster we eventually faced. Erhard expressed full support and appreciation for U.S. policy in defending the free people in Vietnam from Communist domination. He also assured continuation of present financial and technical assistance to Vietnam. He was noncommittal, however, about any additional assistance. Lodge, who had made a masterful presentation, tactfully did not press him.

In light of my experience as coordinator of Greek-Turkish aid in 1947–49, I was concerned to learn from the meeting that U.S. personnel in Vietnam had become involved in combat to the point of occasionally taking command. It had been a basic principle during the guerrilla action in Greece that U.S. forces not be exposed to, or participate in, military action. We had not lost a man in combat, and had been free to withdraw if we found we were supporting an impossible goal. Once we started shooting in Vietnam, I feared, Vietnam would become "our war."

But my thoughts soon returned to European problems. On November 5 the German government advised us of the European unity proposal it had submitted to the European Commission and the five Common Market governments two days earlier. We had been expecting this for a long time, since Erhard had made it clear that it was one of his main objectives. The proposal climaxed months of efforts by Erhard to formulate new ideas for European unity that would win support from other Europeans and the United States. The German proposal focused on step-by-step advances. In the first phase, consultations between governments were to begin as early as possible to facilitate a coordinated policy on important questions of general interest. Prerequisites would be set for the admission of other European countries. Member governments were to be advised by a consultative committee of representatives acting solely in the common interest.

As a means of approaching economic unity, the Federal Republic proposed formation of a customs union among member countries, starting with a 10 percent reduction in internal Common Market tariffs before 1965. Removal of the remaining 20 percent of industrial tariffs was to take place before 1967 if a common agricultural policy could also be foreseen then. Simultaneously with the first reduction of internal tariffs, taxes were to be harmonized at the national level, with national tax frontiers completely eliminated after the transitional period. The harmonization of domestic farm prices, leading to common European prices, was also to be effected in coordination with other market systems.

The German proposal provided for intensified coordination of business cycle policy, economic and financial policy, currencies, and national budget policies. The financial policies of the existing common institutions were to be unified within a reformed European Community, at the same time giving the hitherto purely advisory and nonelected European Parliament full powers. The new community was expected to seek closer relations with nonmember countries in Europe as well as developing countries, and the Kennedy Round was to be brought to a successful conclusion. The German government also proposed a conference of Common Market countries to discuss foreign, defense, and cultural policies, with remaining questions to be taken up by existing European agencies.

The U.S. embassy in Brussels regarded the German plan as an excellent and meaningful set of consistent proposals, neither so revolutionary as to assure their rejection nor so vague as to be meaningless (State Department Bulletin, July 16, 1965). At an appropriate time, the embassy suggested, the United States should state that, though this was a matter for European decision, we considered it a constructive move toward making Europe a more healthy and equal partner. The Brussels memo nonetheless warned that the proposal's success depended entirely on a resolution of the grain price issue, on which the German proposal represented an advance but not a commitment.

When I met Schröder on December 6, I asked him what response the new proposals had received. He replied that there were not yet any definite reactions. The French insisted that agreement must first be reached on "certain outstanding political problems," which Schröder understood to mean a European defense system organized on de Gaulle's terms. He concluded that no meeting should be held until after the MLF had been settled. In fact, the German proposals appeared to arouse little interest among their Common Market addressees.

We had at this time the benefit of a number of high-level American visitors, who always turned up interesting German comment. Henry

Kissinger (1979, 508), who was visiting Bonn as a private citizen, reported to the embassy his talk with Adenauer on November 17. Adenauer, who did "98 per cent of the talking," according to Kissinger, said that U.S.-FRG relations were in a worse mess than at any time since the war, "leading to the destruction of postwar gains in Europe." Adenauer said he thought the MLF should be "thoroughly reviewed" and a final decision on it delayed at least until Autumn 1966. He appeared to agree with most of de Gaulle's criticisms of MLF and explained that, as chancellor, he had agreed to have the question studied only so as not to be accused of having missed a chance to join in nuclear developments.

Adenauer contended that most of his party was with him in opposing MLF. He blamed the United States for forcing the Federal Republic to take anti-French positions, Kissinger reported. Adenauer said atmospherics, which were critical, were now "very sour." Adenauer criticized Schröder for not having treated de Gaulle with proper respect, thus needlessly antagonizing him. In conclusion, Adenauer expressed "great fear" that U.S. policy would force de Gaulle to deal with the Soviets at the expense of Germany and Western Europe as a whole. When Kissinger asked Adenauer why he did not attempt to ameliorate de Gaulle's views, Adenauer said it was because he basically agreed with de Gaulle. The fault was on the other side.

One of the reasons Kissinger was in Bonn was to attend the biannual German-American Conference scheduled for Berlin on November 13–15. This conference as usual included a number of leading Americans, among them former high commissioner to Germany John J. McCloy. As a U.S. official I was ineligible to participate as a member of the conference, but I monitored most of the meetings, entertained many of the participants, and attended the social occasions. I learned that many of the U.S. participants opposed the MLF. Kissinger had made it clear in a personal communication that he did not give a blanket endorsement to the MLF. If queried in Berlin he would say, "Something along the line [the MLF proposal] should be part of allied arrangements, but which modality is chosen depends on so many factors which are constantly changing and hence beyond the knowledge of a private citizen that I do not want to get into details."

I also learned that the day the conference was scheduled to discuss the MLF in Berlin, Foreign Minister Schröder would be defending it on the floor of the Bundestag in Bonn. I called a meeting of the American representatives and, acknowledging that I had no right to tell them what view they should have of the MLF, pointed out that Schröder was on the next day defending it before the Bundestag largely because it was American policy and he thought he was helping us. The debate was of such importance that Schröder's political future was at stake. No matter what their views were on the MLF, I urged them not to attack it in their remarks in the conference. Although some of the participants who opposed MLF later grumbled, no one opposed it that day.

On November 12 I had made an address in Berlin to the Ernst Reuter Society in which I had said that the United States would continue to defend the freedom of West Berlin and to seek ways of bringing about German reunification. I said that since Germany lies at the center of Europe, it is "within a field of magnetic force which grows stronger with every new tie joining Eastern and Western Europe." I urged gradual progress toward increasing these ties. This speech received wide coverage in the Berlin and West German press; a Munich paper credited my magnetic field analogy to the development of a new theory of German reunification.

In its way, Adenauer's interview published February 10, 1965, with C. P. Sulzberger, head of the *New York Times* Foreign Service, was symptomatic of the European doldrums. The interview, which was highly critical of U.S. policy in Europe, created a furor in the German press. It represented Adenauer at his worst—mischievous, even malicious. It clearly showed an underlying anti-American tone, the counterpart of his open Gaullist sympathies. The State Department press officer had denied the former chancellor's reported claim that he and President Kennedy agreed the MRBMs would be developed by the United States for installation in Europe, but that neither the Kennedy nor Johnson administration honored the agreement.

The day Adenauer's interview appeared, I took advantage of a visit to Hamburg to talk to editors, both in a press backgrounder at the consulate and in separate meetings in their offices (memcon, Con Gen Hamburg, Feb. 15, 1965). Hamburg had become the undisputed center of the postwar German press, headquarters of Axel Springer's daily, nationally circulated *Bild Zeitung* and *Die Welt*, as well as the sensationalist radical news magazine *Der Spiegel*, which had recently published my views at length in a verbatim interview, and the influential conservative weekly *Die Zeit*, edited by Countess Marion Dönhoff. Talking to these media leaders gave me a better feel of the current trends of thinking in German political circles on questions regarding U.S. policy.

In my two-hour meeting with Dönhoff and the editors of four other publications, there was considerable discussion of the Adenauer thesis that strategically placed intermediate-range missiles (IRBM) were essential to the security of Western Europe. The editor of *Sonntagsblatt* asked why the Soviets continued to oppose German reunification. Was it fear of a resurgent Germany or of the dismantling of the buffer coalition of Communist states in Eastern Europe? When I replied that it was probably both, he asked why the security threat perceived by the Soviets could not be handled through negotiations. There seemed to be an inverse ratio in West Germany between security and the drive to achieve reunification. During the building of the Wall all thoughts turned toward physical security. Since this now seemed assured, Germans thought it should be used as leverage to achieve such important constructive aims as reunification.

I did not see Helmut Schmidt, who at that time was serving in the Hamburg city government just a few blocks away from where we sat. None of us could anticipate that, some twelve years later, when Schmidt himself was serving as chancellor of the Federal Republic, he would come to take a view quite similar to Adenauer's on MRBMs, eventually leading to the deployment of the American Pershing II—or that today he would be Dönhoff's colleague as copublisher of *Die Zeit*. But in 1965 things looked quite different. I noted that neither the French nor the Low Countries wanted these weapons and that the Italian government was too weak to take a firm stand. The editors showed no interest in the idea either, pointing out that, in the event of war, the missiles on West German soil would automatically draw Soviet nuclear fire. But I made it clear that the United States had not abandoned interest in some form of sea-based MLF in NATO though, as President Johnson said, we were not pushing but waiting for European opinion on the issue to crystallize.

The discussion then focused on possible U.S. troop withdrawals from Germany. I pointed out that the purpose of our recent "big lift" exercises was merely to improve U.S. airlift capability and concerned backup forces, not those holding the front. I pointed out that nothing in our twenty-year record in Germany belied Johnson's pledge that our troops would stay as long as needed and chided anyone who undermined confidence in our partnership by raising the issue. In answer to questions on the utility of the Hallstein Doctrine, I said that it had from a U.S. standpoint worked very well in denying recognition to Cuba but that this was basically a question for the Federal Republic.

Later I discussed the same issues at a separate meeting with Rudolph Augstein, publisher of Der Spiegel and the most outspoken, controversial, and feared of German publishers, and Augstein's top editors. They tended to agree when I pointed out that the French, Belgians, and Dutch would not allow IRBMs on their territory and doubted if the Germans would allow them either. I stated that the Polaris missiles and long-range missiles stationed in America were fully able to knock out the Russian missiles aimed at Europe and that reports of the MLF's death were premature.

The question of troop reduction was raised in connection with the discussion of the Adenauer-Sulzberger interview, and I made it quite clear that the "big lift" operation was never designed for use in Germany, that the United States realized as well as anyone else that under war conditions it would be impossible to fly troops so close to the front lines. I reiterated that this test operation had absolutely nothing to do with any thinking about withdrawing troops now stationed in Germany.

As the discussion turned to U.S. trade with the Soviet bloc and East Germany, I called attention to the insignificance of our East German trade compared with other powers, in particular the Federal Republic. We agreed on the need for coordinating trade policies between West and East. The U.S. embargo on the sale of pipe for a Soviet oil pipeline to Vienna was also discussed briefly, and I acknowledged gratefully that the Federal Republic had complied with our request not to sell, unlike our British allies, who refused to go along with us but whose prices were too high for the Soviets anyway.

When mention was made of de Gaulle's recent discouraging statement on German reunification, I expressed surprise at the praise it had received, considering the consternation when Secretary of State Rusk had offered some related suggestions on the same subject not long before. The Spiegel editors agreed with me and sharply criticized Adenauer's recent statements advocating a "policy of strength and pressure on the Russians." Augstein nonetheless believed we were making inadequate use of our tremendous strength and our position as the key world leader. Like the Germans and the Jews, he said, Americans wanted too much to be loved and expected gratitude for what they had done. The Spiegel editors felt that it was more important to be respected.

At lunch with Axel Springer and his principal aides, I had a brief contretemps with Peter Böhnisch, editor-in-chief of the popular Bild Zeitung, over their recently published interview with Adenauer on possible U.S. troop withdrawals and another story on a presumed deal between the United States and the Soviet Union to permit Soviet withdrawal of forces from East Germany. I denied both stories and said that such sensationalizing was dangerous to the alliance. I also stressed possible American reaction to the constant expressions of distrust on the part of our German allies. I pointed out that some Americans would welcome our pulling out of Europe. If Germans wanted us to stay, the constant questioning of our promises was intolerable. I was reminded, I said, of the wife who had been faithful for twenty years but whose husband began to worry that she might cheat on him five years in the future.

Springer changed the subject by expressing his belief that the United States could accomplish something by using trade as a weapon. I again noted how little trade the United States had with East Germany and the Soviet bloc in general and as other Americans have, defended the United States against implied charges of a double standard on trade with the Russians. I thought we had made a good bargain in our recent deal to obtain much-needed gold in return for surplus wheat and tried to set the affair in perspective by pointing out that the wheat, unlike strategic commodities or technologies, was something the Russians could also get along without or buy from Canada, which at that time was having shipping difficulties. I expressed the further opinion that it was impossible today to bring a nation to its knees by economic pressure anyway, citing the example of Cuba right on the U.S. doorstep, which had survived in spite of all the economic pressure we were bringing to bear.

Springer saved his proposals for solving the German question for after lunch. He suggested two different approaches. The first was simply to demand that the Soviets take their twenty-two divisions out of the East Zone. This would be reiterated in the press and in public statements on all possible occasions. The Soviets, of course, would then demand the withdrawal of American troops, making the situation ripe for negotiations. Springer seemed to feel that we could demand a price for the withdrawal of American troops. On being questioned, he agreed that this was somewhat similar to the Rapacki plan (a Polish proposal made in 1957 by Foreign Minister Adam Rapacki elaborating a suggestion made by Sir Anthony Eden at the 1955 summit meeting for an East-West disengagement based on a demilitarized atomic-weapon free zone, though Central Europe was on both sides of the Iron Curtain).

Springer's second suggested approach to reunification was a three-phase action. First, a European atomic force would be created; second, the present expansion of European economic activity would be continued, increasing the West's economic power; third, the West would offer the Soviets a hidden reparations payment in the amount of DM 100 billion, at the time about $25 billion. There followed a discussion of Adenauer's attitude on Franco-German relations. Bönisch said Adenauer considered himself to be not a Gaullist but a German Gaullist. I reminded those present that the French had clarified de Gaulle's proposals and now agreed on four-power responsibility for the reunification of Germany. Springer was throughout the friendly and gracious host, and the sharp tone he sometimes used with Americans was missing. He put forth his proposals only half-heartedly, as if he did not really believe in them himself. He did not seem too disappointed at my lack of enthusiasm.

After sampling the views of German editors, I had occasion to hear what German business leaders thought at a dinner in my honor in Düsseldorf on March 23 (memcon, Con Gen Düsseldorf, Mar. 25, 1965). It was attended by top leaders of German industry in the Rhine-Ruhr area, Germany's traditional industrial heartland, though it was now coming on hard times. The guest list included Fritz Berg, president of the Bundesverband der Deutschen Industrie (BDI); Ernst Schneider, president of the National Chamber of Commerce; Hans-Gunther Sohl, head of the Thyssen group and president of the German Iron and Steel Institute; Egon Overbeck, president of Mannesmann; and Ernst Wolf Mommsen, president of Phoenix Rheinrohr. The views of this group were of particular interest to me; they represented the current mood of the business community and its opinions on specific issues of the day. Fritz Berg, who was one of my oldest German friends and pro-American, usually acted as spokesman for the group.

Nourished by the prospect of continued European growth and favored by the dollar's unbroken postwar strength, the rising volume of direct American investment was inevitably a subject of conversation. The German guests thought German industry was generally not opposed to direct American investments, although some felt that certain criticisms of specific American companies were justified. I made it clear that German subsidiaries of American companies did not have a tax advantage over their German counterparts.

Currency and foreign exchange were seen by the guests as the most pressing economic problems. All appeared to accept my strong statement on the sincerity of U.S. intentions and the adequacy of U.S. actions to correct the current deficit in our balance of payments. Several in fact expressed the fear that the United States might go too far and cause a shrinking of capital available for Germany. Berg said that he already saw some signs of this. Schneider added that, in his opinion, the principal threat was the weakening position of the pound sterling, on which 40 percent of world trade depended.

Speaking for his peers connected with steel, Hermann Winkhaus, the former president of Mannesmann, stressed the necessity to maintain current production of 140 million tons of coal per year, although consumption was 20 percent below this. His principal suggestion, in which he was joined by the others, was that current oil prices in Germany were excessively low compared with prices in other Common Market countries and that the oil companies should agree on a firm basis to maintain a higher price in Germany over a period of years.

Leaving aside the obstacle of American antitrust laws, I replied that at least seventy companies now produce oil in large quantities in various parts of the world and need to sell it. They would never agree to fixing prices. I urged those present to give a fair trial to the present German system of voluntary quality control, as agreed on by the oil companies and the chancellor. If this should fail, the Federal Republic could then consider mandatory quotas. After a heated debate, it appeared that most of those present accepted this position.

Berg said that German reunification would clearly be impossible to achieve for a long time and questioned the desirability of the frequent "initiatives" being made to this end. They would certainly fail, causing a loss of prestige to the West. Schneider and Sohl expressed the need for some psychological step to support the new generation of Germans in the Eastern Zone. They felt that time was running against the FRG there. Overbeck stressed the need to stop the sniping going on between the allies so that we could reach an agreed policy and maintain personal and trade contacts insofar as possible. I made clear the sincerity of the U.S. desire for German reunification and our willingness to consider any initiative to and help in working it out on a four power basis. After hearing this frank discussion I was in general surprised at the moderation and degree of unanimity expressed by German business leaders. Since they were a tight group who shared values and knew one another well (see Appendix 1), they were able to express themselves freely whenever we talked. I thought this boded well for American interests in Germany. I knew from my frequent contacts with the chairmen of parent companies in the United States, as well as the heads of their

German subsidiaries, that large U.S. firms such as Standard Oil of New Jersey, Ford, IBM, and Mobil were so far doing well.

I was also pleased with my contacts with German businessmen per se, whom I found to be an able, hardworking group. Although a few of the old family firms like Siemens, Krupp, and Flick had survived the war, most of the business leaders were self-made. They had earned their positions in intense competition and were not there, as was often true in England, because of their name or family wealth.

The University of Maryland has for many years operated a European division based in Heidelberg that enables members of U.S. armed forces, mainly in Germany, to complete their higher education. Wilson Elkins, president of the university and a classmate of mine at Oxford, asked me to address their May commencement exercises, scheduled for the Aula, or auditorium, of Heidelberg University, and to receive an honorary degree. Chancellor Erhard had been asked to share the platform.

I had long wanted to make a major speech highlighting my conviction that the efforts of the German people in the postwar period to redeem themselves from the Hitler era deserved recognition. I wanted to emphasize how important it was to encourage their continued assimilation into an increasingly unified Europe—and their cooperation with the United States. I discussed this with Elkins, and he heartily approved. The fact that Erhard would also be speaking would enhance the importance of what I would say.

The essence of the speech (U.S. Information Service, Amemb Bonn, May 30, 1965) was contained in the first sentence. "The time has come, I say, for the world to make up its mind about the Germans." I added, "I say this because there is evidence that many have not yet made up their minds. I say this because I believe that ample grounds for a decision exist." I then recounted what I considered the evidence to be and made a final appeal to the world to "weigh that case on and make up its mind about the Germans." The speech attracted wide publicity, in America as well as in Germany and its thesis was unchallenged. It was included in an American publication of the most significant speeches of that year.

Chancellor Erhard made an unofficial visit to the United States in June 1965 to receive an honorary degree and make various public and private appearances. President Johnson, in a meeting with the chancellor alone without a fixed agenda, assured Erhard that Germany was the most trustworthy of U.S. allies (interpreter's notes, June 4, 1964, Department of State Archives). Erhard responded that a recent German poll gave the United States twenty-four times the votes for the next country as being Germany's most trustworthy ally. After the forthcoming elections in September, he hoped, with a four-year mandate, to be in a stronger position. He proposed that he and the president meet at regular intervals. Johnson agreed that they "must stay in touch." He liked Erhard's concept of a Formed Society, which seemed to him much like his proposed Great Society. They could learn from each other.

Erhard said that a new and clearer concept of the world picture, of a modern and more open world, was needed. They should work together toward such a goal. He liked Johnson's proposals for a new approach to aid to Southeast Asia. Johnson thought that more flexibility was needed in the conduct of foreign policy generally and was determined to keep the alliance intact. The United States would stay in Germany and Europe as long as it was needed.

Johnson asked Erhard to tell him what Germans thought of the war in Vietnam. Erhard replied that they were sympathetic with the U.S. position there. They considered Vietnam a testing ground—Saigon was to them like Berlin. Johnson assured Erhard that he could count on the United States to fulfill its commitments under the SEATO (Southeast Asia Treaty Organization) Pact or any other pact. Otherwise serious doubts about the United States would be raised. In response to Johnson's question to explain the recent hardening of the Soviet line, Erhard replied that this resulted not from strength but from insecurity by the Soviets. Johnson commended Erhard on Germany's recent recognition of Israel, which he realized represented in part a desire to please us.

I was not in Washington for these meetings. When this minute was first made available to me I was pleased with the spirit of frankness and intimacy it represented. No problems between us appeared insurmountable. The future in our relations seemed bright. Little did I realize the sharp turn for the worse the next two meetings would take, as pressure on both heads of state mounted from increasing economic difficulties and, in the case of the United States, a step-up in the tempo of the Vietnam War.

15

German Student Unrest
December 1963–May 1968

$\mathbf{G}$ordon Craig (1982, 184) ascribes the origin of the German university student unrest to two major factors. First, the student population tripled to 900,000, making it difficult for universities to satisfy student needs and precipitating student demands to democratize the traditional hierarchical university system along the lines of the American model, to liberalize the university bureaucracy, and to lessen class size. Second, German students were worried about the growth of conformity in Germany and the absence of opposition to the values of the marketplace and militarism, to German support for U.S. military intervention in Vietnam, and to the growing respectability of former Nazis. Student unrest, long prevalent in Latin America, arose in the United States in the early 1960s as a student reaction to the Vietnam War and was projected into the world scene by the violence at the University of California at Berkeley. It found a ready response among German students.

Student opposition in Germany was led by Students for a Democratic Society (SDS), an offshoot of the Social Democratic party that had broken away when the SPD abandoned its Marxist affiliations in 1959. Starting in 1964 the SDS held classes on apartheid in South Africa, the Vietnam War, and political repression in Iran. Universities and professors largely chose to ignore the student movement, which assisted its growth. The public became alarmed at the student threat, in part because of the conservative interpretations given of it by the German press. Without question, German students were sympathetic to the strong student anti-Vietnam protest in the United States. This was not, I believe, the result of a world student organization but was in imitation of scenes the

German students had seen originating on American television. If American students had taken to the streets in opposition to Vietnam, why should not they?

Student protest was building in Germany during my early months in Bonn, which led me to organize a program of lectures in German universities to try to get the official American point of view across. I did not expect to be able to stop the flood of protest but hoped to blunt its reaction against us. I hoped to clarify genuine misunderstandings of United States policies. Having six children myself, I was concerned with the consequences of an increasing alienation of young people, both in the United States and in Germany. I wanted to explain those U.S. policies, particularly intervention in South Vietnam, that had aroused strong opposition among young Americans as well as young Germans. I decided to speak to the students in all major German universities. This began in late 1963, and by 1966 I had visited almost every German university. I found, however, that the situation would get worse before it got better. I was not unhappy to avoid Frankfurt University, because its students had become the most radical in Germany. As my visits progressed, student alienation and unrest, negligible when I started, increased dramatically. I avoided trouble at the Free University of Berlin by speaking on an apolitical subject. I first encountered heckling and disturbances in Munich, where I managed to cope with it, and later in Göttingen and Cologne. The opposition became worse each time, and I knew the meetings could easily break out into major demonstrations. The results were becoming counterproductive.

The format for my talks was the same in each university. They were advertised in advance by posters, and I spoke in the Aula. I was usually introduced by the rector and answered questions after each speech. At first I was listened to politely, but as my program progressed, questions became increasingly antagonistic. In answering what I considered to be a rhetorical, insincere, or unfriendly question, I always came back hard. I might say, "I can't believe you really mean that," or, "If you will let me explain, I am sure you will conclude that you are wrong." This, I thought, would serve to keep the questioner off-balance and make the questions more reasonable. I always sought smaller, more informal meetings in connection with my main appearance. I particularly enjoyed small sessions in a rathskeller atmosphere.

My first lecture took place on December 10, 1963, at the University of Freiburg, a charming old town at the edge of the Black Forest. I was received by the rector. In German universities, the office of rector rotates among the heads of departments, and I was not surprised to find that the rector was a forester. My topic was bland: "The Atlantic Community in a Time of Challenge." I sought to define the basic elements required for the creation of a community, which we believed existed among the Atlantic nations: our common cultural heritage, the similarity of our national economies, our military strength, and our opposition to Communist totalitarianism. The United States sought a close association with an Atlantic community of equals. I got by easily on the questions and considered that my university visits had gotten off to a good start.

My next visit was to Phillips University in Marburg, a picturesque city on the Lahn River dominated by its fifteenth-century *Schloss*. On January 17, I spoke on "The Goal of American Foreign Policy." I stressed the continuity of U.S. foreign policy based on a consensus among its people. Although the United States unfortunately had to devote much of its efforts to taking care of crisis situations around the world, Americans had the positive goal of building peace and stability by strengthening and unifying the free world.

University visits came faster. On January 18, I spoke to the Fuhrung Academie of the Bundeswehr in Hamburg on "Training for Leadership." On February 14 I gave the same lecture to the students of Johannes Gutenberg University at Mainz. Increasingly, student attention in the question periods turned to U.S. policy in Vietnam. I did not reply defensively but said that we were there to prevent a takeover by a Communist-armed minority. Having helped contain Communist expansion in Europe and the Middle East, we could not refuse help to those fighting for freedom in Vietnam.

This did not always satisfy student questioners. Indeed, I was beginning to be concerned about our Vietnam policy myself, as I learned of the steady increase in our military forces and that U.S. troops were using weapons "to defend themselves." But I did not communicate my doubts to the students. On February 21, 1965, I spoke to the students of Heidelberg University on "The United States Role in the Atlantic Partnership." I emphasized the importance of working toward a united Europe while seeking to form a partnership between Europe and America. In the meantime, all must accept worldwide responsibilities, particularly in aid to developing countries.

When I rose to speak to the members of the Society for Foreign Affairs on "The Atlantic Partnership and European Unity" in the splendid main auditorium of Munich University on May 15, I had no premonition of what was to take place. I had looked forward to my appearance at the university because of my close association with Munich during student days. Since my audience consisted mostly of political scientists, I made my remarks a little more professional than usual. Suddenly I heard a weird moaning sound from the balcony on my left, and looking up I observed a short man wearing a gas mask throwing leaflets down on the audience. I stopped, and in a light vein made a brief appeal to him to allow me to continue speaking. I promised him the first question in the discussion period to follow. He continued his moaning, shouting intermittently, "Vietnam, Vietnam." I then stepped back from the lectern but remained standing. The chairman appealed to the demonstrator, who had been joined in his leaflet-throwing by several other young people sitting near him. There was, however, no diminution. When it became apparent that the disturbing group was not going to stop, a number of students got up, marched around the balcony, seized the leader by the arms, and carried him out, his cohorts following. The other students cheered, and I was able to resume my speech. This was the first serious heckling I was to encounter, but not the last.

The climax of my talks to students came on July 14, when I spoke at Göttingen University on a subject I knew would be particularly provocative. This was my first visit to Göttingen, and I had looked forward to it. Göttingen, in many ways the most prestigious university in Germany, had pioneered in the development of the science of geophysics, in which I had taken my doctorate at Oxford. Before I left Bonn, the German police advised me of an anonymous tip that I would, while in Göttingen, be attacked with swords by three Chinese in ceremonial dress. I knew it was a student prank and made a joke of it, but the police took it seriously. From my arrival in Göttingen to my departure, I was under twenty-four-hour surveillance, and on my return to Bonn I received the report that no attack had occurred.

As my car approached the auditorium in early evening, however, a group of students stood in front, burning a neat pile of copies of my speech. The university had been careful about screening the audience, so there was no disturbance inside the Aula. In my speech, "The Tasks of the Free World Community," I developed the picture of attacks by Communist aggression and subversion in Iran, Greece, Berlin, the Philippines, Laos, Vietnam, and Malaysia. If we were to avoid piecemeal defeat, I declared, we must make it clear to the Communists that these intrusions would always be met as they had been in Korea. In Vietnam, I contended, the conflict was not a "war of liberation," a popular uprising, or a civil war, as some had said. It was a war of stealth waged by troops and weapons brought in from outside.

I had not forgotten the angry students outside. I asked the rector if I could stay and meet with small groups from the demonstrators for as long as they wanted to come. Most of them appeared shy and embarrassed as they came in to talk with me, but they warmed to the discussion. Most seemed sincere in their questioning of U.S. intervention in Vietnam. They saw it as an act of imperialism, suggesting that this was a local war in which Americans had no role. I explained patiently, over and over, why we thought we owed it to the Vietnamese people to help them in their struggle against Communist aggression from outside. We were sure the majority of Vietnamese wanted us there to help save them from subjugation. I pointed out how what we were doing in Vietnam was similar to what we had done to save the Greeks from being drawn behind the iron curtain. When I left the hall about midnight, a sizable group of students remained in front and cheered me as I departed.

At Cologne University, where I spoke on February 7, 1966, I kept my prepared remarks to a minimum and confined myself largely to questions from the audience. I deliberately invited questions on Vietnam, saying: "In Viet Nam we have made it clear, not only to the aggressors in the North but to the whole world, that while we will continue to strive to find a peaceful solution to the conflict, we are determined to honor our commitments." I was hissed when I suggested that recent student demonstrations in Berlin were unrepresentative of the German people.

Although I had expected to be attacked, and indeed had asked for it, the ferocity of the opposition startled me. It was apparent that the comments and questions had been planted. They were aggressive and hostile. I concluded that time was running out on my campaign to talk with German students. They were not there to listen or reason, only to attack me and U.S. policy. Rather than assuage student anger, I was only giving it publicity.

In April 1967 Vice President Hubert Humphrey made a brief stop in Berlin during an official visit to Germany. An acknowledged liberal, he would not have been expected to evoke a hostile student attitude. But eleven students were arrested by the perhaps overly solicitous West Berlin police. The bombs the students were alleged to be planning to throw at Humphrey, and which the press had said were furnished by the Chinese embassy in East Berlin, turned out to be sacks of cold tapioca. But I remember well the tenseness of the situation and the strong press attacks later against the students involved.

The tragic climax of the Berlin unrest occurred only two months afterward, during an official visit by Muhammad Reza Pahlavi, shah of Iran. On June 2, while the shah, who had been a particular object of student protest, was attending an opera, students gathered in the street outside the West Berlin opera to heckle his party and throw things at them. This led to scuffles with the police. After the shah was inside, the police charged the demonstrators, injuring forty-seven, some seriously. Unfortunately, one student, Benno Ohnesorg, was killed by a police bullet.

I remember vividly the masses of angry, belligerent, and sullen students who marched the Berlin streets later that night. A martyr had been created for the student cause. In the absence of a realistic response from the government or university, their movement was captured by extremists. Radical student groups, some organized from East Germany, where all universities were controlled by the governing Socialist Unity party, spread rapidly through the German universities. On April 11, 1968, Rudi Dutschke, himself a refugee from East Germany and a Marxist-Maoist leader of the radical "extraparliamentary opposition," was shot and critically wounded by an unstable housepainter of neo-Nazi sympathies. The militant student left organized demonstrations by some fifty thousand marchers all across Germany. This was a sad era for Germany and the Western world. Although the student movement lacked coherence and leadership, the German universities would be upset and disrupted for years by Stalinist and Maoist-Marxist "red cells" and action groups.

16

U.S.-German Relations in the Doldrums
July–September 1965

Perhaps the best forum in Germany for a political speech during my stay there was Tutzing, south of Munich, where a Protestant adult education agency called the Evangelische Akademie ran a kind of Chautauqua known as the Political Club. On July 16, I spoke there informally, presenting "Some American Thoughts on Current Issues." This address received the most widespread coverage, not only in Germany, but in Western Europe and the United States, of any speech I made during my five years in Germany.

My first theme was aid to developing countries. I said that freedom in the world was indivisible and required a forward strategy in Vietnam and Central America as well as in Berlin. Although Americans did not expect Germany to provide military forces and understood that Germany was already offering substantial development aid, I said, we looked to Germany with its growing resources to help by doing more. My second theme was the future of Europe. I said that we welcomed the steps already taken through NATO, the Common Market, the European Atomic Energy Community (Euratom), and close ties between Germany and France. But we looked forward to the strengthening of free Europe as a whole, its further economic and political integration, and the consolidation of an Atlantic partnership that included the United States.

I then addressed the complex and emotional issue of whether West Berliners should be given passes to visit friends and relatives in East Berlin at Christmas. The United States had approved the arrangement negotiated in late 1964 by the West Berlin government and the East Germans because of its humanitarian aspects, I noted. But we were concerned that they not jeopardize the allies' position in Berlin, since we were responsible for the security of the city. We needed to be fully informed of anything that was going on. Brandt, unfortunately, interpreted this remark as a criticism.

My most important point regarded German reunification; the subject was going through one of its periodic revivals in German public interest as a result of a treaty of friendship and cooperation between the Soviets and the so-called German Democratic Republic. I mentioned that the United States had been accused of putting its search for détente with the Soviet Union ahead of reunification. In reply, I quoted President Johnson's recent statement on this subject to prove that Americans considered that there could be no détente until the artificial division of Germany was removed as a cause of tension in Europe. I commented that the U.S. position on reunification had remained the same since 1945.

I said that on its face the Soviet-GDR treaty was not a cause for serious alarm. It might reflect a more sober, less aggressive policy. It was nothing new but only reaffirmed the Soviet commitment to the division of Germany. We should not be pessimistic about the prospects for German reunification, I said, noting that historic changes were occurring in both Eastern and Western Europe in their relations with each other and with the United States. Their Berlin zone today would seem to be a waning asset to the Soviets. We could at least hope that by increasing contacts with Eastern Europe, we in the West could exert increasing influence, thus modifying the division of Europe and speeding reunification.

It was interesting to observe the reaction of the German press. "McGhee—New Power Alignment in Western Europe Unnecessary—Washington against Bonn-Paris Union—German Problem Remains World Problem"; "McGhee Warns against Pessimism"; "McGhee for European Cooperation"; "McGhee Warns against Fragmented Europe—No Reason for Pessimism concerning German Reunification"; "U.S. Welcomes Bonn-Paris Cooperation—But Treaty Should Not Exclude Others"; "McGhee—Exert Influence over Developments in East."

Editorial comment centered mainly on the question of reunification, with European unity next (daily press summary, Amemb Bonn, July 17, 1965). Few commented as to whether West Germany should play a greater world role. There was also little concern or criticism of my views. Some read me as favoring the Christmas pass arrangements but criticizing Bonn's role in past negotiations. The International Herald Tribune emphasized that I was worried about a Paris-Bonn axis, the

New York Times lead was that I warned against an "Inward-Oriented Europe."

The speech, I believe, emphasized the sensitivity of the German press and people to views expressed in behalf of the U.S. government on German reunification, the German-French relationship, and the closely related question of European unity. Underlying all questions, however, was the degree and direction of the continuing American interest in Germany itself, which all Germans considered the sole basis for their security. This made them sensitive to the role the United States expected them to play in Europe, in meeting such world crises as Vietnam, and in negotiating with the East. I realized more fully than ever before the importance of the U.S. role in Germany and the grave responsibilities it created.

This aroused my earlier concerns that the relationship between our countries had, in broad perspective, remained too long an unnatural, even unhealthy, one. While I felt the Germans should retain close relations with the United States as an ally, I thought that Americans should increase their efforts to get Germans to stand more independently on their own feet.

The origins of Brandt's policy toward the East, known as Ostpolitik, goes back at least as far as 1958, his first year as governing mayor of Berlin. In an address that year to the Royal Institute of International Affairs in London, Brandt declared that the free existence of Berlin depended, among other things, on being a "uniting bond between the inhabitants of both sectors of our disrupted land." Berlin should promote an "open-door policy in human and cultural contacts." The only course was "an unflinching, stubborn struggle for a powerful solution by political action." During the 1961 local elections, Brandt had campaigned on pledges to build relations with the Soviet Union and its satellites insofar as the situation justified, while also keeping counterpressure against Soviet moves. The SPD vote rose 4.5 percent.

In 1961 Brandt had been critical of the Western powers, including the United States, for accepting the loss of East Berlin implicit in the building of the Wall. Brandt himself was accused of cowardice for having accepted the Wall. He had said, "The Wall is there now, and cannot simply be overrun." He concentrated on steps to take to make it "permeable." The erection of the Wall has been described as the main reason for Brandt's subsequent policy of Ostpolitik, for bringing Germany together again by "small steps." In my early meetings with Brandt, he often talked in terms of improving ties with the East—East Berlin, East Germany and the other satellites, and the Soviets—through "small steps." He based them on responses to "human" problems created by the Wall: the separation of families and the deep yearning of West Germans for Christmas passes to visit friends and relatives in the East. He appeared to be encouraged in the evolution of his Ostpolitik policy by his faithful associate Egon Bahr.

I reported Brandt's views, as did others, and Washington became interested in finding out just what Brandt had in mind. I urged that we encourage Brandt to explore further practical applications of his policy, but some in Washington were skeptical. A division arose between those who agreed and those who were skeptical—who feared Brandt and Bahr were going too far too fast. Robert Bowie, at Dean Rusk's suggestion, made a special visit to Bonn to appraise this issue. From all the evidence, however, the State Department continued to accept the policy I recommended.

During Brandt's visit to Washington in May 1964, he had discussed his views on Eastern policy with Dean Rusk and had promised to put some of his thoughts on paper. When I saw him I encouraged him to do so. In late August he forwarded through the U.S. mission in Berlin a paper entitled "Relations with Eastern European States and Peoples" for transmission to Rusk. It proved to be an interesting document, proposing that the Western states engage the Eastern European states in the largest possible volume of communications.

This paper was the beginning. It was not until December 1966, when Brandt took over from Schröder as foreign minister in the Grand Coalition, that Brandt had the opportunity to transform what had largely been his own musings into Germany's foreign policy.

The implied linkage of German performance under the offset agreement with the continued stationing of U.S. troops in Germany became of increasing concern to me. I fully understood the importance of trying to improve the adverse U.S. balance of payments. Germany and other affected nations complained that we were exporting our inflation and thereby increasing theirs. Nevertheless, I viewed the continued presence of a significant U.S. troop level in Germany necessary for the success of NATO in organizing a credible European defense.

During talks with Secretary of Defense McNamara in Washington, I reminded him that, although Erhard was having problems with his budget, the Germans had met their commitments in the past (draft

memcon, Department of State A/CDC/Mr, Apr. 23, 1965). I would oppose any direct linkage of force levels in such a way that lower offset
spending would mean automatic reduction of U.S. forces. McNamara
said we should not do that but must stick to the old formulation of the
offset-troop level linkage "as long as you need them and want them
and make it possible for us to keep them there by meeting the offset."
Without an agreement, McNamara said, German defense spending
would probably not offset more than 20 percent of our balance of payments spending.

I also noted that our present agreement had two years to run and that
there was no reason to be unduly concerned. But McNamara said he
was worried about political signs that the Germans were not going to
follow through on their commitments. I replied by citing a number of
pending German military projects that would go a long way toward
meeting German obligations under the agreement. In light of the budgetary problems Erhard faced, I also expressed my hope that there be
no undue publicity. McNamara agreed but also expressed the view that
the American people must know what was happening.

During my talks with McNamara, I urged that he or the president
relieve German anxieties by stating positively that the United States
would take all necessary steps to stop a Communist attack against
Germany, using the appropriate force, conventional and nuclear.
McNamara promised to make such a statement while in Europe but
emphasized that the Europeans would have to make their full contribution if Europe were to be defended according to a strategy of
flexible response. They should realize that deterrence must, to be
credible, be based on strength, not just statements. He observed that
the Germans were, instead, cutting their military budget by DM 1
billion.

Meanwhile, Secretary of the Treasury Henry Fowler, the cabinet
member most directly responsible for balance of payments problems,
had proposed to McNamara that "we should not rule out considering
reducing U.S. combat forces in Germany—with due regard for all the
implications involved—if this proves necessary in order to maintain
the full offset principle" (letter, McGhee to Fowler, July 20, 1965). Chip
Bohlen, U.S. ambassador to France, agreed with my view that any reduction of U.S. forces in Germany would play directly into French
hands (letter, Charles E. Bohlen to John M. Leddy, Oct. 28, 1965). But
the noose was tightening.

Knowing how serious the president and McNamara considered the increasing U.S. balance of payments problem to be, I became concerned that a German default could raise the issue of U.S. troop withdrawals. This, I thought, could have serious consequences, both in the Federal Republic and NATO-wide. In a meeting with Defense Department representatives in Bonn, September 28–29, German negotiators agreed to examine thoroughly their maximum essential and justifiable procurement from the United States, assuming availability of funds. But since the German government was prohibited by law from submitting an unbalanced budget, it would either have to cut back other budget requests or raise taxes. The negotiators warned that either alternative would incur great political opposition and reminded the Americans that the Bundestag had already voted to fund many of the requests for social programs. A cutback now would require complicated amending legislation. They also pointed out that a cut in funds to cover the large state railway deficit would be politically difficult, since rail transport affected so many people and so much of German industry. They added that the German capital market was too demoralized to provide deficit funds through borrowing, as the law permitted, and that although increased productivity to take up the slack was imaginable, this could be negated by inflation or a decreased investment.

The German negotiators then referred to their defense budget request for 1966. They had originally asked for DM 19.2 billion, a reasonable increase over the 1965 budget of DM 18.3 billion, but the finance ministry was pressing for DM 17.3 billion. The defense budget had clearly lost its momentum. Granted, the German economy was still growing at the high annual rate of 5 percent in real terms, and money was available if the government had the political courage to increase the defense budget at the expense of something else or, even more courageously, to raise taxes. This was the issue that McNamara and Kai-Uwe von Hassel had to face in their November meetings. The prospects for full German payment of the offset commitment looked increasingly grim, the embassy having calculated that by October the shortfall might be as much as 50 percent.

From the beginning of my tour of duty I had taken an interest in seeing if there was anything either the United States or West Germany could do to improve their relations with the USSR. I had communicated often with the U.S. embassy in Moscow and with the State Department on this question, but no concrete conclusions had yet been reached. On December 9, Secretary Rusk and Soviet Foreign Minister Gromyko met on this issue during a luncheon at the Soviet embassy in Washington (memcon, Rusk-Gromyko talks, Dec. 9, 1966, Department of State Archives). The results are worth reporting.

Gromyko said that the Soviet Government attached the greatest importance to a German peace settlement. Until this problem was resolved Europe would continue to be explosive. The crucial points, in Gromyko's opinion, were: Western forces in Berlin and access to Berlin, borders, a nonaggression pact, GDR sovereignty, Western subversive activities in East Berlin, and denuclearization of the two Germanies.

Rusk replied that he saw two roads along which we could proceed. We could seek a final, historically satisfactory solution to the German problem, linked to organizing European security through arrangements between NATO and the Warsaw Pact. This would involve agreement among the vast number of people concerned in a variety of questions, including disarmament and trade. Perhaps, however, this was too soon for such a bold solution. The other approach, Rusk continued, would be to see what could be done with the ordinary people living in the immediate area. Something had already been done in trade and in relations with the East and West Germany to alleviate humanitarian problems, the recent passes for Christmas visits being one example. Perhaps more could be done to make the lives of the people more secure, said Rusk, adding that any move must be based on the judgment of the people living in the two Germanies. Did Gromyko think this possible, Rusk queried.

Gromyko responded that he did not consider judgment the right word in this context. The fact was that there were two German states and the division between them was most profound and almost impossible to overcome. The only approach to reunifying them was through disarming them and promoting mutual understanding between them. The Great Powers should make clear that they would make efforts to facilitate reunification; the method, however, should not be imposed from the outside.

Rusk agreed that there should be no question of a solution imposed "from outside." The United States was prepared to accept the choice made by the German people, including a continuation of the status quo. Gromyko said that Rusk was proposing to mix the Germans together and ask them to make a choice according to U.S. concepts. The USSR's view was that there were two German states. Rusk noted that the Soviets claimed that only the leaders of the two states could speak for the people. The United States believed that the people should have their say, in separate polls.

Gromyko contended that East Germany had already voted. We should let the two German states get together and discuss their problems. In response to Rusk's query, Gromyko said that if he represented East Germany he would try to improve relations with West Germany. Sooner or later East Germany would be recognized. The further the rearmament of West Germany and the fulfillment of MLF went, the more difficult a solution between the two states would be. Both must be in the same position—disarmed.

Rusk commented that in his view the only reason the United States and the Soviet Union maintained such huge forces was because they both feared they would have to fight a war over Germany. If the German problem could be solved, the way toward disarmament would be open. The United States did not ally itself with the Soviet Union to battle Hitler just to fight a Third World war over the German question. Gromyko agreed that some aspects of a German peace settlement could be made without disarmament in Europe and a denuclearization of the two Germanies. Rusk repeated that reunification was subject to the will of the German people. Nobody knew what factors would influence their decision, he said, but he thought national feelings would prevail, just as they would in the United States or Soviet Union.

Although this exchange was inconclusive, it revealed the basic division between the United States and the Soviet Union over the German question. The Soviets, according to Gromyko, were unwilling to consider any alternative to a negotiation between a disarmed West Germany and a legitimized East Germany represented by the Communist hierarchy there. We, by contrast, were sure that free separate polls in the two countries would both favor a German reunification based on German nationalism. There appeared to be no hope of bridging this gap.

1966

February 17–18	The NATO Nuclear Planning Group is formed
February 22	Great Britain reduces its obligations "east of Suez"
March 7	France announces it will leave NATO July 1, 1966, creating a NATO crisis
March 21–23	Ludwig Erhard is elected chairman of the CDU party congress
May 13	The congress of the German Trade Union Federation (DGB) votes against any emergency legislation
July 4–6	The Political Advisory Committee of the Warsaw Pact proposes a European Security Conference
September 15	Chief of the chancellor's office asks Erhard to be relieved of his duties
October 27	All FDP ministers in Erhard's cabinet resign
November 10	The CDU/CSU faction nominates Kurt Georg Kiesinger to succeed Erhard; coalition negotiations begin
November 27	The negotiating commissions of the CDU/CSU and SPD agree on a Grand Coalition
November 30	Chancellor Erhard resigns
December 1	Kurt Georg Kiesinger (CDU) elected chancellor as head of the Grand Coalition
December 13	Chancellor Kiesinger makes his government declaration
December 21	A Franco-German agreement is reached on the status of French troops in Germany after France's departure from NATO

Erhard Is in Trouble
December 1965–
October 1966

Erhard's visit to Washington on December 21–22, 1965, was based on his desire to discuss the nuclear problem with President Johnson, though it would soon be clear that Johnson's main concern was quite different. Erhard told Johnson that Germany was confident that American nuclear superiority would deter any full-scale invasion. But German leaders feared that if this represented only "a very small gap" the Warsaw Pact states might be tempted into thinking they could engage in small operations against the West without fear of nuclear retaliation.

The German government still hoped that sufficient European NATO countries could agree to an MLF to make it feasible. German leaders, however, were also interested in exploring other proposals, including a nuclear freeze or even, as proposed by the Poles, a reduction in nuclear weapons. In anticipation of the Erhard visit, one high-level German-American group had proposed that Germans consider renouncing any right of control over nuclear weapons. This group believed that such a move would at once enhance German prestige, particularly in the nonaligned world; show the fallacy in Communist charges of persisting German aggression; and provide more effective opportunities for an active German policy toward the Eastern Bloc.

Johnson's top agenda item was pressure on Erhard for more tangible support of U.S. policy on Vietnam and the U.S. effort there. After the president's dinner in Erhard's honor, Johnson took Erhard, George Ball, and myself up to a small, darkened room in the upper reaches of the White House. He began the meeting by noting that de Gaulle and the Soviets knew well that the United States had an unwavering commitment to defend Europe. Nevertheless, the United States was also obliged to honor its commitment in Vietnam, he added meaningfully. We had not yet, however, worked out how we were going to do that. If we withdrew we would be breaking a commitment and our word would no longer be respected, Johnson emphasized. We could not accept a defeat. The Vietnam conflict was beginning to put a drain on the U.S. budget, which would necessitate an increase, Johnson continued. This would make more difficult U.S. efforts to cure the balance of payments problem. He therefore expected the Federal Republic to make another payment that month under the offset agreement to maintain the quarterly U.S. government balance and preserve international confidence in the dollar.

Chancellor Erhard explained that he had been forced to pare his own budget by 10 percent after the 1965 election. He had even resorted to such extreme measures as repealing legislation already on the books. This was not to say that the FRG did not want to fulfill its commitment, Erhard said, reiterating his willingness to talk about the matter but reminding Johnson of the considerable difficulties Germany faced. Erhard said that he "felt ashamed" that there could never be equality in the contributions of the two countries to their joint efforts. He "intended to stand by our agreements," but he also had to "find ways and means." He pointed out that the balance of payments between the two countries was running in favor of the United States.

Erhard admitted that he could not say when Germany could pay. He must first balance his budget, and since reserves were unavailable, new reserves had to be created. "This does not mean," he said, "that we are withdrawing from the offset arrangements. Our defense minister has made certain suggestions." Erhard repeated that his government was thinking of sending a group of medical volunteers to Vietnam. If it were possible under German recruitment laws, he added, he would send two labor battalions the president asked for too.

Johnson then proceeded to apply his well-known treatment to Erhard. The demands of the Vietnam conflict and the strains they made on him were telling. His tall, rangy figure towered over the comparatively small figure of the chancellor. Gesticulating and speaking in a strong, strident voice, Johnson alternately wheedled and threatened. He put his whole body into his demands. I was shocked by the emotion and vehemence behind his argument. "Now we're going to find out who our friends are," he said. He recounted all we had done for Germany. Now was the time for Germany to pay us back, he declared. We badly needed the help and public support of our allies for our policy and war effort, he emphasized. We needed tangible, if only nonmilitary, aid. We expected Germany to take the lead by giving the most, Johnson announced with increasing conviction. Ball and I exchanged furtive glances of dismay and tried to slow him down.

In my view, Johnson had greatly overplayed his hand. Erhard, who appeared increasingly uncomfortable, verging on fright, must have had a very mixed reaction to the man who had sought his friendship scarcely two years earlier when Erhard visited Johnson's ranch.

The following day, Chancellor Erhard, Gerhard Schröder, and other German representatives met with Secretary of State Rusk and a large American group. There was a broad discussion of world problems such as normally occurs between two close allies. The particular subjects discussed were: problems between NATO and France, the Common Market and the Kennedy Round, Vietnam, space exploration, and finance.

On December 21, the two leaders issued a joint communiqué covering the results of their meeting. It said that close political and military cooperation was necessary among member nations of NATO, which the two countries would make every effort to maintain and strengthen. The Federal Republic and other interested partners in the alliance should find an appropriate way to participate in nuclear defense. Both countries upheld the principle of nuclear nonproliferation, denying that NATO was a cause of nuclear proliferation. They agreed to cooperate in space exploration, including a joint project to launch a German-built satellite. Both agreed to pursue all opportunities for achieving the common objective of peaceful German reunification as soon as possible on the basis of self-determination, including West Berlin. They noted that relaxation of tensions required progress in improving relations with Eastern Europe. They agreed to seek progress toward a united Europe and success in the Kennedy Round.

President Johnson expressed appreciation for substantial German aid in Vietnam. Chancellor Erhard said Germany would continue to assist in the cause of freedom. Both agreed that aid to developing countries must be increased. Both also reaffirmed that offset payments were of great value to both countries and should be fully executed and continued. The U.S. Great Society and the German Formed Society had much in common and should be the subject of a joint sharing of experience. Effective consultation between the two countries must be continued.

In their final meeting, the president asked Erhard if he was happy with the communiqué. Erhard responded that he was. Johnson assured

Erhard that he had read and agreed with the paper Erhard had given him on nuclear sharing, which detailed Germany's concerns and expectations in this field. He then asked for a $100 million payment under the offset agreement before the end of the year, now only ten days away, and for a $50 million German contribution to the Asian effort. Erhard replied that he would honor German commitments and would expedite military purchases. He reiterated, however, that he had his own budgetary problems. Erhard promised only $30 million to the Asian effort. At the appropriate time he would raise this to $50 million, payable over ten years.

Johnson emphasized the extreme budgetary problem he faced as a result of the war in Vietnam. He might have to go to Congress for an additional $125 billion. He urged Erhard to send to Vietnam the two hundred medical men and one-thousand-man construction battalion they had discussed earlier. Erhard reminded Johnson of the legal difficulty posed by the latter but promised he would throw his influence behind it. Erhard suggested Johnson visit Germany in 1966. Johnson replied that he was very busy, but added that he would be pleased to get an invitation.

In the face of rumors that the United States was considering abandoning the MLF, Rusk wrote a letter to Schröder on January 14 assuring him that the United States was prepared to move ahead without France but not on an exclusive U.S.-German basis. The letter highlighted the importance of British and Italian participation. Although the message was calculated to let the Germans down lightly, it obviously reflected a declining U.S. expectation that the conditions required for MLF's success could be met. President Johnson himself was clearly prepared to abandon it. Indeed, if Germany was the only interested power, the idea would only bring more trouble to the NATO alliance than it brought comfort to the Germans. It was disappointing that so much well-intentioned effort had been wasted and embarrassing for us and the Germans, particularly Schröder and Erhard. There was, however, no alternative, and I was glad to see the matter ended.

Perhaps to assuage the Europeans Secretary Rusk said in a speech in Cleveland on March 6: "If the European countries wish to play a larger role, possibly as a collective entity, in sharing the burdens and responsibilities of NATO defense," the United States would be receptive. This was an important statement, although it aroused little interest at the time and was not elaborated further by our government. European

NATO allies, moreover, have never responded. The issue of a collective European voice in NATO has been discussed back and forth without resolution to this day.

A possible consequence of a unified European role in NATO would, of course, be to give Europe a much stronger voice in NATO affairs. Matters taken up in the NATO Council have always been discussed by all parties before a decision is taken. If a European decision were already made, the area for discussion with the United States would be limited. On the other hand, such an arrangement could play an important role in defining the European position on defense matters and facilitating a U.S.-European consensus. If the Europeanization of the NATO members included nuclear matters, the consequences would likely be the creation of an independent European nuclear force based on the British and French nuclear arsenals. This would undoubtedly provoke opposition from those European countries fearing possible French hegemony and by France itself, which would prefer European acceptance of its force de frappe.

On the conventional side, the grouping of European countries within NATO could facilitate not only a European defense policy, including strategy, but even a European army. Without integrating forces, European and American commanders could be integrated at various command levels and perhaps rotated as SACEUR (Supreme Allied Commander Europe). I wrote to Secretary Rusk suggesting consideration of these questions pointing out that in a meeting with me on March 24 Jean Monnet had urged encouragement of inter-European cooperation in the foreign policy and defense fields corresponding to that achieved in the economic field in the EEC.

When Johnson finally dismissed the MLF in early 1966, the question of European participation in nuclear decision-making remained unresolved. Only the United States and West Germany were really interested. At least temporarily, it was settled by the creation of the NATO Nuclear Planning Group, an idea of McNamara's. For the first time, the other NATO members were given full information about U.S. nuclear forces and allowed to participate in planning for their deployment.

Meanwhile, Europe and NATO struggled to adjust to the difficult changes forced by de Gaulle's decision to expel the alliance's military organization from France and its command from Fontainebleau, near Paris, where it had been located since 1949. Brussels was chosen as new NATO headquarters, and logistical rearrangement through the Channel ports began. The Germans did their best to adjust to the new situation, which was made easier by French forces remaining in southern Germany.

On March 4, 1966, I wrote to Chancellor Erhard summarizing our government's views on the many different issues arising out of de Gaulle's actions vis-à-vis NATO (letter, Am Emb Bonn, Mar. 4, 1966). The United States considered it critical that it and Germany act in concert in these matters and wanted its position to be very clear.

We considered the French action against U.S. bases in France or against NATO as being against NATO as a whole. We stood committed to NATO as embodied in the 1949 treaty and would not be willing to substitute a system of bilateral security commitments. We wished to develop contingency planning with the other thirteen to maintain, no matter what France did, NATO's defensive capability, including a "forward strategy" on an integrated basis and relocating essential facilities abandoned on French soil. We would in consultation with our allies try to facilitate French full return to NATO.

Erhard's victory in the September 1965 elections had represented a major triumph, not just for him personally but for his party. He had always had to contend with bitter opposition from the pro-Gaullist clique in his party's ranks. But the economic recession that followed his election and was to be the principal reason for his decline came as a complete surprise. Because it was unrelated to any general European or worldwide recession, it was blamed on excessive government spending. Erhard was attacked in the Bundestag for large military purchases under the U.S. offset agreement, for heavy spending to bail out and modernize the national railways, and for huge subsidies to German farmers. A trade deficit was predicted, as was an increase in unemployment despite 700,000 unfilled jobs. At the same time, the Bundestag had recently voted to increase government pensions by 30 percent. Always wary of recessions and inflation, Germans expected leadership from Erhard that was not forthcoming, although he did attempt to cut expenditures by announcing a 10 percent cut in the 1966 budget.

Other factors also worked against Erhard. The neo-Nazi National Democratic party (NPD) crested at 8 percent in the 1966 state elections in Hesse and Bavaria, representing a reflection on the Erhard government. The discontent of the miners in the Ruhr's declining coal industry resulted in an almost 50 percent increase in SPD seats.

There had been an alarming run of sixty-six accidents among the controversial F-104 Starfighter planes the Germans had acquired from the United States. Both the Americans and the British were demanding purchase of military equipment to the full value of their balance of payments to offset the cost of maintaining their forces in Germany. Both former chancellor Adenauer and Federal President Lübke were supporting the idea of a Grand Coalition of the two major parties, CDU and SPD, and demands for a new government to solve the economic crisis were growing.

During the summer of 1966 discussions on the U.S.-German offset agreement moved toward a crisis, coming to a head during Erhard's visit to Washington in mid-September. The unpopular war in Vietnam was diminishing Johnson's credibility and popular support and exacerbating his budgetary and balance of payments problems. For his part, Erhard was fighting for his political life in the face of an increasingly threatening recession and budget crisis. The two men's problems intersected in their differences over the offset agreement.

I had been in Washington during my home leave in July and had discussed the offset question with both President Johnson and Secretary of Defense McNamara. It was clear that their position had hardened. As the time for the Erhard-Johnson meeting approached, I became increasingly apprehensive. I queried Erhard's office to see if he would like to discuss with me what position he might take in Washington, so I could help prepare the way. I was informed that he did not want to discuss the matter with anyone until he saw Johnson himself. In a sense, he wanted to "throw himself on Johnson's mercy." Had I seen him, I would have warned him not to expect any.

As the visit approached, Erhard's advisers became apprehensive. General Julius Klein, who often acted as a useful high-level go-between, told an embassy official on September 13 that Erhard had asked him what the reaction would be if a diplomatic illness caused the trip to be cancelled. Klein said that he had told Erhard that he would be finished, both in the United States and in Germany. Erhard reportedly agreed. When I arrived in Washington a few days before Erhard, I requested, as usual, a meeting with Johnson. For the first time I was told that this would be impossible because the president was spending a few days at his ranch. So I prepared a memorandum for the president on the meeting, which I was later assured he read before his meeting with Erhard. It read in part as follows:

September 22, 1966
Memo for the President
Subject: Your Meeting with Chancellor
Erhard, Sept. 26–27

Your meeting with Erhard next week will be the most critical one you have had with the German leader.

The meeting takes place against the backdrop of deterioration in U.S.-German relations, characterized by a fading confidence on the Germans' part in the firmness of our commitments to them and Europe by a feeling that they are not being given the consideration by us they feel is due them as an important and loyal ally. We should set as our primary goal the restoration of mutual confidence and ease in our relationship.

We must also take into account Erhard's weakened internal political position. This restricts his freedom in making concessions to us. Also, an obvious failure for Erhard in the talks could bring down his government. Rightly or wrongly the Germans—including the Chancellor—believe that he has a special relationship with you. If we let him down now he—or his successor—could draw the conclusion that too intimate a relationship with us is not a political asset—perhaps even a liability. This will not go unnoticed in other countries.

We should, therefore, not press the Chancellor too hard on his vulnerable points, should be prepared without sacrificing vital interests to make accommodation with him, and should try to assume at least the appearance of a successful meeting.

This is, in my judgment, a time to be generous. In so doing we can help assure retaining Germany as a valuable ally.

I predict that he will in private throw himself on your mercy, citing Germany's past performance as a loyal ally.

I argued strongly that Johnson consider sympathetically Erhard's probable request to stretch out offset payments and substitute debt repayment and purchases of U.S. bonds. In particular, I advised against reducing U.S. troops to meet the offset. I also urged that a joint commission be established to examine these repayment possibilities and recommend specific offset targets and force levels, stating, "If agreement can be obtained on force reductions in this way, they could be made with much less repercussion." I added, "We should not press the Chancellor to accept any public formula which rules out forever any multilateral NATO or European nuclear forces. It would be wise, however, to inform Erhard confidentially we regard the MLF/ANF as unlikely of achievement."

The climax of the ensuing discussions came during an all-day confrontation in the State Department. Robert McNamara represented the president; Kai-Uwe von Hassel spoke for the chancellor. Hassel, the perfect gentleman, soft-spoken with a well-modulated voice, was no match for McNamara. McNamara, always confident and quick to respond with the right fact or figure, spoke in rapid staccato phrases. He was able to inject a note of the United States's moral right to offset payments, whereas Hassel, asking for leniency in fulfilling an acknowledged obligation, was disadvantaged. Hassel became increasingly embarrassed and finally appeared to give up.

The crucial issue was whether to allow Germany to buy medium-term U.S. Treasury bonds as a substitute for an immediate cash purchase of military equipment and services. Although it represented an equivalent dollar payment, the purchase of bonds was, of course, not as satisfactory to the United States as was a final, cold-cash sale: the funds invested in bonds would eventually have to be repaid to the German government. The U.S. side was unyielding on this point. The final discussions took place at 11 A.M. on September 26 in a fateful "four-eyes" meeting between the president and Erhard at the White House. The only record comes from informal notes taken by Johnson's interpreter now in the State Department files.

Erhard observed that the two were meeting in arduous times. Both of them were dealing with difficult problems. People were searching to find ways to assess blame, but the two of them were, of course, used to that. They were expecting progress, which he hoped would be possible. He could assure the president that Germany would "stay the course and cooperate with the U.S.," the close ties between the two countries being a stabilizing factor all around the world. The German tendency to "lean toward France" was being pursued by a small but vocal minority, Erhard stated. Reconciliation between Germany and France was important; without it no progress could be made toward the economic and political unity of Europe. Erhard said that he did not, however, believe that Europe could be built on a bilateral German-French base.

Together our governments faced two basic problems, he observed—offset payments and U.S. troop levels. The former were due on June 30, 1967. At that time, some new formula had to be found for a follow-up agreement. American troops were very important to Germany, providing protection and a guarantee of future security, he acknowledged. Confidence in the United States was not lacking, but Germans needed to know where they stood, how they would be protected under a non-proliferation treaty, and what voice they would have in nuclear affairs. It was not just a question of military hardware.

President Johnson said he agreed with the chancellor's formulation of the problems they faced. He felt affection for Erhard and wanted to help him. Erhard interposed that the Germans appreciated the loyalty of the Americans in fulfilling their commitments in Vietnam and wanted to help us, adding, a little self-servingly, that whoever succeeded him might take a different view of loyalty to the United States. But meeting the current offset obligation put the Germans in a difficult economic situation, he continued. The German economy's growth curve currently had flattened. The necessity to reduce the national budget had required post facto cuts in thirty appropriations. His government had also been forced to enact a special price stability law that was just then taking effect. Then came Erhard's punch line. It would be impossible to fulfill all of the financial obligations under the present agreement. The German government would stand by its promises, but it needed more time. Erhard said that the German Central Bank was helping. (We knew that he was in contact with bank president Karl Blessing, who was in Washington at the time, but reportedly without success.) Erhard promised that the Federal Republic would pay the equivalent of an additional $250 million during the remainder of calendar year 1966 against $450 million in U.S. Treasury bills they were to purchase by then under the two-year offset agreement.

This left $450 million due on June 30, 1967. Erhard said that Germany would do all it could to reduce the shortfall, which would then be included in the follow-up military offset budget. He reminded Johnson that it was customary for businessmen who could not meet all of their obligations to roll the balance over in another loan. In defense of his plea for leniency, he cited German efforts to protect the dollar through purchase of so-called Roosa Bonds and engaging in "swaps." The Federal Republic had not sold dollars or bought gold since 1962. He added that Germany currently had an unfavorable trade balance with the United States of $800–$900 million a year and that the Federal Republic had previously paid some outstanding government-to-government debts before they were due.

President Johnson agreed with Erhard that the two principal problems were the offset and the level of U.S. forces in Germany. He explained, however, that his financial problems were greater than Erhard's. He was unclear on the essence of Erhard's remarks. In the past he had always taken the Germans' words for granted. If Germany could not keep its commitments it would put the United States in a serious situation, one he would have to look at carefully. This would in effect nullify the existing agreement, which would be disheartening. He added that Chancellor Erhard must be aware of the difficult situation he faced on troop levels. How, he asked, would he be able to defend himself against criticism in the face of what Erhard had told him? Could the Federal Republic not offer more cooperation in space projects or increased purchases of U.S. government bonds?

Johnson repeated that he understood the chancellor's problems and wanted to help him as a friend. He did not, however, want to see a situation created that might have regrettable results for both countries. He suggested that they refer the problem to economic and military experts on both sides. Although he undoubtedly had in mind the trilateral committee, he did not spell this out.

Erhard could only reply that it was bitter to hear the president say that he could not trust the German word. There was no reason to doubt the Germans' sincerity and loyalty, he declared. They would pay all they owed. All they asked was an extension. Erhard acquiesced in the referral of the offset problem to experts. Before he left, Erhard again urged the president to visit Germany in 1966, but Johnson was noncommittal. In the end, Erhard agreed that the final communiqué would obligate Germany to meet the full offset through mid-1967.

I saw Erhard as he came out of the meeting. He looked utterly dejected. I felt genuinely sorry for him. No one knew, of course, that Erhard's government would fall within a few weeks and that he would be forced to resign from the chancellorship.

In his memoirs Johnson (1971, 308) wrote that he had decided on a multilateral approach to the offset-U.S. force reduction problem in August and had asked John J. McCloy to represent the United States when Johnson was in New York in October to discuss European policy. Immediately after Erhard's visit, on October 7, 1966, Johnson set up a trilateral committee to resolve a number of related problems: the U.S.-German offset agreement; the equivalent British-German agreement, which had only recently been strengthened to full offset; and Sen. Mike Mansfield's resolution, already introduced with considerable support, calling for the United States to begin withdrawing forces from Europe.

Johnson chose to treat these problems together since they involved all three countries and could not be handled separately in Bonn and London, and he appointed John J. McCloy, the highly respected former U.S. high commissioner to Germany, to chair the trilateral committee.

Chancellor Erhard had outlined his views on the future of the offset agreement in a May 15, 1966, letter to Johnson in which he suggested that consideration be given to payments for other types of purchases in addition to those for purchase of military equipment and services. In his letter of August 31, 1965 (Dept. State no. 3), Rusk had advised Schröder that the United States had begun to look into the possibility of handling on a trilateral basis the closely related balance of payments problems affecting the Federal Republic, the United Kingdom, and the United States.

Johnson had no trouble persuading Prime Minister Harold Wilson of Britain, whose government was in desperate straits, to join the committee. Erhard was initially reluctant to join, but agreed during the meeting with Johnson in Washington. It was nonetheless late January 1967 before the Germans could join in the work of the committee, and by that time Erhard was no longer chancellor.

Meanwhile, on October 15, 1966, I had met Karl Carstens to sound him out on how the government, still under Erhard, proposed to deal with the offset. He told me confidentially that there would be an effort to obtain an additional DM 2 billion ($500 million) in appropriations to help meet the prospective $892 million deficit in offset payments for the period ending June 30, 1967. The money was to be raised as a supplement to both the 1966 and 1967 budgets and would presumably enable the Government to collect the $892 million, it was hoped from social insurance reserve funds, and deposit it as an arms purchase account in the U.S. Treasury by the deadline. This would be recorded as a capital receipt for the United States and a capital outflow for the Federal Republic, with the corresponding salutary effect on the U.S. balance of payments. It was understood, however, that this transaction would not relieve the German government of the obligation to pay for the associated $214 million worth of arms orders.

There may not have been a real meeting of the minds on this point. It seemed likely that, if the Germans agreed to prepay, they would do so only on the clear understanding that at least an equivalent amount of their offset obligation, and probably orders as well, would thereby be *extinguished*. But the United States was not prepared to agree to such a cancellation of offset obligations, instead regarding this payment as an advance deposit. This point needed to be clarified. In early November, I addressed some suggestions for a compromise settlement to McCloy (Amemb Bonn, Nov. 4, 1966).

During previous negotiations over force levels, the U.S. position had always been that they should be determined by the allies "on the basis of security considerations," broadly construed. McCloy's committee did not set long-term figures for the number of U.S. and British troops to be stationed in Europe under NATO. The principal issue was the number of U.S. aircraft to be brought home under a limited rotation plan, which was confined to a dual basing of one division. McCloy proposed bringing home 144 aircraft. The Germans argued for at least 76. McCloy compromised on 96.

An agreement between the three governments was finally reached on April 28, 1967. Under its terms, the Germans themselves were to determine how much military equipment they would buy from Britain and the United States to meet NATO force goals. The settlement of accounts for the remaining balance of payments deficits incurred by American and British troops in Germany was to be achieved by fiscal means, as mutually agreed. For the United States, German purchase of medium-term U.S. Treasury bonds was deemed acceptable as long as the United States continued to hold Germany's gold.

1967

January 27	Agreement on the peaceful research and use of the universe signed; put in force 10/10/67
January 31	The FRG and Rumania take up diplomatic relations
February 22	Fritz Erler, SPD Bundestag chairman, dies
April 6	An SPD-FDP senate under Heinrich Alberts formed in Berlin
April 12	Chancellor Kiesinger delivers government declaration on the German question
April 19	Konrad Adenauer dies in Rhöndorf
May 11	Great Britain, Ireland, and Denmark apply for EEC membership; France opposes, creating a Community crisis
May 15	Kennedy Round of tariff negotiations successfully concluded
May 22–23	The CDU party conference elects Kurt Kiesinger chairman
May 27–June 4	Shah of Iran visits the FRG and West Berlin
June 2	A police officer kills student Benno Ohnesorg during a protest demonstration against the shah's visit in West Berlin
June 5–10	The "Six Day War" between Israel and the Arab states starts

June 17	The People's Republic of China detonates its first hydrogen bomb
June 23–25	President Johnson meets Soviet Premier Alexei Kosygin in Glassboro, New Jersey
December 13–14	The Harmel Report on NATO's future tasks recommends a "two pillar doctrine" based on military security and détente

18

The Grand Coalition Comes to Power October 1966– January 1967

When it became known in Germany that Johnson and McNamara had refused to give Erhard the relief he sought despite his strong plea, Erhard suffered a severe political setback. Of what value was the presumed high regard in which he had always been held by Americans, Germans asked? On October 27, after Erhard had proposed an unpopular tax increase largely to meet the offset payment, the FDP's Erich Mende, deputy chancellor and junior partner in Erhard's coalition, withdrew his party from the government. Although Mende was personally fond of Erhard, he was alarmed at the prospect of a recession and wanted to avoid responsibility for it. After rejecting the alternatives of a new coalition with the small FDP or a grand coalition with the opposition SPD, Erhard announced on November 2 that he was ready to resign if another government could be formed. He was not even offered the presidency as a face-saver.

Erhard's fall came as a great shock to the U.S. government. Since democratic government had begun in Germany the United States had dealt with a succession of conservative governments. Although Erhard differed personally from Adenauer and did not agree with him on many ancillary policies, such as relations with France, both represented a reliable line of economic conservatism and pro-Europe, pro-NATO, pro-U.S., and anti-Communist policy. The United States had felt comfortable with these leaders, particularly Erhard, who was, somewhat to his disadvantage, considered "our man."

But the mood of Germany's political parties and leaders was changing. People were reacting against the rigid policies of the Adenauer-Erhard era. Some believed they had followed the U.S. line too closely, that they had allowed themselves to be overly influenced by the United States's great power confrontation with the Soviet Union and by its uncertain war in Vietnam. There had been little progress in Germany's Eastern policy and none toward German reunification. Adenauer was quoted as saying that Erhard's Eastern European policy had not been active enough and that he must go. Erhard's coolness toward de Gaulle had created bitter enmities, not just on the part of Adenauer but also of Strauss and other influential German Gaullists. Erhard had even failed in the area he knew best—economics.

There was a general feeling that only something as dramatic as a Grand Coalition could solve the smoldering budget crisis. On November 10 the SPD proposed talks on the selection of a new chancellor. After seventeen years of SPD opposition to CDU governments, there was a growing consensus in Bonn that the SPD could not be confined to the fringes of a new coalition. Willy Brandt, leader of the SPD, had gained increasing recognition both for his competence as governing mayor of Berlin and as the exponent of a fresh new look toward the East—Ostpolitik. His advocacy of small humanitarian steps, as exemplified by his successful Christmas passes between East and West Berlin, had increased his popular image. He was a good listener. His statements were all sufficiently vague to give hope to people who interpreted them in different lights. He would be a popular choice as foreign minister to succeed the more private Gerhard Schröder.

The post of chancellor was ultimately bestowed by the coalition on Kurt-Georg Kiesinger, who had been "in exile" from Bonn since 1958. For many years the leading foreign affairs spokesman for the CDU in the Bundestag, he had returned to become minister-president of his beloved native Baden-Württemberg after losing his bid to become foreign minister in 1958. He had filled the role of minister-president with great success, proving himself an excellent administrator. He also brought to everything he did a natural grace and dignity, an eloquence of style, that won him a large following. He was a scholarly, thoughtful man who beamed integrity and goodwill. His natural friendliness was extended to the many Americans living in the Stuttgart area and was reciprocated. Kiesinger's Nazi associations had been minimal and were largely forgiven him.

The parliamentary situation during the change in government was volatile. After the four FDP cabinet ministers withdrew on October 27, Erhard governed with a weak "caretaker" minority government while the CDU decided between Rainer Barzel and Kiesinger. On November

8 the Bundestag, including some CDU members, voted against Erhard 255 to 246, but Erhard refused to resign. Kiesinger was selected the CDU candidate on November 10. Erich Mende was still deciding between FDP coalition with Kiesinger, which would have a strong 294-vote majority, or with Brandt with only a 3-vote margin.

Brandt later said that he would have "considered [this] a good thing—if it had been possible" (Binder 1975, 219). Aware that West Berlin had fifteen Social Democratic deputies and one Free Democrat, which would have provided a respectable SPD-FDP majority, he revived the idea of granting full voting rights to the Berlin deputies. Brandt's question was discussed in a meeting of the Bonn group, which included the U.S., British, and French ambassadors as well as Karl Carstens for the FRG. In addition to abiding by the legal reasoning for the original decision of 1949, the group agreed that a change of status at the time of elections would have put the three powers in the position of changing the rules in the middle of a game, in effect granting votes to the SPD and the FPD. This we correctly considered would be tantamount to intervention.

At the same time, we did not want to raise any unnecessary issue that could affect the election even slightly. Since no change was being made, we considered a statement unnecessary. I had always been so conscious of the danger that the U.S. embassy could be accused of favoritism in an election that I never let embassy personnel bet on German elections or predict their outcome, even secretly, to the State Department. The Bonn Group decided that the three embassies would volunteer nothing; if questioned the group would say only that there would be no change in the existing voting procedures. We did not see how such a statement could invite any criticism.

But even the best laid plans of mice and men can go awry. On the eve of the final voting for chancellor, Brandt intimated, during a speech in Hamburg, that he might be able to use the votes of the Berlin SPD deputies for his election. This provoked a press request to the U.S. embassy, probably the only embassy open at the time. To the best of my knowledge this request was answered in accordance with the Bonn Group's decision; it was stated only that there would be no change. This led Brandt—who reportedly was furious—to accuse the U.S. embassy of meddling in German affairs by denying West Berliners the right to participate in the vote.

Brandt's position, which did not evolve into an official protest, would not appear justified under the circumstances. A story that I was never able to verify, however, might explain why he felt he had been misled. A medium-level State Department official, himself of German origin, had been visiting in Berlin a short time before and, in confidential discussions with SPD party members, either said or gave the impression that under certain circumstances the United States would be willing to support the granting of full powers to the Berlin deputies. It is possible that Brandt might have honestly felt that he had been let down by the United States. In any event, Brandt later gave evidence that he harbored a resentment over this affair.

The next day serious discussions of a "big coalition" began between the CDU's Kiesinger and Herbert Wehner of the SPD. Mende was greatly disappointed, but since he opposed increasing taxes, he could not form a coalition with Kiesinger, and without the Berlin votes he lacked the strength to form a coalition with Brandt. The final deal on the Grand Coalition was reached at 3 A.M. on November 26.

Both Brandt and Kiesinger had always been popular with Americans. I welcomed their selection to their new posts. The embassy had supported Brandt's experiment with Ostpolitik, and we all looked forward to working with him. Since my first visit to Baden-Württemberg, I had developed a high regard and a friendly feeling for Kiesinger. He appeared in every way a real gentleman, and his warm, expansive smile was irresistible. I looked forward to working with him as chancellor. I understood that there would be changes in German policies to which we had grown accustomed. His expected turn to de Gaulle and greater independence from us did not bother me. I felt that the German-French rapprochement was a good thing per se and that lessening dependence on the United States was long overdue. I welcomed the beginning of our relations with the new government and the challenges it would represent to me and the U.S. government.

With Erhard's fall, Johnson and the key cabinet members who had been involved in the recent U.S.-German negotiations must have engaged in some soul-searching. I happened to be in Washington on leave when Erhard paid his first visit to Washington after leaving office. Johnson, who I believe was genuinely fond of Erhard, gave a luncheon in Erhard's honor at which he made some warm and complimentary remarks. I sat on one side of the president, Erhard on the other. "Do you think, George, that we were responsible for Erhard's fall?" Johnson asked me during a lull in the proceedings. Although I realized that it was not what he wanted to hear, I could only reply, "Well, Mr. President, he fell for a number of reasons, mostly due to his own shortcomings. There's no question, however, that the results of that last meeting contributed." Johnson did not reply, but a mutual friend later confided that Johnson had commented that I "told him things that he didn't like to hear."

Apart from Kiesinger and Brandt, the Grand Coalition cabinet included an impressive array of talents from both the CDU-CSU and the SPD. Gerhard Schröder, who was shifted to defense minister, was a reliable known quantity. As minister of finance Franz Josef Strauss brought both energy and a sense of order into the government's effort to improve the faltering German economy. He worked surprisingly well with the talented new minister of economics, Karl Schiller, a top-notch professional economist with a quick mind and a gift for explaining complex problems. Georg Leber, who had risen to leadership in the German labor movement through the building and lumber unions and who later headed the Defense Ministry, became minister of transport. Gustav Heinemann, whose talent and prestige led him to the presidency of Germany in 1969, was appointed minister of justice. Carlo Schmid, an SPD leader in Foreign Affairs and a brilliant speaker, became head of Länder Affairs.

The new chancellor, Kurt-Georg Kiesinger, was, like his predecessors, a Christian Democrat. He had made his reputation in the 1950s as an authoritative parliamentary supporter of Adenauer's foreign policy. As might have been expected, there had been a lull in our embassy contacts with the government during the time required to form the new administration. The Christmas season had also intervened, a period taken seriously by Germans, despite politics. It was necessary, of course, to blend both the policies and leaders of the two parties, which had been in implacable opposition during the entire postwar period. Although 80 abstentions and negative votes were cast by members of the two coalition parties, the final vote in the Bundestag was an overwhelming 340 to 109, and the coalition parties had 468 votes against 50 for the FDP.

Kiesinger's inaugural statement on December 13 highlighted the grim German economic situation, the principal factor behind the change of government that brought him to the chancellorship. He acknowleged that 700,000 West Germans were unemployed and 340,000 more were working part-time, the first time in over a decade that employment had been a problem in Germany. He promised a further cut in government expenditures but warned that this would still leave a deficit of DM 3 billion in the coming year. The states and municipalities would be urged to reduce their expenditures, and bank loans would be limited. He called for a controlled expansion of the economy in light of the meager 2 percent increase in national income in 1966, along with a reduction in investment and building activity.

Kiesinger's second theme was foreign policy. He promised to continue the policies toward the Federal Republic's Western allies that had characterized both the Adenauer and Erhard administrations. But he also emphasized, for the first time in West Germany's postwar history, that his government would pursue establishment of diplomatic relations with Eastern European countries "wherever possible."

Deemphasis on relations with the United States was a major consideration for the new government. Kiesinger made it clear that his government would not be running to the United States to solve its problems. He had initially been vague about an early visit to the United States, seeming to prefer to wait until after Johnson's expected visit to Europe that spring. His first foreign trip, on January 13–14, was to France. Nonetheless, on his first day back Kiesinger asked me to call so he could report on his visit (telegram, Amemb Bonn to Secstate, Jan. 16, 1967). I was the first ambassador to be so invited. It soon became evident that both he and Willy Brandt, who had taken over as foreign minister in the new government, wanted early invitations to visit Washington.

In reporting to me on his meeting with de Gaulle, Kiesinger said that his objective had been to revive the Franco-German treaty without creating any "twilight areas" of uncertainty. He had had a clear discussion with de Gaulle on the relations between both of their countries and the United States. De Gaulle had professed respect for the United States but had considered the country so powerful that it could not help "dominating." Even though this was intended in a "friendly way," France would not submit. While continuing its ties and alliances with the United States, France would carry out an independent policy, de Gaulle had told Kiesinger.

In reply, Kiesinger said he had agreed with de Gaulle that the United States had its own interests (which it would be "stupid" of us not to stick with as a guide to our actions). The problem was to determine the extent to which U.S. interests coincided with those of individual countries and of Europe as a whole. At the peak of the Cold War interests had corresponded closely. Perhaps there was a difference now. We should talk about it, Kiesinger had urged, making it clear to de Gaulle that Germany's position differed from France's. Germany would continue to support an integrated NATO and the presence of U.S. troops in Europe and would cooperate with the United States to this end. He had agreed with de Gaulle, however, that Europe must increase its contribution toward "the molding of its fate."

According to Kiesinger, his exchange with de Gaulle contained little debate or extended discussion; de Gaulle had recognized that Germany's position and attitude differed from his own. Kiesinger interpreted this to mean that de Gaulle expected that the Germans would retain their traditional ties "for the time being" but would eventually accept the French view. The two leaders agreed that cooperation under the Franco-German treaty need not be handicapped by their respective attitudes toward the United States.

De Gaulle had emphasized the importance of a policy of détente in Europe. The present confrontation in Europe must be reduced "step by step." This was a thorny problem, but it would be less difficult now than in the future to get the Soviets to agree to détente—including increased economic and cultural exchanges, de Gaulle had said. France needed a period of peace in order to develop its country. Kiesinger had replied that Germany also sought détente in Europe. They had agreed that this was the only way to preserve peace. Germany hoped, however, that throughout the process its allies would keep German reunification in mind. Kiesinger realized that the solution could not be "figured out now" but had stressed that it should not be left entirely to the future. Kiesinger had told de Gaulle that he could not accept France's belief that German reunification must wait until complete détente had occurred, at which time it would come automatically. The Germans were not willing "to pursue détente just for détente's sake." He believed that every peaceful opportunity should be seized to further reunification.

On February 27, 1967, Kiesinger, perhaps inadvertently, used the word "complicity" in connection with the initiation of the Nuclear Non-Proliferation Treaty (NPT) by the United States and the Soviet Union. President Johnson reportedly was furious. At a large luncheon tendered for visiting NATO Secretary General Manlio Brosio, at which a number of German journalists and I were present, Kiesinger attempted to correct his faux pas. Turning to me, he said to all that in recent weeks he had stressed the desirability of renewing broad discussions with the United States on common problems we faced as a framework for more specific issues under negotiation. He had by no means intended to criticize Americans, he added, noting that Germany also had responsibilities in connection with the precipitation of discussions of the NPT.

At this juncture the Grand Coalition government appeared to me to be still "shaking down." It was too early to predict just where United States relations with the new regime would end up. Although dramatic changes were occurring, I did not consider them all bad.

19

The Nuclear
Non-Proliferation Treaty
January–April 1967

$\mathbf{T}$he Nuclear Non-Proliferation Treaty, one of the most important accomplishments in the widely supported effort to limit and control the use of nuclear weapons, was a revealing test of the German-American relationship. It was signed on July 1, 1968, by three nuclear powers—the United States, Great Britain, and the Soviet Union—and more than fifty other nations, not including Germany, which did not sign until November 1969. France and China, both of which had conducted nuclear tests and developed nuclear weapons, did not sign; neither did a number of non-nuclear countries, some of which were in various stages in the development of nuclear capability. In 1974 India joined those who had tested a nuclear bomb. By 1985, 192 non-nuclear nations had adhered to the treaty.

Under the terms of the NPT, the non-nuclear countries forswore nuclear weapons and the nuclear signatory powers agreed to share nuclear technology, work for general nuclear disarmament, and "seek to achieve the discontinuance of all nuclear weapons for all times." In view of Germany's role in two world wars and West Germany's reputation in nuclear science, it was clear from the treaty's inception that the Federal Republic was an important potential signatory.

Considering that the Federal Republic has since become the home of one of the world's most active and best-organized antinuclear movements, it is illuminating to recall how Germans looked at their nuclear opportunities and objectives twenty years ago. The Germans understood that they could never become a nuclear power, and they had no desire to. From a purely practical standpoint, to build a nuclear bomb they would have to conduct nuclear tests, which could be easily detected and could lead to immediate retaliation by the USSR and almost all other nations who would never tolerate a German "finger on the nuclear trigger." Nonetheless, the Germans sought certain assurances about the treaty's impact on their security, economy, and international status: that it not hinder creation of an MLF or European nuclear force; that it not handicap their participating in nuclear development for peaceful purposes; and that it not enhance the international status of East Germany, a concern they had already expressed at the time of the Limited Test Ban Treaty.

By the time the Grand Coalition government came to power, considerable progress had been made on the NPT, and on December 20 I was able to deliver to Kiesinger and Brandt a complete draft of the text, together with certain interpretive comments furnished me by the State Department. On January 11, 1967, we were advised that the West German cabinet had agreed to the NPT in principle. I knew, however, that this was only the beginning and that many roadblocks lay ahead. Another eighteen months went by before the final signing.

During my meeting with Brandt on January 10, I had attempted to refute certain false allegations about the NPT that had appeared in the German press (telegram, Amemb Bonn to Secstate, 7962, Jan. 10, 1967). Apart from requesting an official statement outlining the U.S. interpretation of the treaty, Brandt appeared very relaxed about the NPT. He was unconcerned about the effect of the treaty on a European nuclear force or on GDR attendance at a conference pursuant to the agreement. He seemed, characteristically, more concerned about issues likely to be raised by the non-nuclear countries, particularly the neutrals. Could we make some statement that the nuclear powers would not use nuclear weapons as a threat against them?, he asked.

In order to inform Washington where the NPT stood in Germany, I sent a report to the State Department on January 17. I noted that the West German Cabinet had on January 11 agreed in principle to join the NPT enterprise. This did not mean, however, that U.S. problems with the Germans on this issue were over. In the Cabinet, Schröder, Strauss, and even Kiesinger could be expected to continue to oppose the NPT through the device of seeking clarification changes. The chancellor's comments to the press on January 16 were not positive, and he expressed to me his concern at the possible adverse effect of the NPT on European political integration.

I was concerned by reports of rumors in German political circles that we had already reached agreement with the Soviets and that there were secret codicils and side agreements. The basic weakness of the U.S. position lay in our not being able to tell the Germans that we had discussed with the Soviets the effect of the treaty on a possible European nuclear force in the event of European political integration. This open option had emerged as one of the principal German preoccupations in connection with the NPT. The Germans feared that we wanted to keep them from participating in a nuclear force of any kind.

On January 13, Kurt Birrenbach, chairman of the supervisory board of August Thyssen-Hutte, Christian Democratic member of the Bundestag, and an important factor in German-American relations, raised a new problem (telegram, Amemb Bonn to Secstate, 8150, Jan. 13, 1967). He told me that he believed that the first sentence of Article I, which prohibited "any transfer whatsoever," precluded the transfer of existing nuclear weapons to a successor European force. I advised him of our contrary view, but he was not convinced. The use of the term indirect had, as German Ambassador Heinrich Knappstein pointed out to the State Department, also raised apprehensions. It was not that the Germans considered European political integration to be imminent; but they did not want to promise their traditional enemy never to join a united Europe having its own nuclear force. If the Soviets signed the treaty without a clarification on this issue, the Germans feared that the Soviets might raise it later, even threatening a casus belli out of it.

I recognized that if we were to get a treaty, we had to stick to the principle that what is not prohibited is permitted. I pointed out to the State Department that any unclarity would cost us an increasing price in good relations as we tried to get a German signature. To minimize this risk, I suggested an early statement of how we understood the treaty in a letter from Rusk to Brandt, with the additional assurance that our interpretation would be made public at an appropriate time, particularly if the Soviets should contend that the treaty prohibited a European nuclear force.

Doubts and questions were being asked by a number of German Cabinet officials with a legitimate interest in NPT. An able career officer, Ambassador Swidbert Schnippenkötter, who had been appointed to the position of disarmament representative, coordinated the activities arising out of NPT within the German government. The capable federal minister of scientific research, Gerhard Stoltenberg, also played an active role. The questions raised by all concerned, however, whether genuine or based on efforts to "show off" or have a say in an important decision, resulted in endless duplication and confusion. There was a tendency to question all of our explanations and to use them as a basis for new questions.

In my meeting with Chancellor Kiesinger on January 16 (telegram, Amemb Bonn to Secstate, 8224, Jan. 16, 1967), he had raised the questions uppermost in his mind. I had reported that my recent visit to Washington had shown three issues of foremost concern to those I talked with: the NPT, progress in relations with Eastern Europe, and a successful Kennedy Round. After going over material recently furnished by the German government, I asked Kiesinger what his particular problems with the NPT were. I pointed out that nuclear explosions were probably not practicable in a densely populated country like Germany and that there were no restrictions on peaceful uses.

Kiesinger responded that his principal concern lay in the possible effect of the treaty on the development of European political unification. This could, he said, develop in various ways—for instance, as a federation or as a confederation. Former Minister of Foreign Affairs Walter Hallstein, in particular, was greatly disturbed over this factor and had told Kiesinger so in a recent meeting. Kiesinger hoped that this aspect of the treaty could be made clear.

I pointed out that in our view the present wording of the draft treaty would not preclude a European nuclear force under the political control of a European federation, confederation, or unitary state and also assuming that a single control over foreign and security policy emerged. In the transitional arrangements that might occur until then, a wide variety of cooperative nuclear arrangements were possible, assuming the nuclear forces involved remained under the political control of a present possessor government or governments. Any nuclear weapons arrangements that the Germans now had with the United States would also, in theory, be possible with either France, Britain, or both. Kiesinger expressed his gratitude for this explanation.

Minister of Science Gerhard Stoltenberg, who was principally concerned with the scientific and industrial aspects of the treaty, was a highly intelligent man whom I considered should be taken seriously. In my first talk with him he presented Germany's objections so powerfully and, I believed, so fairly, that I knew we were in trouble. Without seeking permission, I advised the State Department that I was flying back that evening for consultations. Later, at lunch at the embassy on February 21, Stoltenberg described the intensive negotiations going on within the German government between the Foreign, Economics, Defense, and Science ministries, not to mention the Chancellery (telegram,

Am Emb Bonn, 9804, Feb. 21, 1967). It was his impression that the principal issues remaining were the potential obstacles to development and use of nuclear energy for peaceful purposes embodied in the safeguards envisioned in the NPT's Article III.

The Germans were concerned not so much with the present international inspection policy and methods under conditions where inspection was voluntary but with what the constraints would be like under a greatly enlarged responsibility with mandatory inspection. He observed that the existing international inspection agency, the International Atomic Energy Agency (IAEA) in Vienna, was a "little U.N." with both Communist and neutralist members. He feared that it might, in the future, adopt policies contrary to the interests of the Western industrialized nations engaged in development of nuclear energy for peaceful uses. He was also concerned that IAEA inspection might require that inspectors understand the technological concepts underlying the installations, thus increasing the danger of industrial espionage.

Stoltenberg considered it significant that the nuclear powers excluded inspection of their own nuclear programs for military use. He said it was even more difficult for the non-nuclear powers to accept the nuclear powers' exclusion of their installations for peaceful use. Although Stoltenberg understood that we might accept inspection, we both understood that the Soviet Union would not. He was concerned that the nuclear powers would have a competitive advantage in the development of nuclear reactors and other industrial and commercial applications if we were to join the Soviet Union and reject inspection, too.

The Germans did not believe that the Eastern European countries would, in the foreseeable future, be competitors in peaceful use applications. But the Soviet Union could by the 1970s reach a competitive technological position. Because Soviet exports could be made on a political rather than an economic basis, the Soviet Union could become a significant rival in world markets. I advised Stoltenberg that, in our own experience, opportunities for industrial espionage under IAEA inspection were minimal.

Since France would not adhere to the NPT, Stoltenberg also feared that problems might arise in the future with regard to Europewide cooperation in nuclear affairs, particularly in fuel supply and reprocessing. I pointed out that neither we nor the Soviets had indicated any desire to eliminate Euratom, whatever the other countries did with respect to IAEA standards. Stoltenberg accepted fully the U.S. argument that technical "spin-off" on the weapons side was negligible. He did not raise the question of possible discrimination in the use of nuclear explosions.

Stoltenberg clearly saw West Germany as a major potential competitor in the field of nuclear development for peaceful use. He did not want the Federal Republic handicapped by NPT-engendered espionage—or unnecessary constraints. On the basis of our discussion, I asked the State Department to continue furnishing me comprehensive reviews of the safeguards issue. One important conclusion they revealed was that the technical nature of the IAEA inspections did not permit the inspectors access to information of commercial value. I explained to Stoltenberg that U.S. experience with IAEA on "peaceful uses," which we had put under their inspection, had not given competitors any advantage. On the basis of data I received I was able to explain convincingly that the NPT would not adversely affect recent arrangements for fuel supply and reprocessing within the European community.

The United States agreed with the Germans that no problem in the "peaceful uses" field would be created by technological "spin-off" in the nuclear weapons field. I pointed out that the United States already complied with proposed NPT safeguards in its current bilateral supply agreements with West Germany, Italy, and the Netherlands. The United States required no information or knowledge of nuclear research and development from the recipient countries. For good and accepted reasons, it was true that the treaty prohibited nuclear explosions by non-nuclear states. President Johnson had, however, offered appropriate nuclear services to non-nuclear nations on a nondiscriminatory basis, subject only to prevailing international safeguards. In any event, West Germany, because of its population density, would probably provide few opportunities for peaceful nuclear explosions. These explanations seemed to help, but we still had far to go.

The Grand Coalition came into office promising change in foreign policy, particularly Eastern policy. Delivering this promise proved to be harder than anticipated. The coalition itself, which had brought together sharp protagonists, was a new and untried method, an experiment. Brandt had already made a name for himself as the originator of Ostpolitik. Kiesinger, who had had considerable foreign experience in the Foreign Office and the Bundestag, had coordinated Franco-German cultural exchanges, and had participated in many early European unity meetings, saw Brandt as a political competitor. Kiesinger wanted to be his own Foreign Minister and reportedly did so, largely, in secret through individuals high in the Foreign Office hierarchy. Brandt headed a ministry that had been run by the CDU for twenty years; most of the diplomats had in one way or another become closely bound to the CDU. Kiesinger had allowed Brandt to call on de Gaulle in December, but Brandt felt that the Foreign Office had undercut his initial attempts to develop an Ostpolitik.

In a telegram to Secretary of State Rusk on June 30, 1967 (Amemb Bonn, 15466), I summarized my observations on the Brandt-Kiesinger relationship. I could find no major difficulties on points of substance. There were shadings of difference, Brandt being less reserved on the NPT and apparently more eager than Kiesinger to see the United Kingdom enter the Common Market. In general, where such minor differences existed, Brandt accommodated himself to Kiesinger's views. It was, moreover, Herbert Wehner, Brandt's deputy as chairman of the SPD, who normally negotiated with Kiesinger to resolve differences between the two parties rather than Brandt. As a result, and also because of his frequent absences from Bonn, the style Brandt had developed tended to weaken his voice in the formulation of foreign policy.

In pursuit of its major concern over East-West relations, in January the German government established diplomatic relations with Rumania, the most independent of the Soviet bloc countries. In April Kiesinger and Brandt, acting together and following Erhard's lead, made sixteen proposals to the GDR for consideration at the Annual Congress of the Socialist Unity party (SED), ruler of the GDR. In addition to increased trade, West Germany, with Kiesinger and Brandt acting together, proposed technological cooperation, youth exchanges, free passage for newspapers, the easing of travel restrictions, and more frequent visits across the Berlin Wall between relatives. Brandt said over the radio that the purpose of these proposals was "to make the lives of people more bearable, as long as the division of Germany exists." East Germany prime minister, Willi Stoph, rejected the proposals in May by demanding full recognition of the GDR and other unacceptable conditions.

The USSR also struck back with accusations that the Kiesinger-Brandt government's Eastern policy was an attempt to undermine the solidarity of the Socialist bloc. The Soviets were not ready for détente in the East and made every effort to block it. Ostpolitik seemed dead in its tracks, a nonstarter. It was impossible for Brandt to put forward any live blueprint for Ostpolitik, including what he hoped to achieve—and when.

Nevertheless, 75 percent of West Germans said in polls that they favored Ostpolitik as they understood it.

Because Brandt was expected to be the architect of the new Eastern policy I was anxious to obtain from him a preview of what he hoped to accomplish. Negotiations were already underway with Rumania and Czechoslovakia, and negotiations with Hungary and Bulgaria were in the works. It was obvious that the principal stumbling block would be the Berlin clause, prescribing participation by West Berlin in all West German international agreements. Brandt urged that the Allies respond favorably to Germany's proposal for an "automatic Berlin clause," making clear that the Allies had asked the West German government to assume certain responsibilities for West Berlin in its relations with other nations.

I agreed fully with Brandt that we should support—as we had already done in consultations with Britain and France—the German proposal for a new Berlin clause procedure. In the meantime, President Johnson had spoken out strongly in favor of movement in East-West relations. The United States, as well as Germany under the Grand Coalition, was eager to make progress in relations with the East. The opportunities, however, were just not there. In July 1968 Germany restored relations with Yugoslavia, but the Soviet invasion of Czechoslovakia in August put relations with the East in a deep chill.

Then there was Poland. Premier József Cyrankiewicz of Poland had argued in a recent interview that it was better for the Poles to have as neighbors people who recognized their border than people who did not. This, of course, was another way of saying that East Germany had recognized the Oder-Neisse line, defined at Potsdam in 1945 as the provisional Polish-German border, whereas the Federal Republic had not. Brandt said that he considered it critical that the German people know about the international situation affecting their Eastern border— namely, what position West Germany's various allies took on the Oder-Neisse border, which effectively consigned a third of prewar Germany to postwar Poland.

I replied that the U.S. official position was unchanged: that Americans still held that the final delineation of the German border must await the peace treaty with Germany that had been pending since the end of World War II. I admitted that this was not a substantive position. Although we did not wish to get ahead of Germany, I said we would support any flexibility the Germans chose to exhibit in their attitude toward their borders.

Contrary to custom, Chancellor and Mrs. Kiesinger dined with my wife and myself alone on March 2. In our private discussions after dinner, Kiesinger advised me that the budgetary and financial situation when he took over the chancellorship was much worse than he had expected. Although the government had reasonable hopes that the severe restrictive measures on the budgetary side, accompanied by certain countercyclical measures to stimulate the economy, would work, there would be serious problems if they did not. In this context, he noted with some regret the almost complete independence of the German central banking system.

Kiesinger expressed moderate optimism about the FRG's Eastern European policy, noting, however, that the Soviets and the East Germans were trying to slow up West Germany's establishment of diplomatic relations with the other Eastern European countries. I assured him that the FRG could count on full U.S. support of its efforts in this direction. What his government was doing was consistent with what we had favored for some time. He was glad to accept my offer of a stepped-up exchange between our two governments of political analyses affecting Eastern Europe. He remarked that Soviet policy toward Germany remained ambivalent but that a process of change was undoubtedly going on; even the GDR was changing. The younger generation there was acquiring a certain pride in its accomplishments, though less in the system itself. This would not handicap reunification efforts but help them, Kiesinger declared.

Kiesinger was most anxious that the recent misinterpretations in the press of certain of his statements calling for increased consultation between the United States and West Germany be clarified. He had not intended to criticize U.S. policy but to stress that both the United States and Germany must seek to develop through mutual discussions a broader framework for cooperation. This was, I believed, evidence of Kiesinger's persistent search for a broader intellectual base for German foreign policy and his relations with the United States. As a thoughtful, sophisticated man and political leader, he sought to avoid short-term improvisations and reactions. He was beginning to show, also, what would emerge more clearly later—the inherent conflict between his Gaullist leanings and his relations with the other European states and America.

In late February, having become increasingly concerned with the doldrums in which U.S.-German relations seemed to be floundering, I informed Rusk that we were in a difficult stage in our relations with the Federal Republic, where fears of American disinterest and abandonment were reaching disturbing proportions. Although this sentiment was based more on emotion than on facts, this was small comfort. I told him we had to understand what lay beneath this emotion and to consider steps to reverse the trend (telegram, Amemb Bonn, 9959, Feb. 25, 1967).

As I saw it, Germans were troubled because they did not see clearly the future role to which they felt entitled. During the past year they had witnessed a weakening of NATO, which they regarded as the keystone of the established order and the basis for their security. They saw many mutual interests emerging between the United States and the Soviet Union that they felt would realign the pattern of postwar security. They wanted increasingly to pursue their own national interests and establish a more favorable position in the world community. Although they were unable to define just what this position should be, they were suddenly fearful that if they did not act swiftly, the two great powers would decide Germany's destiny between them. In short, they felt "boxed in."

I added that we had begun our relations with the new government under a number of handicaps. First and foremost was the fall of the Erhard government, both because of its close ties to the United States and our presumed connection with its demise. The offset issue, which had been central to Erhard's problems, also raised questions about how closely we continued to identify European security with our own. Although the new government said little about it, I assumed that they resented deeply having to pay the current offset in light of the serious budgetary problems they had inherited. In addition, there was the increasing conviction that the United States had lost interest in Germany and Europe because of its preoccupation with Southeast Asia.

I nonetheless believed we had made progress in establishing good relations with the Grand Coalition. Kiesinger and Brandt were to us well-known, sympathetic quantities. They had made it clear that, despite their bow to the French, they wished to improve understanding with Washington. Unfortunately, their efforts in this direction had been thwarted to date by the highly negative German reaction to the NPT—a reaction that reflected all of the attitudes mentioned above. There was a particular feeling of frustration that the United States had not adequately consulted Germany before presenting it with the NPT as a fait accompli, without taking into account possible adverse effects on German and European interests. Despite our best efforts, Germans persisted in regarding the NPT as part of a new pattern of world organization, secretly worked out and imposed by the two superpowers. I mentioned to Rusk Chancellor Kiesinger's hopes that German-U.S. discussions could go beyond specific points of disagreement to broader and more positive aspects of common policy as well. I believed he had in mind that the United States should try to inform the German government what its long-term plans were.

Kiesinger was a man of high intelligence who sought an overall conceptual framework within which to place particular policy aspects. It was evident that Kiesinger strongly desired, at firsthand, an exposure to the president's personal thinking for the future. I therefore proposed that I be permitted to tell Kiesinger that the president wished to come to Germany but that in the absence of a firm decision this should not preclude an early Kiesinger visit to the United States. I would assure him that he would be warmly welcomed. I urged that the United States provide answers to the seemingly endless questions raised by the Germans, both in public and private, on the NPT. Finally, I urged that we offer full support to the German government in its Eastern policies and engage in in-depth discussions with German leaders regarding our long-range views on Western security and the future of NATO.

Unfortunately, my recommendations to Rusk reached the press in Washington, with disquieting results. Media coverage implied that the proposal for an invitation had not originated with Johnson but from me, because Kiesinger "has in recent statements appeared to be asking for" a visit, as one report put it. I urged a clear extension of an invitation to Kiesinger, subject to a suitable time being worked out, of which the press would be quickly advised. Fortunately, Johnson's visit to Bonn to attend the funeral of Konrad Adenauer in April served to take the pressure off for a Kiesinger visit. It eventually came in August.

Following a helpful early March visit by Ambassador William Foster, director of the U.S. Arms Control and Disarmament Agency, the most intractable issue remaining in the negotiations with Germany over the NPT appeared to be the question of possible industrial espionage under IAEA inspections pursuant to Article III. Other officials reported a widespread suspicion in Germany that the whole purpose of the United States in proposing the NPT was to gain a stranglehold over the German nuclear industry so that American industry could achieve a world monopoly.

On March 10 I advised the State Department of this problem and expressed the view that it resulted from Germans' lack of knowledge and experience with IAEA inspections, which limited discussions to a simplistic level (telegram, Am Emb Bonn, 10558). I proposed that an expert, someone like the chief IAEA inspector in Vienna, visit the European capitals involved and meet with the North Atlantic Council (NAC) to explain how the system worked.

On April 10 Secretary of State Rusk, during a visit to Bonn, met with Foreign Minister Brandt. The two had a full discussion on NPT (Amemb Bonn files). Rusk expressed his understanding that, after twenty-five amendments to the treaty that the United States had made as a result of German suggestions, most German objectives had been met. Brandt promised to present the treaty to the Bundestag, but with only a general discussion—not the text. He would stress the importance of nuclear power compliance with the preamble of the NPT; to its being limited in time, say to five years; and that vertical as well as horizontal proliferation should be limited.

Brandt also expressed his concern over the effect of the NPT on the alliance and on disarmament. Rusk pointed out the dangers of limiting the duration of the NPT. NATO members could begin to withdraw in 1969, and a change in the status of NATO might trigger the invocation of the NPT withdrawal clause. Brandt emphasized the negative effect on internal German politics of there being no possibility of withdrawal after a given time, if necessary, to take advantage of "peaceful uses." Others would want assurance that the nuclear powers would not increase their arsenals. Neither Brandt nor Rusk felt that the effect of Articles I and II on Europewide nuclear arrangements presented an insuperable obstacle.

When I met with Karl Carstens on April 18, he reported that several problems had emerged over the NPT negotiations during a meeting of the German National Security Council earlier that day. They centered on the strong feeling that the term of the treaty should be limited, concern over the possible adverse impact of NPT on NATO nuclear arrangements, and the possible adverse consequences of undertaking such an obligation with the Soviet Union. The Soviets could use the treaty as a basis for false allegations of German violations, German leaders feared.

In reply, I pointed out that the Soviets acquired no unilateral policy rights under the treaty and that the other signatories would defend Germany. As a signatory Germany would also be better able to defend itself and to improve relations with Eastern Europe. I did not obtain any clear feeling as to the tenor of NPT discussions within the government. I suspected that the differences in view represented were too great to permit a consensus.

On May 23 I had a discussion on NPT developments with FRG disarmament negotiator Schnippenkötter (telegram, Amemb Bonn to Secstate, 14095, May 24, 1967). Germany, according to Schnippenkötter, wanted an article on safeguards. Since they were under controls, they would like to see others subject to similar inspection. The Communist countries of Eastern Europe resented the USSR's refusal to submit to inspection. This should strengthen the United States and others who wanted to modify Moscow's position on safeguards. Perhaps this was one of the reasons, if it were true, behind the rumor that the USSR sought to avoid a debate through the tabling of a final U.S.-Soviet draft. The current Soviet objective might really be not the NPT but to keep the pot boiling, perhaps for years, as a disintegrating influence within NATO. They might also seek a prolonged discussion as a weapon against Germany. Schnippenkötter felt, however, that Germany's present position was good, since it could not be accused of blocking the treaty.

According to Schnippenkötter, the general reaction against the NPT had subsided in Germany. The only question remaining was how long the treaty would endure. Germany was satisfied with the provisions of the U.S. draft on peaceful uses. There were those—including the chancellor—who sought a limited duration treaty as a matter of principle, regardless of substance. In essence, Kiesinger's view was based on an unwillingness to commit "future German generations" to a treaty the full consequence of which could not now be foreseen and which would exist in a world of changing conditions—that is, the possible termination of NATO. In a sense, limiting the treaty's duration was intended to take care of unforeseen contingencies.

Prospects for German ratification of NPT still remained uncertain, although certain German objections out of the large number raised had been met. Other important issues remained, however, and a general sullen reluctance seemed to pervade the outlook of the key German actors, particularly Kiesinger. Most were genuinely concerned over their pet complaints. No one was willing to start a movement toward acceptance of the treaty draft as it stood, fearing criticism later.

20

Establishing New Relations
April–September 1967

Ameeting between Kiesinger and Johnson was to come sooner than I imagined, though not exactly in the way I might have wished. On April 19, 1967, Konrad Adenauer died. His death had been expected at any time, but I will always remember hearing the news over the radio-phone in my car in Bonn. I proceeded to Rhöndorf to offer both official and personal condolences, and was received by Adenauer's son Paul, who had been living with him during his last years. After a few words of sympathy to members of the family, I departed.

After his retirement, Adenauer had been given a small office in the Bundestag building, where he took care of correspondence, worked on his memoirs, and cultivated his unceasing vendetta against Erhard. I called on him every few months to keep in touch. Adenauer took the occasion of the CDU celebration of his eighty-ninth birthday to point out his own feeling that West German foreign policy was in decline. Few people came to see him, which disappointed him. Visitors toward the end found him downcast and resentful against both Kennedy and de Gaulle. In his last speech, on February 16, 1967, he urged the creation of a United Europe, excluding the Soviet Union, and a European nuclear Third Force to counter the American and Soviet nuclear monopoly. Adenauer's mind remained active to the end. His final meeting was with Kiesinger on April 3.

Three days after Adenauer's death, the official ceremonies for the great man began. His body was taken by boat to Bad Godesberg. It rested there for a night before being taken to the Cologne Cathedral, where Cardinal Frings conducted the funeral service before most heads of state, including de Gaulle and Johnson. I well remember the eerie sight, like a scene from a Wagnerian opera, as the funeral boat passed my embassy office in the mist, the casket and a small group of mourners in view. For Germany, it represented the end of an era.

Adenauer's death precipitated Johnson's only presidential trip to Europe and his first official meeting with Kiesinger. The Johnson visit I had hoped for two years before had long been eclipsed by the Vietnam War. The meeting with Kiesinger helped put to rest some of the tension that had arisen over who would visit first and when, but questions still remained.

Arranged on such short notice, Johnson's visit accomplished little of significance apart from paying tribute to the creator of postwar Germany. As usual, Johnson came with a large entourage—too large in my view—which created considerable confusion. Like Kennedy in 1963, Johnson elected for security reasons to stay in the house of Deputy Chief of Mission Martin Hillenbrand on the Rhine. The official in charge of the advance party was the worst of such functionaries, who are invariably drunk with their own power and arrogant and demanding, I hope beyond the president's knowledge or desire. He ordered wall-to-wall carpeting installed on overtime in the bathroom the president would use and curtains to cover all bookcases. The president did not like to look at books, he said. He also threatened to have the Hillenbrands fired for suggesting that he and his helpers refrain from dropping cigarette ashes on their silver. A special State Department administrative official was along to hand out funds so members of the party could purchase presents to take home.

Johnson attended all of the funeral functions, the high point of which was the impressive mass at the Cologne Cathedral and the reception that followed. A whole pew of Secret Service men sat behind him. Johnson displayed his usual energy and attention to detail, exchanging pleasantries with the other heads of state in attendance, most of whom he knew, and I introduced him to the important German dignitaries present. There was no opportunity, however—nor was it the occasion—for serious discussion. Johnson himself seemed ill at ease. The German press was positive in reporting Johnson's presence, which, however, did not compare to Kennedy's.

On April 26 President Johnson met privately with Kiesinger with only an interpreter present. Their conversation covered the familiar ground of current problems. Both promised strong support for the Kennedy Round, which was successfully concluded the following month.

They also pledged support for the efforts being made to reform the International Monetary Fund (IMF), including adequate reserve creation. Discussion of the Non-Proliferation Treaty was not so satisfactory since Kiesinger still had a number of reservations, which kept him from giving final approval during the remainder of his chancellorship.

A key issue for discussion was the controversial U.S. troop rotation proposal. The Germans were apprehensive that it would result in a decrease in the effectiveness of U.S. forces in Germany and the beginning of further withdrawals, since much pressure was being placed on Johnson. In response to Kiesinger's questions, Johnson assured him that the modest reduction envisaged would not seriously reduce the capability of our forces. Troops deployed would remain committed to return to Germany, and we would work to reduce the redeployment time. The plan would have the advantage to both countries of reducing our balance of payments drain—hence the offset. We planned to remove 144 strike aircraft (one-half of our total). Ground forces could in the event of an emergency be returned in thirty days, air forces in ten days.

Meanwhile, according to plan, Rusk and I spent two and a half hours with Brandt (telegram, Amemb Bonn to Secstate, 12848, Apr. 26, 1967). Rusk pointed out the great importance the NPT could play in averting the danger of proliferation. He emphasized the role that Germany could play in getting as broadly based an agreement as possible. He was worried that if there were no NPT, India, for example, might deem it necessary to create an atomic capability, in which case Pakistan would follow suit, and that if Israel began a nuclear weapons program, the Arab states would try to do likewise. Rusk told Brandt that he thought we had now taken care of most of the German objections to the treaty draft.

Brandt replied humorously that Prime Minister Harold Wilson of Britain had told him that the Americans had made fifty-two amendments to the treaty as a result of German suggestions. This was an exaggeration, but not a ridiculously big one. We had, in fact, made twenty-five changes at the Germans' request. Brandt said he would stress the treaty's importance as part of the worldwide effort to limit nuclear weapons when he presented it to the Bundestag. He would also assure the Bundestag that, under the treaty, the non-nuclear nations would press the nuclear powers for compliance with the injunction in the preamble to control the arms race and reduce their nuclear arsenals. He thought it would be much easier, both in Germany and Italy, if the NPT were limited to, say, five years. He also thought it would be helpful if it could be made clear that nuclear as well as non-nuclear nations were obliged to limit proliferation in any form.

President Johnson and Secretary of State Rusk departed later that day, precluding an in-depth discussion on the overall results of the meetings. Kiesinger and Johnson released separate, rather bland, communiqués. Kiesinger emphasized his pleasure both in "getting to know" Johnson and with the results of their conversation, which was in an "atmosphere of mutual trust and confidence." For his part, Johnson expressed pleasure at being able to reaffirm the friendship between the two countries. "We have not made any hard and fast decisions here today," the communiqué read, but it announced the chancellor's agreement to an early visit to America. Subjects that would be discussed included NPT, trade and monetary matters, U.S. troop deployments, and general questions of security and prosperity of the two nations.

How the chemistry of the meeting between these two proud and independent-minded men worked, I could not really tell, not having been with them alone. Press reports for the next two days, however, were not positive. Although no critical editorial comment on the results of the top-level meeting were voiced, there was an undertone of "wait and see," even a suggestion that little had been accomplished. There were rumors in press circles that rapport between the two was not perfect.

I reported to the State Department that it was important to get to the press and to other influential circles a positive assessment of the president's talks with the chancellor. The principal points of emphasis should be: the establishment of good personal rapport between the two; the president's invitation to the chancellor for an early visit to Washington; a better U.S. understanding of the German attitude on NPT; and real progress in the tripartite talks.

I was frankly concerned about the results of the meeting. It had been hastily arranged and held under the pall of the funeral of a great man. I looked forward to the time when Kiesinger and Johnson could have a meeting under proper circumstances. Unfortunately, the uncertainty of the Johnson-Kiesinger relationship was to linger as late as March 1968. Johnson did not mention Kiesinger in his memoirs.

On the country's biggest domestic issue, its economic and budget policies, the government was showing progress. This I had learned on May 18 when I asked Franz Josef Strauss, the new government's finance minister, to lunch alone with me at the embassy (telegram, Amemb

Bonn to Secstate, 13865, May 18, 1967). Conservative, a prototype Bavarian, Strauss had been a good scholar in the University of Munich and had served in the German army in World War II. He was known for his pro-Gaullist views and his support for a strong German defense. His ambition clearly was to become chancellor of Germany. Strauss had been Kiesinger's principal supporter for the chancellorship. It was natural that he be offered a key cabinet post.

In his first six months in his new office Strauss had been doing well in turning the German economy around. I was interested to hear his views on future prospects. Strauss felt that the Grand Coalition government was working quite well. Indeed, the present German political situation afforded no alternative. If either of the coalition partners were to create difficulties or withdraw without due cause, that party would lose public support. A dissolution of the coalition would have to be followed by new elections, in which case Strauss felt the margin of the CDU/CSU over the SPD would be small. Neither could obtain a majority. The FDP, after a poor recent performance at its party meeting in Hanover, was not considered a suitable coalition partner for the CDU/CSU, and an SPD/FDP coalition would be too weak. There would, therefore, be no alternative except a resumption of the Grand Coalition. Strauss did not feel that the CDU/CSU had gained appreciable strength as a result of the coalition.

When he took over his current office, Strauss told me, he had been urged to balance the budget by drastic cuts accompanied by higher taxes. He had disappointed such extremists by not doing so, since this would only have worsened an already severe deflation. Unable to balance the budget, he had been forced to borrow approximately DM 8 billion to cover the year's deficit; this he said had been accomplished with little difficulty. Next year, however, because of built-in increases in the social legislation, he expected the deficit to rise to DM 12 billion. He had thus decided to aim for a budget cut of DM 10 billion starting the next year, which could be accomplished only through a change in social legislation. He thought he could accomplish this, with SPD approval, if he could show that his changes were distributed fairly between lower and higher income groups. He opposed tax increases but was willing to see repeal of certain tax concessions and other forms of subsidy. He did not believe it would be necessary to reduce the defense budget. In fact, he hoped for a small, though probably tiny, increase. I pointed out the important psychological effect such an increase would have on the United States and other NATO countries in maintaining force levels.

Strauss saw no reason why the new financial arrangement between the Bundesbank and the United States to help neutralize American military foreign exchange expenditures in Germany could not continue. (The new version of offset involved German purchase of medium-term U.S. bonds.) In the future Germany would buy such arms as it needed, although this could not of course fully answer the offset problem. Strauss left no doubt of the need to keep NATO forces at approximately the present levels.

I reported to the State Department how relaxed Strauss had seemed. It occurred to me that one reason for this was his satisfaction that the government was now pursuing a foreign policy along lines he had previously advocated. This included greater independence vis-à-vis the United States, improved relations with France, and greater emphasis on the European rather than the Atlantic framework. I considered that the positions taken by Strauss during the conversation did not generally conflict with current U.S. policies. Without a doubt, however, he remained the strongest opponent of the NPT within the government. His comments on military subjects—rotation, offset, and the Bundeswehr— were on the whole encouraging. Perhaps the most significant of Strauss's comments on economic problems was his acceptance of the need for a delay in the economic upturn. (This had come to be called the "beginning of the end of the downturn of the upturn.")

On May 30, 1967, only hours before the expiration of President Johnson's authority under the Trade Expansion Act, which had passed as a result of President Kennedy's initiative in 1963, the United States signed an agreement which formalized the successful conclusion to what had come to be called the Kennedy Round of trade negotiations. The enabling legislation permitted the president to cut tariffs up to 50 percent in return for equal benefits from the recipient countries. Fifteen countries, including those comprising the Common Market, took part in the talks, which had been held sporadically in Geneva starting in 1964. Four countries took part in a special category and some two dozen additional countries contributed to the discussion, making a total of forty-four participants.

Hard bargaining continued until the final negotiations. Neither the United States nor any other country got everything it wanted. Near the end, the United Kingdom had stiffened its position on chemicals, steel, and grains. Japan had held out on several food commodities and aid to developing countries, and the Common Market had opposed opening its market to grains. Germany, as one of the leading world trading countries, with two-thirds of its business outside the Common Market, was from the beginning a staunch supporter of the Kennedy Round. Although Erhard's enthusiasm was matched neither by Adenauer, who had little interest in economic issues, nor by Kiesinger, who generally deferred to de Gaulle's opposition to the Geneva negotiations, all three chancellors gave support. There were, of course, differences between German and U.S. interests, which were reflected in their respective negotiating positions. One issue was the degree to which Germany attempted to influence the French, another the influence of Germany's membership in the Common Market and the sensitivity of the German agricultural community to imports of U.S. grain and other foodstuffs.

In the end President Johnson accepted the negotiating package agreed upon as being the best that could be achieved under the circumstances. It included concessions received and made by the United States totaling $8 billion. The great effort that had been made to promote increased international trade had been well worthwhile.

At a lunch meeting on June 26, I learned Helmut Schmidt's opinions on progress in Germany. Again in Bonn after a tour in the city government of his native Hamburg, the future chancellor was currently Social Democratic floor leader in the Bundestag. Although he had already shown leadership qualities, his later rise to party leadership and to the chancellorship could not then have been predicted. Schmidt told me how the government was planning to cut expenditures by DM 7 billion and raise another DM 7 billion by increasing taxes and public borrowing. Since the increase in taxes would fall mainly on low income brackets, partly through increased social security contributions, Schmidt admitted that he and Brandt had reluctantly concluded that the new measures must be accompanied by a decrease in the defense budget.

Now that the SPD was finally in the government, Schmidt believed it politically impossible for his party to cut social spending without corresponding cuts in defense. For the first time, pensioners would have to pay taxes on their income and would receive only a 4 percent increase in the coming year's payments rather than the 8 percent originally provided for. He assumed that the trade unions and the party rank-and-file would revolt if defense were not cut. Unfortunately, Germans did not assign defense expenditures a high priority, he noted.

I told him that a German defense reduction would be viewed critically in the United States, and would weaken the government's efforts to maintain present U.S. force levels in Germany. In place of the modest increase in the defense budget that had been tentatively planned for 1968, the budget he described would result in an actual decrease below the 1967 level. The United States would not understand this, in light of its own recent increases, I told him, nor would Germany's NATO allies, who were already doing more pro rata than the Germans.

Given the growing distance between German and American positions, I continued to think about a summit-level visit between Kiesinger and Johnson. It had become one of the principal issues between them and consequently an irritant in itself. Kiesinger complained about a lack of "quality" in U.S. consultations with him, which tended to take the form, he thought, of our informing the German government after our decisions had been taken. He also complained that U.S. consultations with him personally were not on important and global subjects but only on specific bilateral issues. He gave me as examples the type of discussions held in Prince Bernhard's Bilderberg meetings, which we had attended together.

In order to meet his concerns I suggested to the State Department that, when he came to Washington, there be an informal meeting in some quiet place that would include a few elder statesmen like Dean Acheson and Jack McCloy, a few key cabinet members, the vice president, and perhaps the president himself, if at all possible. The agenda should be far-ranging, including such topics as the future of the NATO alliance. After the chancellor's return, I suggested that there continue a regular exchange of personal letters between him and the president to follow up on topics they had discussed in Washington (telegram, Amemb Bonn to Secstate, 13635, May 12, 1967).

Rusk replied to my reports that "the way to consult is to consult," and that the Germans had not come to us for consultation except on the "German question" (letter, Rusk to McGhee on consultation, June 26, 1967, Department of State Archives). Most governments, including the Germans, seemed to wait for some initiative from us before they reacted, he said. The German government did not give the impression that "their Foreign Office was thinking about world problems, generating ideas about them, and letting other governments know what they are," he added. He also pointed out the difficulties of changing decisions once made under our interdepartmental system. He referred to the division of powers between the government and the Congress. If we were to consider the views of others, we needed concrete suggestions early in the process, he reminded me.

The visit, so long discussed and delayed, finally occurred, and on August 15 Johnson received Kiesinger in a welcoming ceremony at the White House (*State Department Bulletin*, Aug. 15, 1968). After a warm greeting Johnson referred to the long and close association between the two countries, to the U.S. commitment "to work with you in the great task of ending the artificial division of your country," and to looking forward to exchanging views and ideas during their meeting.

In his response Kiesinger, while pledging German support to NATO as an instrument of peace, called for a common pursuit of a policy of détente to overcome conflicts and create a climate of trust and cooperation that would guarantee a lasting peace. He spoke of efforts to unify Western Europe and strengthen relations with the East, citing as Germany's one great obstacle its continued division. The meeting was off to a good start.

In remarks to the press, Johnson emphasized the importance of minimizing troop reductions and in concluding the Non-Proliferation Treaty. Kiesinger stated that although he was known as a chancellor who wanted to make an independent policy, he pledged continuing friendship and cooperation with the United States. In his toast following the dinner he gave in Kiesinger's honor, President Johnson expressed appreciation for Kiesinger's candidness, understanding, good advice, and counsel. Kiesinger in turn thanked the president for his clear-sightedness and sense of responsibility during their frank and friendly talks.

The extended discussions between Kiesinger and Johnson, and between Brandt, Rusk, and other U.S. officials, produced few surprises and almost no important differences apart from Kiesinger's continuing reluctance to approve the NPT. If the conclusions reached did not meet Kiesinger's ambitious expectations, they at least relieved tensions between the two leaders and paved an easier path in the relations between the two countries.

The joint statement issued by Johnson and Kiesinger at the close of talks on August 16 highlighted common goals: the maintenance of peace through NATO; the relaxation of tensions as a step toward ending the division of Europe; further efforts to unify Western Europe; and strengthening development assistance to other peoples in the world.

Following the chancellor's visit to Washington, I sensed that a major improvement had occurred in U.S. relations with Germany. I began revising the pessimistic view I had expressed only six months earlier. When I reported to the State Department on September 9 (telegram, Amemb Bonn to Secstate, 2654, Sept. 9, 1967), I said that German-American relations were characterized by a pervading calm, an absence of controversial issues. I pointed out that offset and related troop rotation problems had—pending the German decision on reduction of forces—been resolved. The NPT, while still not a happy prospect for the Federal Republic, had been recast to meet the Germans' most acute objections, and other countries were now willing to take the lead in seeking further gains.

I reported that German emotional resentment against the United States had been reduced substantially. The Kennedy Round and international liquidity problem had been settled to mutual satisfaction. There was no acute concern over U.S. investment in Germany. A recent American purchase of a large German firm had gone unnoticed. The German government appeared satisfied that consultation was adequate. While the initial delay in arranging a meeting between the president and Kiesinger had itself been a source of instability, one could now say that a new period in German-American relations—one long in the making—had begun.

I thought that the principal characteristic of the new period was a clearer separation, but not necessarily a divergence, of German policy from our own. The Germans knew they remained dependent on us for defense. There was, however, no present military pressure from the East, and they were thus in a position to concentrate on problems where the United States was less important. For the German government and people, the overriding concern was the economic recession and resultant budgetary squeeze, a field outside direct U.S. influence. Deeply alarmed by their first real postwar economic turndown, they were looking out for themselves.

Their second most pressing concern, I believed, was the German Question, the development of a more hopeful relationship between the Federal Republic and the Communist countries, including East Germany. Because of our importance in an eventual European settlement, the Germans wished to work with us toward this goal. But they appeared to have concluded that too close an association with us could handicap rather than assist their relations with Eastern Europe. They looked to the French, their closest European ally, as a more natural and effective partner in that enterprise.

Western security, particularly the German contribution to it, probably ranked third among German concerns; and here the position of the United States remained paramount, being the subject of our closest bilateral consultations. The chancellor had made a serious effort to remove some of the emotion from German relations with both France and the United States by being friendly toward, but independent of, both. He had disassociated himself from both French policy regarding NATO and U.S. policy in Vietnam. Kiesinger had said that the Germans would no longer look to the United States to solve all of its problems. I predicted there would be less closeness in our relations but also, in the long run, less potential tension and fewer recriminations.

There were, nonetheless, possible areas of future difficulty. We had in the past encouraged the FRG to seek better relations with the Soviets, Eastern Europe, and East Germany. In doing so, we had suggested no limits as to how far we thought they could safely go without endangering Western security. We had shown signs of unease when Kiesinger had hinted that a reunited Germany might be neutral and when Brandt suggested that NATO might disappear. But we had not, I thought, said what would be acceptable in the way of a European settlement.

Should the East seem ready for movement and the Germans respond, I feared misunderstanding might arise between us as to how far the FRG could and should go. This was, I thought, something we must discuss with the Germans. The planned rotation of U.S. troops in Germany had caused no serious disquiet in Germany. A more extensive reduction in our presence, however, would likely exact a strain in our relations and a decrease in U.S. influence in Germany. German troop reductions, which seemed inevitable, could cause additional stress on our side. We should work closely to minimize such reductions and their impact.

I believed that further concentration of U.S. investment in German industry, particularly in petroleum, might entail serious problems. The U.S. government should consult our oil companies closely on this possibility. We should take advantage of our favorable relations with Germany to increase cooperation in the social-environmental field in transportation, in research and coproduction in advanced fields such as space technology, and through consultation at all levels to avoid troubles before they arise. Finally, I urged continuing direct exchanges between the president and the chancellor.

Following my review, I asked the embassy staff to help me analyze more deeply the East-West issue in order to determine the extent to which the United States should be concerned about German dealings with the East. I observed that a hallmark of the Kiesinger-Brandt foreign policy was its flexible, dynamic approach to Germany's Eastern neighbors. On interlocking fronts, the new government was seeking a reconciliation with the Soviet Union, diplomatic ties with the smaller countries of Eastern Europe, and "humanitarian" contacts with East Germany. This tended to bring Bonn's policy more in line with U.S. policy and addressed the deep-felt desire of the German people for some progress in relations with the other Germany. I noted that the U.S. government had up to that point generally endorsed the initiatives taken by the German government in this field and had made no effort to set limits on the Germans as to either procedure or substance.

West German preoccupation with all-German affairs was essentially a holding operation; "humanitarian" contacts served largely to prevent a further widening between the two Germanies, in the absence of any short-term movement toward reunification. While giving general support, I said, the United States should continue to let the Germans set the pace on what was an inter-German matter. Our main concern should be that adequate arrangements be made to fulfill Allied responsibilities in Berlin. I saw no dangers in West German efforts to strengthen its ties with the small countries of Eastern Europe. Although increased German influence would be desirable, I saw no opportunities for drastic change. We should not tell the Germans what they should give up in such matters as the Oder-Neisse.

Although the United States would welcome Germany's achievement of better bilateral understandings with the USSR, leading to fewer Soviet anxieties about Germany, prospects for sweeping change seemed unlikely. The Soviets obviously preferred the status quo. But it impressed me that the field of European security presented a significant potential for misunderstandings between ourselves and the Germans on Eastern policy. I pointed out that such issues as mutual troop reductions and exchange of military observers had traditionally been a matter of NATO and four-power concern. But I also believed that the German initiative for mutual renunciations of force with the Eastern European countries merited continuing U.S. support.

Although both the United States and Germany had supported measures to prevent surprise attack, such as an exchange of military observers, I did not believe the Germans should be given license to act
in the matter on behalf of the NATO alliance. I thought the same should
apply to discussions on mutual reduction of foreign troops, noting that
the Germans had shown no interest in earlier Polish proposals for a
Central European arms limitation zone, to which the United States
objected. I added that the United States should make it clear to the
Germans that it did not believe the time propitious for their consideration of any Soviet proposal for a united neutralized Germany.

Jean Monnet and Max Kohnstamm were in Bonn on October 12 and
joined me at breakfast for a tour d'horizon of Europe's problems (telegram, Amemb Bonn to Secstate, 4109, Oct. 12, 1967). Monnet was no
longer exclusively preoccupied with the question of British entry into
the EEC but appeared to be concentrating on moving through the par-
liaments of the six members the June 15 resolutions of his Action Committee on the establishment of a formal structure for a working
relationship of equals between Western Europe and the United States.
Monnet remained as convinced as ever that a process of European
unification was underway but that it would be lengthy and was unlikely
to be as orderly as many had originally supposed. The United States
was, perhaps, too impatient for more concrete evidence of progress.
Unity would come as political problems were gradually delegated to
experts in a competent European bureaucracy. This, rather than political union, would best facilitate unity in the future, the next field of
activity being monetary policy.

I pointed out to Monnet that on some problems Europe still seemed
to be unable to reach a unified view. I cited the recent Middle East
crisis as an example. Monnet did not dispute this but observed the
growing Western European unity toward Eastern Europe. Within the
framework of whatever unity was ultimately achieved, he thought that
the present individual countries—like individual American states—
would always have their particular interests and points of view, which
they would wish to be free to express.

As for Europe's relations with the United States, Monnet criticized
the Harmel Exercise because it was essentially an Atlantic—rather than
a European partnership with the United States—approach to common
problems. (The Harmel Exercise was a study by a committee appointed
by NATO and chaired by Foreign Minister Pierre Harmel of Belgium to

study proposals made by the Warsaw Pact countries and European Communists for an approach to all-European security. The committee report placed increased emphasis on creating a more stable relationship between Western and Eastern Europe, including mutual and balanced force reductions [MBFR].) The United States, he thought, still loomed so large that it should not inject itself into the development of European policy. In answer to my question about the Harmel proposal for a European caucus, Monnet said that this had not succeeded because of French obstruction and the issue of British entry, which made any basic European consensus impossible just then.

In general Monnet and Kohnstamm were optimistic about Europe's development, citing the European Parliament's willingness to support the Action Committee's June 15 resolutions. Europe was organizing itself, gradually and pragmatically, and Monnet saw no cause for impatience.

1968

January 1	Value-added tax is introduced in the FRG
January 30	Walter Scheel takes over the chairmanship of the FDP from Eric Mende
January 31	The FRG and Yugoslavia establish diplomatic relations; Vietcong Tet Offensive begins in South Vietnam
March 11	Chancellor Kiesinger gives his first state-of-the-nation address
March 21	SPD conference reelects Willy Brandt chairman
April 3	The Bundestag passes legislation adjusting the German coal mining industry
April 11	SDS leader Rudi Dutschke is seriously injured; widespread student unrest emerges
May 13	May unrest in Paris peaks
May 29	Bundestag passes criminal law reforms
May 30	Bundestag overwhelmingly passes the emergency law, giving the executive branch wider powers

21

East-West Relations and Other Business November 1967– February 1968

On November 15, 1967, I called on Kiesinger principally to discuss Germany's relations with the East (telegram, Am Emb Bonn, 5213). I queried him regarding a press statement he had made November 3 when, after repeating the standard German line that no final agreement on the Oder-Neisse border could be reached except through a peace treaty, he said: "That does not exclude, for example, that joint discussions of such a solution acceptable to both peoples could be arranged before such a peace treaty." The chancellor replied that he saw nothing to prevent such discussions, the purpose of which would be "just to build up a little more trust." He was aware that the Poles did not consider the matter a subject for discussion. Poland was unwilling even to accept a German offer of mutual declarations against the use of force, which Poland felt would weaken its case against Germany as a threat.

According to Kiesinger, the Federal Republic had to direct its efforts not just to the Communist countries but to convincing the whole world that, although West Germans would exercise their rights they were seeking solutions in a responsible way on the basis of justice for all. In so doing, he said, they recognized fully that the first step must be détente with the East. Unification, he acknowledged, could not precede détente. Kiesinger judged that the government should have moved more quickly to establish relations with Hungary, and perhaps other countries, before Walter Ulbricht, East Germany's Communist party leader, made his expected counterattack against Bonn's new overtures to the East.

In response to my query about rumors that Germany might move toward reestablishing diplomatic relations with Yugoslavia, after breaking them off when Yugoslavia recognized East Germany, Kiesinger replied that the majority of his party was not yet prepared for such a step. He himself was less worried at such an apparent breach in Bonn's traditional policy of nonrecognition for countries that recognized East Germany. But he admitted that it would be a great defeat if India, for example, established relations with East Germany on the basis of such a precedent.

He was pessimistic about overall prospects for improving East-West relations but thought that Germans must continue to try. Many changes, Kiesinger felt, would take place within the next five to ten years that might favor their cause. But he was skeptical of prospects for immediate success and was concerned that people might end up accusing the government of having raised "illusions" and ending up in a "dead end." He fully supported the policy that he and Brandt had developed, which was based on the desire to move forward without expectation of early results. This policy, he said, was not seriously contested within the party.

I advised Kiesinger that the United States had followed the efforts of his government in East-West relations closely and found nothing to take exception to. His policy matched ours in attempting to build bridges to the East, although we were then handicapped in our own efforts. Kiesinger commented that he did not think we could do much under the circumstances. He assured me that Germany would, of course, not undertake any action with the Soviets affecting the United States without first consulting fully with us. I confirmed that this was particularly important to us where U.S. forces were involved, for example, with respect to proposals for mutual force reduction.

As a follow-up to my discussion with Kiesinger on East-West relations, I met Brandt on November 28, who briefed me on his recent talks with the Soviet Ambassador to West Germany, Semyon Tsarapkin (telegram, Amemb Bonn to Secstate, 5661, Nov. 28, 1967). According to Brandt, the Soviets seemed to mean business and used the phrase "renunciation of force" as an umbrella under which they would discuss everything involving the Federal Republic and Eastern Europe. This included the Oder-Neisse issue, the validity of the 1938 Munich agreement with respect to the postwar German-Czech border, atomic weapons, East Germany, and Berlin. Nor had Tsarapkin made an issue of West Germany's ties with NATO or the West.

Brandt concluded from his discussion with Tsarapkin that the Soviets wanted to move forward with further talks. He considered that the most important agenda topics for any ensuing discussions would be renunciation of force, relations between the two Germanies, and relations with Eastern Europe. Brandt said that he considered it important that the three powers display again, as they had not done in recent years, interest in certain aspects of the German problem. They should show interest in attempting to bring about at least limited progress. The Soviets should be advised that if progress were made in direct talks between the GDR and FRG, the three powers would be willing to do something about European security, including such questions as mutual troop reductions.

I reported to the State Department that I believed that the conversation with Tsarapkin was highly revealing of Brandt's whole approach to European security issues with the Soviet Union (telegram, Amemb Bonn to Secstate, 5708, Nov. 29, 1967). From his account, it was clear that the Soviets had offered nothing that would suggest any basic change in their attitude toward Germany or the German problem. They had so far talked specifically only about agreements on the renunciation of force. The completion of such an agreement between West and East Germany was, as Brandt reported it, the key that could open the door to a general improvement in Bonn's relations with the East. Tsarapkin did not, however, indicate what this improvement meant in concrete terms. The sweetener he offered—the only new point—was that the completion of such an agreement need not entail recognition of East Germany.

Brandt's optimistic assessment that the Soviets "seem to mean business" and "want to move forward" appeared to me to be based mostly on hope. In light of Brandt's approach to the East German regime during the period he was governing mayor of Berlin, his attitude was not, however, surprising. He tended to think in general terms. He was persistently optimistic as to what could be achieved in a pragmatic way through "small steps"—minor advances of opportunity centering largely around "humanitarian" gains for the West Berliners. The negotiating details were of less interest to him. He appeared to minimize the obstacles. His great achievement was the "pass agreements." Even though these agreements brought no real progress on the German question, the German public compared Brandt's efforts favorably with the "stand pat" attitude of the Erhard government.

As foreign minister in the Grand Coalition government, Brandt faced a serious problem in maintaining his own and his party's prestige and his own influence within his party. The SPD's main hope for political profit from its present role was to get credit for progress in relations with the East. To the extent, therefore, that a stalemate persisted in relations with Moscow and East Berlin and no new Eastern countries were taken into camp, SPD confidence in both Brandt and the Grand Coalition declined apace.

It seemed to me that Brandt had at least to create an impression of potential progress. A large element of the tactical in Brandt's present outlook toward the East flavored his interpretation of his conversations with Tsarapkin. He thought that talks with the Soviets would last two years—that is, past the 1969 elections. He cast himself in the key role— one in which he showed persistence, but patience and reasonableness, in his approach to the central problem of Germany and Europe. Brandt's tactics also contained a broader aspect, I inferred. Kiesinger himself had suggested that Germany's Eastern policy must be directed not only at the Eastern states but also to the "people of the world"—to prove the goodwill and peaceful intentions of the Federal Republic. To this extent Brandt and Kiesinger were likely to agree to pursue talks with Tsarapkin.

The United States should also, I believed, consider this to be the preferable German posture toward the Eastern question. I believed that the Brandt-Tsarapkin conversation certainly introduced the possibility of some new and welcome flux in German-Soviet relations but thought it unlikely that such talks would in themselves produce any basic changes in Soviet policy toward Germany. The Soviets would continue to follow their own timetable. They would continue to work for the acceptance of two German states and to defer to the interests of their East German ally. Brandt would be misguided if he thought he could divide Moscow from East Berlin.

What seemed to me likelier to change—indeed what had changed over the past months—was the German demand for reunification through a unified German government based on self-determination. As their dialogue with the Soviets progressed, I thought that West Germans, in response to a friendlier attitude from Moscow, might be willing to accept a modus vivendi with East Germany along the lines that the Soviets had long been seeking: acceptance of East Germany as a legitimate state with special connections to the Federal Republic. In this event, an improvement in relations between Bonn and Moscow seemed feasible. I thought it likely that a trade agreement, air service between Moscow and Frankfurt, and the like might be achieved. But I believed that the underlying basis of any change would be Bonn's acceptance of Germany's division rather than any steps toward ending it.

I believed, moreover, that the U.S. attitude toward Brandt's efforts should continue to be one of confidence and support. It was important that the FRG have the opportunity to discover for itself the potential offered by direct conversations with the Soviets. As I had often pointed out, improvement in bilateral relations between Bonn and Moscow need not be contrary to U.S. interests.

We must expect that the Soviets would try to use their talks with Brandt to weaken NATO and confidence between the United States and Germany. It seemed to me, however, that we could rely on Brandt and the Kiesinger government as a whole to be cautious in talking with the Soviets on any matters directly affecting German or Western security. Brandt and Kiesinger had both said they would keep in close touch with the United States and with NATO and would take no steps involving U.S. interests without prior consultation. This would probably provide the assurance the United States needed. Americans should, I believed, continue to make quite clear—as I did with Brandt—that they welcomed German initiatives with the East, that they had no concern over their contacts up to that point, and that they had full confidence as to German efforts in the future.

In *Years of Upheaval* (1982, 143–45) Henry Kissinger records his first meeting with Willy Brandt in the 1950s when Brandt was the mayor of embattled Berlin. He characterized Brandt as "bluff, strong, outgoing, and at the same time oddly remote from the drama in which he was a principal actor," responding more to intuition than logic. American inaction over the Soviet building of the Berlin Wall, Kissinger believes, had convinced Brandt that America and NATO could not be relied on to achieve the easing of Germany's divisions. This led Brandt to abandon Adenauer's rigid anti-Sovietism in favor of a determined effort to reduce tensions and suspicions between East and West, which Kissinger describes as sometimes "verging on neutralism." Kissinger states that Brandt found a way to "live with the partition of Germany." He relinquished claims to Germany's eastern territories while putting his own ideas forward "as a means to achieve German unity." Kissinger writes, however, that Brandt had neither the stamina nor intellectual force to manage the forces he had unleashed. He had in fact become their prisoner. He had contributed to a "race for Moscow" on the part of the United States and the other allies.

Kissinger saw Egon Bahr not as pro-Soviet but rather as an old-fashioned German nationalist, and the intellectual driving force behind Brandt's Ostpolitik. He credited Bahr for the German treaties with the USSR, Poland, and East Germany, as well as the Quadripartite Agreement of 1971 on Berlin. Bahr actively encouraged "separate approaches" by others to Moscow, confident he could exploit them to achieve Germany's national goals. Bahr had become convinced that America's loss of strategic prominence forced Germany to "seek safety in reduction of tensions with the East." Kissinger sees in this the implication by Bahr that Europe's interest might lie in separating itself from the United States and accommodating itself to Soviet power, camouflaged as closer East-West economic relations.

In my own evaluation of Bahr I never questioned his loyalty to his country or thought him biased in favor of the USSR. I would characterize him as a tactician grasping at every opportunity for national gain, perhaps for the reasons described by Kissinger. This would permit Germany to accept American and NATO support when it was to their advantage, while avoiding long-range commitments that would impair their ability to make advantageous arrangements with Eastern Europe and the Soviet Union. Although such an approach by the German government would not preclude us from negotiating with the government on particular issues, it represented a departure from relations we had become accustomed to on the basis of a close alliance between the two countries.

George Ball, in his exposition for an American foreign policy in *Diplomacy for a Crowded World* (1976, 109–10), cites the origins of German Ostpolitik as de Gaulle's "flirtation" with the Soviet Union and withdrawal from NATO, together with the increasing U.S. obsession with Vietnam. With the Grand Coalition came a relaxation of Adenauer's rigid pro-Western and anti-Soviet attitude. This led in 1969 to Brandt's full-blown Ostpolitik, and to the Soviet and Polish treaties of 1970 recognizing the territorial status quo resulting from the wars, and to the recognition of East Germany.

Ball states that in 1970 he felt the disenchantment prevailing in Washington, shared by President Nixon and Secretary of State Kissinger, that "excessive preoccupation" by Bonn with Ostpolitik was leading the Germans to believe the Cold War was over and to a return to emphasis in Germany of traditional ties to the East. Although he did not doubt that Brandt was "a man of the West," Ball worried that Brandt's successors might not be so committed. On balance he considered that the Soviets gained from Ostpolitik through a recognition of the status quo, although he admitted the value of the Quadripartite Treaty of 1972, which Ostpolitik made possible in assuring allied access to Berlin.

I did not have these fears in 1968 and do not believe they have materialized. Ostpolitik has brought about a more realistic and workable relationship between East and West in Central Europe. No German chancellor succeeding Brandt has been less cautious toward the East. No movement in either East or West today challenges the status quo Ostpolitik has helped create in Central Europe. Ostpolitik averted armed conflict and bought time until the evolution taking place within both blocs permitted a temporary truce to become a permanent peace.

The perennial problem of the offset continued. I called on Brandt on February 20, 1968, to make clear to him how serious the United States was about the program Johnson had proposed on January 1 for redressing the U.S. balance of payments (telegram, Amemb Bonn to Secstate, 9568, Feb. 20, 1968). We were considering a number of border tax adjustments, I emphasized. It was our sincere desire that this be accomplished without restricting trade. The ability to do what we had to do and at the same time stave off protectionist measures in Congress, however, would depend in large degree on assistance from trading partners. In particular, we hoped that countries with a surplus, including West Germany, would take appropriate measures to increase imports and encourage the flow of long-term investment capital abroad.

In connection with the offset, the objective for the fiscal year 1968–69 remained a full neutralization of the foreign exchange losses resulting from U.S. forces in Germany, a total of $775 million. Although the final negotiation, which lay ahead, would be between the Bundesbank and the U.S. Treasury, I hoped that the German government would support U.S. objectives with the Bundesbank in whatever way was appropriate. We agreed that this could be achieved largely through German purchase of medium-term securities. Brandt made no comment.

I also told Brandt that the United States was concerned by recent allegations in the German press of American misgivings over German Eastern policy. I assured him that this was not the case. In the past we had stressed the importance of continued four-power responsibility and the risks of any bilateral Soviet-German negotiations on Berlin. We felt that Brandt had adequately assured us on this point. Otherwise, we welcomed direct discussions between the Germans and the Soviets on questions outstanding between them, as well as continued German efforts to improve relations with Eastern Europe and the recent reestablishment of relations with Yugoslavia. We had every confidence that the German government would continue to keep us advised of their discussions with the Soviets and would consult with us in connection with any matter involving allied interests.

I asked Brandt what new moves he contemplated in the East-West arena, in particular what answer the German government proposed to make to the Soviet memo of January 29 on mutual renunciation of force. Brandt said that some in the German government wanted to say, in effect, "Since there are so many issues on which we do not agree, we must exchange mutual renunciations of force in order to avoid conflict." His own view and that of the Foreign Office was more to the effect that, "Because we disagree we must discuss the areas of our disagreement with a view to reaching some solution, not necessarily in the short-term but in the long-term." He said he was considering a complete statement of reasonable German positions on all subjects related to Eastern policy for presentation to the Russians. He thought that such a move would eliminate the danger that the Soviets might exploit their own interpretation of talks for propaganda purposes. He also believed that such a paper could provide a basis for further exchanges of views.

Brandt considered it significant that Soviet Ambassador Tsarapkin had never conditioned mutual force renunciation on a prior resolution of the issues raised by the Soviets in their note. Brandt thought that there was an opportunity for progress which, even in the absence of an overall agreement, could reduce the potential danger of existing differences. He thought it possible, for example, that the Germans might be able to tell the Poles that they would accept the present western Polish border until the matter could be considered in connection with an overall peace treaty. I told Brandt that such an approach seemed to me to be headed in the right direction.

I then asked Brandt if a final decision had been made about the Bundestag defense committee's rumored meeting in Berlin. Given four-power agreements on the demilitarization of the city, I always considered such meetings an unnecessary provocation to the Soviets, who could be expected to protest vigorously. Brandt too raised his hands in obvious disapproval of the idea. He had taken up the issue with Eugen Gerstenmaier, Speaker of the Bundestag, and found that the decision had already been made. But it appeared that the committee would meet only for the day and would reserve discussion of military matters until the members returned to Bonn. Brandt assured me that this would not happen again. I mentioned that, although we had not advised the Germans to drop the meeting and although neither of us would wish to appear to be backtracking in the face of Soviet threats, I thought his attitude was a wise one.

Two days after talking to Brandt, I had a long meeting with Kurt Kiesinger at my request (telegram, Amemb Bonn to Secstate, 9894, Feb. 22, 1968). This was my first opportunity to talk with him since his meeting with de Gaulle in Paris the week before. Kiesinger was feeling friendly and expansive and carried the discussion well beyond the time allotted. He told me that, as usual in such Franco-German meetings, he and de Gaulle had disputed over their respective views toward the United States. This time he believed he had "won some ground." Whereas de Gaulle had stressed the great power of the United States, which he said constituted a threat to other countries, Kiesinger had referred to the power of the Soviet Union as a much more dangerous threat.

Though de Gaulle had told him he could not understand the German attitude toward NATO, Kiesinger continued, he had accepted the fact that Germany wished to "practice" NATO. De Gaulle had also said that he fully understood the German desire for the continued presence of American forces in Europe and appreciated the value of the NATO alliance. Apparently de Gaulle had even agreed that NATO could be abandoned only if the threat to Europe were removed, which he did not consider to be the case. Unless something "quite unforeseeable" arose, de Gaulle had told Kiesinger, France would not leave NATO. Kiesinger told me that he had repeated to de Gaulle the words "quite unforeseeable" for confirmation, which he thought was a stronger expression than de Gaulle had previously used.

Kiesinger said that he had emphasized, as he had in the past, that there could not be full Franco-German cooperation as long as de Gaulle continued to make public anti-American statements. He also said he told de Gaulle that such statements lost him much public support in Germany. Kiesinger said he had then told de Gaulle that he did not believe France and the United States to be far apart in their visions of Europe's future, because the United States, like Germany and France, wanted a strong and united Europe, which would constitute a stabilizing factor in the world. If Europe could be united in agreement with the United States, Europe could do its share in coping with free world problems. He said de Gaulle had apologized in a sense for the categorical language he customarily used. It was necessitated by the French internal political situation, de Gaulle had claimed. He needed the Communist support he could get by charging that Britain was "a satellite of the U.S." Kiesinger believed that domestic politics played an important role in de Gaulle's thinking, because de Gaulle had given Kiesinger a similar explanation of his position several months earlier.

With respect to U.K. entry into the Common Market, Kiesinger advised me that "we stick with our position"—that is, that there should be a "beginning of negotiations with the U.K. on entry." Of course de Gaulle opposed this. But Kiesinger pushed him in Paris to permit a start. De Gaulle had been willing to state, both privately to Kiesinger and in a joint communiqué, that both countries welcomed in principle the entry of other countries, mentioning specifically the United Kingdom.

I expressed my appreciation to Kiesinger for his strong statement of support for U.S. policy on Vietnam before his party's governing committee on February 20. Kiesinger had warned the CDU against criticizing the United States on Vietnam and against lecturing other people generally, stating that the United States was the country most strongly engaged for peace and freedom all over the world. He insisted that the Federal Republic should support U.S. policy. In the case of Vietnam, humanitarian aid for the suffering population constituted the best German contribution, Kiesinger had said at the meeting.

Kiesinger confirmed that he had repeated this statement in a public speech made the previous evening in Hamburg. In his judgment there was really no anti-American feeling in Germany. He quoted a recent poll showing that 69 percent favored particularly good relations with the United States, whereas only 13 percent opposed this. According to Kiesinger, most Germans also believed that the United States should stay in Vietnam. What feeling there was in Germany on this question was really a general "antiwar" feeling, he said, rather than hostility to the U.S. effort in Vietnam. This had led to the capture by extremist groups of some opponents of the war. The chancellor referred to another recent poll taken in leading Western countries on the relative value of preventing cancer, eliminating war, reducing unemployment, achieving long life, and reducing working hours. It showed that German and American views on these questions were almost identical, closer than any other two nations.

During our conversation Kiesinger outlined his broad views on the future of Europe. He believed that the alternatives were what he called an Atlantic imperium, or an Atlantic partnership. The imperium would consist of Western Europe, which I assumed meant NATO Europe, the United States, and, presumably, Canada, in confrontation with the Soviet Union, Eastern Europe, and possibly the People's Republic of China. These two great blocs would be firmly constructed, with no political leeway for Europe. The point of contact between the two would be the Eastern border of Germany. France would oppose such a solution because the French identity would disappear. Germany would oppose it because of the confrontation it would generate on Germany's eastern border, which would be a permanent danger to world peace. In Kiesinger's view, it would be better if "some distance could be put" between the superpower antagonists. He believed that the imperium concept could materialize only in the unlikely event of Soviet-Chinese solidarity.

Kiesinger made it clear that he preferred creation of a Europe that was a friendly partner of the United States. Europe would in such a case follow a European policy, he said, but in harmony with the United States. He thought that the harmony would be assured by the common interests of both sides, which would constitute a durable tie "for a long time" in ensuring that Europe would not fall under Soviet domination. Under such a concept, Europe would not be a third force, Kiesinger said; it was too small to be one anyway. Instead, it would function as a bridge between the two superpower antagonists. It was interesting to see how much importance Kiesinger attached to the conception of his foreign policy goals in global terms. He seemed to lose confidence when he failed to find a general policy framework for individual decisions.

The subject of Eastern policy arose when Kiesinger said that he had complained to de Gaulle that "you ask us to recognize the Oder-Neisse line as do others." Germany could not make such an "advance payment" unless there were a "grand design of a European order," he had told de Gaulle. The French see little possibility for short-term progress in the East. In the long-run revolutionary process, however, Kiesinger believed that Western Europe could exert a beneficial influence on Eastern Europe. De Gaulle had advised him to go ahead in his efforts to improve relations with the East. In particular, he hoped Germany would go faster with Poland. At no time, however, did de Gaulle propose an Eastern policy that could be considered contrary to U.S. interests.

I took this opportunity to assure Chancellor Kiesinger that the U.S. government did not, contrary to recent press speculation, have any misgivings over Germany's Eastern policy. Secretary Rusk had emphasized to Brandt in Brussels the importance of three-power responsibility in West Berlin and the possible pitfalls of a bilateral Soviet-German approach to Berlin. We had no evidence, however, that Brandt had considered such action. Kiesinger confirmed that this was the case.

I also said that we wished to set at rest any fears on his part that we had concern over German-Soviet discussions, as represented by the Brandt-Tsarapkin talks. Kiesinger interjected that he was "not impressed with these talks." He favored a mutual renunciation of force with the Eastern countries; the Soviet talks up to this point, however, had been only preliminary. He was by no means willing to pay the price the Soviets demanded for mutual renunciation of force.

I observed that press accounts of Kiesinger's meeting with de Gaulle had built it up as creating a basis for a new European approach to world problems. Had this possibility been discussed in any detail? Kiesinger minimized such a conclusion, saying, "For the time being we cannot do many things." Any reports to the contrary were incorrect. At no time had de Gaulle mentioned the possibility of German neutrality, which I reminded Kiesinger had been raised in the French paper. Indeed, he did not believe that de Gaulle saw this as a possibility.

This meeting revealed, I thought, some interesting nuances and developments. Kiesinger genuinely believed that he had helped induce some favorable changes in de Gaulle's thinking toward the United States, NATO, and even British entry into the Common Market. He expressed sympathy for the U.S. position in Vietnam and scoffed at there being any serious anti-Americanism in Germany. Pursuing his emphasis on large concepts, Kiesinger had presented an interesting analysis of overall East-West relations, and an attitude toward German Eastern policy that I could assure him corresponded closely to U.S. policy. To me the overall tone of this exchange, which I considered an important one, had been reassuring.

22

End of a Mission
March–May 1968

I next saw Chancellor Kiesinger on March 22, 1968 (telegram, Am Emb Bonn, 9894). He was visibly upset about reports of "worries and doubts about the President and his government" from "recent German visitors to Washington." He was worried about the form in which these doubts were expressed as well as their content. I could not believe the reports to be accurate and told him so.

This unfortunate situation appeared to reflect the chancellor's lack of confidence in the United States. But it also reflected the irresponsibility, even malice, of the German visitors he had talked to, perhaps even the carelessness or bad intentions of certain American officials and their subordinates who had briefed them. Germans of high rank in business, in the Bundestag, and on the periphery of government frequently visited Washington, in total more than all other Western Europeans. In order to have something "juicy" to report on their return, they had, I was sure, exaggerated or reported as fact mere hearsay. I had checked on similar reports received earlier and had found no substance to them.

"Evidently our recent actions have not been understood in Washington," Kiesinger said. German visitors were told "by someone close to the President" that "the President felt cheated by Kiesinger." "As long as I am Chancellor I will steer the course that I discussed with the President when I met with him last year." Moreover, he had not, as alleged in Washington, engaged in any conspiracy with the Communists. It was true that he was trying to improve relations with the Eastern countries; he was not, however, trying to "woo the Reds," as had been charged in Washington, Kiesinger said to me.

It had also supposedly been said in Washington that Kiesinger had knowledge of, and had acquiesced in, conversations between SPD officials and representatives of the Italian Community party. He had heard the reproach that the "SPD was the real master" of coalition Eastern policy and that the chancellor merely followed. He wanted to make it clear that the government's policy was his policy. He was not moving to the left; the SPD was moving to the right. Forces in the SPD were trying to push the government into a different policy, but he had blocked this. This was an accusation the SPD would later make against Helmut Schmidt. Brandt himself had given him no reason for doubt, although Kiesinger did not like the SPD attitude toward Vietnam. Kiesinger emphasized that he had no desire to play the role of "school master to Americans." This role, curiously enough, is that to which Schmidt referred when he became chancellor. Perhaps the Germans, considering themselves the originators of what is called Realpolitik, felt an obligation to educate the less experienced Americans.

Kiesinger continued that he had also heard from German visitors to Washington accusations that he was following a Gaullist policy. He had been accused of making a secret agreement with de Gaulle at their last meeting. As he told me when he returned from that meeting, he was unhappy that France had left NATO.

Kiesinger referred to his "Atlantic imperium" concept, which he had outlined on March 11 in his speech to the Bundestag. Certain sections of the American press and American individuals appeared to have misunderstood him. Birrenbach, for example, had heard that Jack McCloy was disturbed. Perhaps his choice of the word *imperium* was a mistake. Some might as a result consider what he had said to be Gaullism. He had hesitated, however, to use the word *community*, since he did not feel it to be accurate.

I assured Kiesinger that the views reported to him conformed neither with those I had encountered in my recent visit to Washington, nor with any reports from the embassy or comments in messages from the government. No one suspected him of collusion with the Communists. He appeared somewhat assuaged, but it was clear that he believed what his recent visitors had told him. He did not identify, nor did I ask him to name, the personalities involved.

It was probably no coincidence that the same subject came up again on April 3 during my last meeting with Ludwig Erhard, who had just returned from a trip to the United States (telegram, Amemb Bonn to Secstate, 10419, Apr. 4, 1968). It was a sad occasion for me. I recalled my many meetings with him as chancellor and the great blow of his fall from power and hasty removal from office. He had been an outstanding economics minister, and German prosperity—self-evident everywhere—was in large measure due to his efforts. He remained a loyal friend of the United States, even though I felt that it had, in the end, let him down. He thought it likely, he said, that the 1969 election results would be such that the Grand Coalition—toward which he remained adamantly opposed—would have to be continued.

In response to my question about his trip to the United States, Erhard spoke warmly about his meeting with President Johnson, but immediately began to reiterate the view he had already expressed in a recent interview that there was serious concern in the United States about German policy. He did not attribute this view to any particular U.S. official. In fact, he said, government officials were naturally cautious in discussing relations with a friendly country. His views represented a distillation of impressions he had obtained in talking to a great number of prominent Americans. It was difficult to put his finger precisely on what had caused this deterioration, he said, but he believed that much of the blame fell on the German side. He cited the use of such phrases as "complicity between the U.S. and the U.S.S.R." and the "Atlantic imperium," by government leaders in Bonn, as well as their repeated emphasis on Europe as a separate and independent entity, their tendency to lean heavily on France, and their criticism of U.S. policy in Vietnam, especially by the SPD, as contributing factors.

I noted that Kiesinger had spoken warmly about relations with the United States before the Bundestag the day before. I expressed some concern that if people got the impression we were critical of German policy, this in itself could lead to a deterioration in relations between the two countries. Erhard agreed. He admitted that he had been "not quite innocent" in contesting privately the chancellor's positive statement on U.S.-German relations in the Bundestag.

I asked Erhard whether it would be helpful if, in connection with the security aspects of the NPT, the United States were to make a strong statement reaffirming its NATO assurances and guarantees. Erhard doubted whether this would do the trick, because such a statement would not affect the text of the treaty as it now stood. He said that he had not counted noses but had the impression that the present text was unacceptable to a majority of his party. Nor did he think it could be taken for granted that the treaty in its present form would be ratified by the Bundestag. He believed that extraneous considerations would play an important role, such as the fear that passage would result in a loss of votes to the extreme rightist NPD. Without going into detail, he suggested that further changes in the text of the treaty were necessary to make a convincing case that there would be no deleterious effects on Germany's security and access to nuclear technologies for peaceful uses.

I asked Erhard whether the government's Eastern policy tended to create friction within the coalition. He thought that the general direction of this policy created no problems. He recalled that his government had already initiated a flexible policy toward Eastern Europe, that trade relations had been normalized with Eastern Europe and that diplomatic relations with Rumania had been assured before his resignation. German leadership maintained a genuine desire to normalize relations with Poland and the USSR, spurred by hopes that this would lead to progress toward German unity. The problem for the CDU/CSU was not, therefore, the general direction of the policy but that the SPD, in its desire for "successes" in this field, wanted to move too far and too fast. The SPD tended to boast about imaginary successes, he argued. Some of its members even wanted to attribute current domestic changes in Czechoslovakia to Germany's new Eastern policy. He thought that this was sheer nonsense. The real debate within the coalition, declared Erhard, was over relations with East Germany, where coalition partners had a clear difference of opinion.

Erhard remarked that his opposition to the CDU/CSU-SPD coalition was well known. He felt that it would have been far preferable for Germany to move toward a two-party system. During his tenure there had been a strong tendency in this direction that had now been reversed. At least one and possibly two additional parties would be represented in the next Bundestag, meaning that the CDU/CSU could not win an absolute majority in the next federal election. The CDU would probably lose some seats and the SPD would lose even more. Numerically, a CDU/CSU-FDP coalition might be possible, but the FDP, under its present leadership, tended more toward the SPD. It was unlikely that the SPD and FDP together would have a majority. Consequently, much to his regret, Erhard acknowledged that the Grand Coalition seemed likely to have to be continued beyond the 1969 elections.

Erhard was in good form. He had enjoyed his trip to the United States and was flattered by the attention President Johnson had shown him.

His principal interests at this stage appeared to be criticizing his successor and justifying his role as chancellor. Except for such occasional exercises, he appeared to have withdrawn from active politics, devoting much of his time to lecturing on economic subjects abroad, including, he hoped, in America.

On April 4 concern for the future of the NPT led me to Rainer Barzel, the CDU floor leader in the Bundestag. Barzel was anxious over parliamentary support for the NPT. But I was anxious myself to see just where the NPT stood.

Although foreign policy was the chancellor's ultimate responsibility, it was Barzel's role to shepherd the treaty through the Bundestag. He now told me that he had no majority in his caucus for the NPT as it stood. He needed help in interpreting the treaty, particularly from a psychological standpoint, to the German public. What he thought was needed was something that would make the right headlines in Axel Springer's mass-circulation *Bild Zeitung*. He hoped that the United States would take the occasion of the upcoming debate of the NPT in the United Nations General Assembly to make a strong statement clarifying the U.S. position. In particular, he hoped that we would give assurances on technological and fuel supply problems, show an understanding of the European problem, and give some type of reassurance on the security aspects. What he thought might be called for was a U.S. statement to the effect that all countries who had relied in the past on the U.S. nuclear guarantee could continue to do so.

I took advantage of my final visit with Barzel to raise a few other points, for which his position of fraction leader provided insight. In response to my query, Barzel said that he and Helmut Schmidt, fraction leader for the SPD, were continuing their close collaboration. He did not foresee any difficulties, following the SPD Nuremberg convention, in maintaining the coalition. He had just finished talking with Schmidt about the emergency legislation, the passage of which he viewed optimistically. I thanked him for the strong line the CDU had taken in the recent Bundestag debate on Vietnam. Barzel replied that the CDU thought it was particularly important at this juncture—which was not long after the Tet Offensive and the U.S. decision to deescalate the war and pursue peace talks in Paris—that President Johnson be given freedom to handle the fluid situation in Vietnam without the handicap of advice from others.

On April 26, two weeks after I left Germany, Arthur Goldberg, the

U.S. representative to the United Nations General Assembly, deposited the text of the NPT. The seven-year negotiating process was over. Although no time limit was set on the treaty, as Germany and other nations had desired, Article VIII provided for a review conference to begin in five years, with a view to assuring that the purposes of the preamble and the provisions of the treaty were being realized. The preamble set as goals the cessation of the nuclear arms race, the discontinuance of all nuclear tests, the elimination of nuclear weapons and the means of their delivery, and a treaty on general and complete disarmament. These goals represented some of the most important objectives laid out by Willy Brandt as foreign minister.

During the treaty negotiations, the United States had helped bring about many changes to strengthen the treaty and meet particular issues raised by West Germany and other members of the Committee on Disarmament. Article IV had been strengthened to protect and promote peaceful uses. Article V had been added in order to ensure that non-nuclear countries would be offered nuclear explosive services for peaceful uses at low cost under appropriate international procedures. Article VI had been added to bind the parties to "seek to end the nuclear arms race at an early date and to seek effective nuclear disarmament."

During the period of the Grand Coalition with the SPD, Kiesinger and his party delayed signing the NPT. But on November 13, 1969, only two weeks after Brandt was elected chancellor and Kiesinger and the CDU were eliminated from the government, Brandt announced that he was prepared to sign after receiving appropriate assurances from Washington and Moscow. The assurances were given, and Brandt signed on November 17, 1969. Germany was safely within the NPT fold.

By that time, there was also a new president in the White House and a new American ambassador in Bonn. Since all good things must come to an end, both my wife and I sensed as my fifth year in Germany drew to a close that the time had arrived to return home. Five years was a long time to remain at any post, and I had become increasingly concerned at losing contact with my country during this period of travail—the effects of the long Vietnam War on U.S. college students and the riots of disaffected black youths in the inner cities. During a visit to Washington, I had conveyed this to both Rusk and Johnson, suggesting an assignment in the State Department.

Having heard through the State Department grapevine that Henry Cabot Lodge, then serving as ambassador-at-large, was seeking an overseas assignment during the forthcoming election period, I suggested to Rusk the possibility of swapping jobs with Lodge. With his broad experience and the prestige of having been a senator and a vice presidential candidate, I knew he would be highly acceptable to the Germans. One day I received a cryptic call from Rusk, which, for security reasons, consisted of the message, "The switch you proposed has been approved. Do the necessaries." It took me a moment to figure out what he meant, but when I did I said, "Fine, I believe I can finish everything up in twenty-four hours. It can be announced tomorrow."

Host government approval of a new ambassador normally takes a week or so. But this would obviously be an easy case, and I was anxious to avoid the usual press leaks of ambassadorial changes, which can give rise to embarrassing speculation about why the change is being made. Official German approval was obtained that very day, and the announcement was made the following day in Washington and Bonn. Everyone involved was happy. Both Lodge and the State Department were agreeable to my staying long enough to make my farewells and for my children to finish the school year.

Rightly or wrongly, farewells have become such an important aspect of an ambassador's tour of duty that he and his family would feel cheated without them. Although strenuous, they are worth every moment, particularly when one has been on post as long as we were and has developed such a warm feeling for the country and its people. During our last weeks, we paid our farewell visits, in seven separate trips, to all ten of the German *Länder* and to Berlin. In each state and city state, the mayor or governor tendered us a luncheon or dinner—in Berlin, Mayor Schutz. There Cecilia and I hosted a convivial buffet dance at the lovely U.S. Army guest house overlooking the Wannsee, and military ceremonies were held in my honor. I had been briefed to flex my toes periodically to keep my blood circulation going and so prevent fainting from standing motionless for about twenty minutes.

In Bonn there were in all sixteen farewell dinners, luncheons, or receptions, as many as time permitted. On one memorable evening the entire embassy staff took over a Rhine steamer for dinner and dancing. A reception was given by the press corps. A number of dinners were hosted by fellow ambassadors. Several parties were given by friends in neighboring cities within easy driving distance of Bonn, and we were able to sleep in the car on the way home. A high point of our entertainment was the luncheon given us by President Lübke, who made very generous parting comments. On the evening before our departure,

Chancellor Kiesinger extended a formal state dinner. His farewell remarks, which were warm and friendly, touched me deeply. It provided
a heartening finishing touch for the end of a long tour of duty which
Cecilia and I had accepted as a great challenge, had thoroughly enjoyed,
and felt was fully worth the effort we had made. This is a feeling I hold
even more strongly today, as I conclude this account of an important
segment of the close U.S.-German postwar relationship, which will I
am sure continue to be an essential element in the structure of world
peace.

23

Postlude
May 1968–
September 1969

The Grand Coalition came into power in 1966 largely as a result of the severe economic recession that Erhard had been unable to turn around. By 1966, 700,000 people were unemployed, a situation that had been considered impossible in Germany. Starting with a projected deficit for 1967 of DM 3 billion, the new government managed to balance the budget. By the end of 1968 the recession was over, unemployment was down, and industrial growth was up 6 percent.

The neo-Nazi NPD, an index of political malaise, reached the peak of its strength in 1968, winning 16 percent of the votes in Kiesinger's own state of Baden-Würtemburg. Kiesinger had succeeded by 1968 in strengthening Franco-German ties, and East-West relations, under the stimulus of Willy Brandt, had received an impetus that resulted in the establishment of diplomatic relations with Rumania and trade relations with Czechoslovakia in 1967, and the restoration of diplomatic relations with Yugoslavia in 1968. But further improvements came to an abrupt halt with the Soviet invasion of Czechoslovakia in August 1968. Kiesinger pursued a balanced policy of détente and supported NATO and the maintenance of U.S. troop levels in Germany.

Despite Kiesinger and Brandt's repeated efforts little progress was made with the Communist government of East Germany. The sixteen proposals put forward in April 1967 to Prime Minister Willi Stoph of the GDR, which constituted an extension of Brandt's "small steps" policy, fell on deaf ears. The GDR continued to oppose any movement toward reunification. A virtual stalemate in GDR-FRG relations ensued, despite occasional lip service to the idea of German unity by Communist party leader Walter Ulbricht and Kiesinger's renewed offer to the USSR and the GDR of a mutual renunciation of force agreement.

Student unrest had increased in June 1967, was further intensified in April 1968, and remained a serious problem during the entire period of the Grand Coalition. Kiesinger favored strong measures to deal with it. The student movement became principally associated with the question of special legislation to take care of an emergency threatening democratic order.

The CDU suffered a setback when Gerhard Schröder was defeated in his bid for the federal German presidency in 1969. Free Democratic party chairman Walter Scheel threw the support of his party behind SPD candidate Gustav Heinemann, presaging a shift toward an SPD/FDP coalition. The SPD, which had experienced a loss at the polls as a member of the coalition with the Christian Democrats, was becoming increasingly disenchanted with continuing a coalition government with the CDU as the two parties faced the September 1969 national elections. Kiesinger campaigned on the government's record of ending the recession and its accomplishments in Eastern policy. He criticized Brandt's willingness to accept the Non-Proliferation Treaty, which Germany had still not recognized. The political charisma of Brandt as SPD leader plus the organizing ability of Wehner led, however, to an increase in votes for the SPD (from 39.2 percent to 40.7 percent), whereas the CDU vote held virtually steady. Kiesinger, whom President Nixon had mistakenly congratulated as winner (as Schmidt curiously enough did with Ford a few years later), waited too long to approach the FDP as a coalition partner, permitting Brandt, who had moved quickly, to make such a deal with Scheel. The new SPD/FDP coalition came in with a majority of only twelve votes.

Kiesinger, bitterly disappointed, ceased to be a power in German politics. Many historians have characterized both him and his coalition as failures. He has, I believe, been denied the credit he was due for the very real accomplishments of his coalition, not the least of which was making such an improbable combination work at all. I have good memories of Kiesinger as a gentleman and as a fair and reasonable man with whom to discuss problems and negotiate. I only regret that his relations with the Johnson administration were marred by his original Gaullist tendency, the difficulties encountered in arranging a visit between him and Johnson, and Kiesinger's opposition to the Non-Proliferation Treaty in which the U.S. government had placed such high hopes. To me Kiesinger always demonstrated great courtesy and consideration. He combined charm with frankness and real powers of analysis. Until his recent death I always saw him during his regular visits to the United States.

Willy Brandt had at last become chancellor. He now had the great opportunity for which he had labored so long. It was true that he paid a high price to the Free Democrats—the Foreign Ministry for Scheel plus four other ministries out of fifteen for the FDP's 9 percent of the votes. Brandt was to serve as chancellor for nearly five years, until forced to resign on May 6, 1974. These were, however, fulfilling and productive years; Brandt became a world figure and received the Nobel Peace Prize for the fruition of his goal of many years, his policy of Ostpolitik.

What about Germany's relations with the United States in recent years? Some Americans have seen a lessening of American ties during the consecutive SPD-led administrations of Chancellors Brandt and Schmidt between 1969 and 1983. Schmidt, though friendly to America, did indulge in much unfortunate personal criticism of President Jimmy Carter. But these perceptions appear exaggerated, as demonstrated by Helmut Kohl's election in 1983 and the reelection in West Berlin in 1985 of the city's first Christian Democratic government since World War II. Kohl, who is considerably to the right of center and is almost as blatantly pro-American as Erhard, was able to lead the Bundestag to accept the new U.S. medium-range Pershing II and cruise missiles, originally proposed by Chancellor Helmut Schmidt, in the face of determined opposition from the SPD, Schmidt's party. These missiles are, of course, now scheduled for removal under the recent U.S.-USSR INF agreement. At this writing, the openly anti-American Greens appear to have peaked. The SPD, although opposed to medium-range missiles, subsequently adopted a conciliatory, pro-NATO resolution at its May 1984 convention in Essen.

Polls have been taken regularly over many years on the question of which nation West Germany should choose to cooperate most closely with. Support for the United States peaked at 90 percent in 1963, the year of Kennedy's spectacular visit to Germany, but has not been below 80 percent in thirty years. Over the same period, France has climbed to 70 percent and Britain has fallen from 70 to 60 percent. The Soviet Union, however, has never exceeded 50 percent.

Commentators suggest that most German opposition to the United States in recent years is not so much anti-Americanism, which would mean something visceral, emotional, and of lasting duration. Rather it seems to come from ad hoc opposition to particular U.S. leaders, policies, or postures. Many Germans see Americans as having created in recent years an unnecessary atmosphere of confrontation with the Soviets. President Reagan, particularly over the issue of German pipe for the Soviet gas pipeline to Europe and in his apparent willingness at the 1986 Reykjavík summit to dispense with nuclear deterrence for Europe, has been considered by many Germans as a unilateralist, prone to take action before consulting NATO allies. The Reagan administration is also viewed by the peace marchers as overly reliant on military means, particularly nuclear weapons.

But I believe that the attitude of the mass of Germans toward America is little changed since I was there in 1963–68. We still have the same shared interests and cultural heritage. We still profit mutually from our extensive bilateral trade and investment. The Germans see in U.S. military power, particularly its nuclear strength, the only real basis for their security. Americans, on the other hand, see in West Germany the only hope for effectively resisting a Soviet attack against Europe or Soviet efforts to extend its political influence by intimidation, even assuming our own all-out help in the common defense. No, I believe the present ties between West Germany and the United States result from coincidences of history and shared interest which, fortunately for both of us, have survived the inexorable changes in the relations between nations. I believe the momentum created by these ties is a powerful force assuring their continuation.

My experience with the Germans persuades me that we are fortunate to have as our ally—in the dangerous zone of transition between East and West—such a united and determined people who can always be counted on to defend their country. It behooves Americans, I believe, to pay close attention to the well-known mood changes in Germany. We must take into account the impact in our respective attitudes flowing from differences in history and geography.

The long German border with the Communist bloc, where Germans face every day the most modern weapons in the hands of an implacable enemy, contrasts sharply with our isolation beyond the broad Atlantic. Americans must respect the fact that the Germans are continuing to make every effort to assume their responsibilities as respected members of an increasingly integrated Europe. This will require increased flexibility in what Americans expect from their bilateral relations with Germany.

The only real danger the United States faces in our present relationship with West Germany, I believe, lies in overemphasizing our confrontation with the Soviet Union as the determinant in our policy toward Germany and U.S. insensitivity to valid German anxieties arising out of their unique situation. The controversy in 1985 over President Reagan's and Chancellor Kohl's visit to the Bitburg Cemetery shows that misunderstandings between the United States and West Germany can still arise, particularly when old wounds are inadvertently opened. Americans must have patience in seeking common policies with the Germans, through negotiating issues as they arise on a basis of equality and respecting their national pride and patriotism. In this way Americans can, I believe, assure a continuing relationship between the two countries that can immensely benefit us both and assure peace in the world.

Hunting in Germany

I found that the best way to understand and develop close, friendly relations with German business leaders was through hunting. Having hunted in the United States, I was happy to be invited to try my hand in Germany. Hunting in Germany is a highly formalized, serious affair, quite different from hunting in the United States. In America many people have hunted at one time or another; one needs only to buy a hunting license, get a gun, and obtain permission to hunt in season or to poach on some farmer's land. In Germany, however, a sharp division exists between hunters and nonhunters. The subject was so complex that the U.S. Army Europe provided a manual, *Guide to Hunting in Germany*, for official American personnel.

Potential hunters are normally required to attend ten to fifteen lectures and do classwork covering all aspects of hunting, weapons, safety, laws, game, customs, and so on. The applicant must then pass an oral examination by three to six experienced hunters and officials; the whole process takes at least a year. A *Jagdhaftpflichtversicherungsschein*, or insurance policy, is also required.

Hunting lands in Germany are divided into *Reviers*, or aggregates of 1,000–2,000 acres, which are leased, usually for nine years for small game and twelve years for large game, from one or a number of landowners grouped together in a *Gemeinde*, a township, to whom this is an important source of income. Lessees can be individuals, hunting groups, or corporations. They have certain law enforcement obligations and can invite guests. The trophy, consisting of headbones only, is removed as a gift to the guest hunter. The meat, however, is customarily

263

sold by the lessee as a contribution toward the expenses of the hunt. Even in hunts where the host is a large corporation, the guest receives no meat.

Over the years dress has become an important, highly formalized aspect of hunting. The color of all articles of clothing, including such accessories as ties, socks, gloves, and handkerchiefs, must be forest green. The hunter must be aware of unacceptable variations of color. The shape of the hat, the length of the jacket, the neck of the sweater— all must conform to tradition; to dress otherwise is to be recognized as a gauche new hunter. Warm clothes, raincoats, and waterproof boots are also required.

Selecting one's gun is particularly important; a different caliber and bullet weight are required for each of the principal animals shot with a rifle: the red, fallow, and roe deer, the wild boar, the chamois, and the mouflon. I generally used an Austrian rifle, an 8 by 57 mm. caliber Walther that I had acquired when stationed in Turkey. It was a light gun but because of this was more sporting. For a time I used a more powerful rifle, a .300 Weatherby magnum, which had an interesting story. Shotguns are used for rabbits and birds but are forbidden in hunting cloven-footed game.

I owed the Weatherby to a social conversation with a German industrialist about a forthcoming hunt. My Walther was not powerful enough, he said. He would send me a .300 Weatherby. I resisted, but he sent me one anyway. The U.S. consul in Düsseldorf warned me later that he had heard rumors that my benefactor, in discussions with other industrialists, had bragged that "he had the inside track with the American ambassador." I had better be wary. It happened that Jack McCloy, who was in Bonn for a visit, said that he had been given an unwanted gun by the same man under the same circumstances. Not long afterward, I was a luncheon guest of this individual at his home. I took the gun along and had my driver give it to his house man. Neither of us referred to the incident again.

Hunting has been practiced in Germany for many centuries and has come to be surrounded by many traditions. Most German words involved in hunting have a special nickname that all seasoned hunters use. Before hunting, hunters wish one another well by saying "Waldmannsheil," (good luck), the response to which is "Waldmannsdank" (thank you). A successful hunter is told "Gratulieren" (congratulations). Broken branches of particular pine trees are used for special hunting signals. A branch dipped in the blood of the slain animal is laid on a knife or hat and offered the successful hunter, who sits briefly on the ground to pay respects to the fallen animal before the game is dressed. This ritual is called the *Totenwache*, or death watch. Any failure to fulfill these formalities is considered a serious breach of etiquette.

Bugles are used to signal the start, progress, and finish of a hunt. At day's end, the game is laid out on the ground in relative rank, ranging from red deer down to small birds. A bugle call that has been used for centuries is given in turn for each group. One always walks around game, never over it. Deer are hunted either by stalking or from a *hoch-sitz*, an elevated blind. Often the hunt is aided by simulated animal calls or by huntsmen who drive the game toward the hunters. Wounding an animal is a serious affair; the hunter must search for it, usually with all in his group. If the wounded animal is not found by evening, the search is resumed the following morning. A pall is cast over the hunt. After an Aachen coal mine owner wounded an animal on a hunt I was on, his wife recounted that he had a nightmare in which the animal appeared and accused him. He had had heart trouble, and she actually feared for his life. The next year, on the same hunt, I asked my host about him. He replied, "Oh, he wasn't invited this year—a nervous fellow, you know."

As a consequence, I became conscious of the necessity to take my time to aim at a vulnerable spot before firing. Often to the guide's annoyance, I would wait as much as a quarter-hour after he had given approval to shoot. A stranger to the country and a diplomat, I did not want to incur criticism for being a bad shot and wounding game. I practiced my marksmanship at a U.S. Army range near Bonn before every hunt and had my guns calibrated for the trajectory of the bullet at different distances. This I would measure optically for each sighting before shooting. A 150 grain bullet, for example, would without compensation strike 3.9 inches low at one hundred yards. In a broadside shot, which, for a deer, should be two-thirds up the body directly above the front leg, this could be the difference between success or failure.

I fired many shotgun shots in hunting hare and pheasant and other birds. But since I took killing my larger game without wounding any so seriously, I fired, during my five years of hunting in Germany, only six rifle shots. All in all, I brought home only five cloven-hoofed trophies: two *hirsch* (red deer) and a chamois from Austria, and two roebucks (roe deer) from the Rhineland. My first hirsch, which I stalked, was a mature male, which I killed cleanly with my first shot at extreme range against a setting sun. The next year my first shot was a clear miss, which led the animal, leaving no wound. The chamois I shot after spending the night with the chief hunter at a lodge in the snowdrifts ten thousand feet up. After waiting twenty minutes to shoot, during which he grew increasingly impatient, I got a clean hit at a hundred meters. The chamois plunged immediately off the crag it was on. I also hit the two roe deer squarely. Five trophies, from six rifle bullets, were all I had to show for my five years of hunting larger game in Germany.

But the reward from hunting in Germany was not just in the shooting of game. Hunting provided the best way of getting close to German men in their own natural setting—permitting the development of an intimacy not easily established otherwise. The hunts in which I participated included the leading German industrialists. My host for two seasons was Hans-Günther Sohl, like me a geologist by training, who was president of Thyssen, the largest steel company in Germany. Sohl, with whom I have kept in touch over the years, became a close friend during my five years in Germany. The company lodge was on the idyllic Jägersee near St. Johann im Pongau, south of Salzburg.

One season we were joined by Kurt Birrenbach, who chaired both Thyssen and the Bundestag Foreign Relations Committee. At each hunt there were eight to ten leading Ruhr businessmen. In our luncheon and dinner conversations and late into the night over brandy before a roaring fire, I achieved a much deeper understanding of the German man in his elemental state—hunting.

I also valued my experiences on two hunts with Heinrich Müller, chief executive officer of the DEMAG company of Duisburg, a manufacturing firm for heavy industry. DEMAG had a delightful lodge high up over the Rhine in the Damscheid und Oberweseler Hochwald. To the first hunt he invited sixteen guests, most of them industrialists from Düsseldorf, as well as men from his own firm and a few diplomats. I shot my roebuck from a hochsitz. Müller later advised me that the hunt netted four red deer, one wild boar, two foxes, and a hare.

Müller ran a meticulous hunt, sending each guest a "General Guide for the Shoot" in advance. It cautioned against shooting the lead animal in a group or any stag red deer. It provided rules of engagement with the game, safety precautions, and the meaning of bugle calls. The group was most congenial, and under Müller's gentle direction our many discussions were both pleasant and valuable.

There were other hunts—several for roebuck along the Rhine and for hare, foxes, and pheasants. I participated in one pheasant hunt, hosted by President Lübke, with other members of the diplomatic corps. It was an all-day affair with an elaborate champagne luncheon on a wooded estate near Bonn and provided a pleasant milieu for a group that was otherwise often stuffy. I have fond memories of hunting in Germany.

An Ambassador's Statistical Summary May 16, 1963– May 21, 1968

It may interest the reader to see a summary of the activities of an American ambassador and spouse in their line of duty. Since I incline personally to a factual and statistical approach, I asked my staff to analyze our schedule during my five years in Germany. Bonn is not a typical post, since the embassy is also responsible politically for Berlin and the U.S. brigade there; for the three major NATO commands and 250,000 American military personnel with dependents in Germany; and for a large CIA group with responsibilities going beyond Germany. Germany is also a key NATO ally and the leading industrial country of the Common Market. With the largest embassy staff except perhaps the U.S. embassy in wartime Vietnam, Bonn could be regarded as one of America's most important embassies.

The basic duty of an ambassador is to represent the president of the United States with the host government. During the five years under review, I participated in 344 meetings with senior West German officials, including 24 with President Lübke, and 96 with the three chancellors, including 14 with Adenauer, 65 with Erhard, and 15 with Kiesinger. I held 39 meetings with Foreign Minister Brandt and 29 with Foreign Minister Schröder, 64 with Under Secretary Carstens, and 117 with other ministers and their subordinates. A typical meeting averaged an hour.

Official visits occupied much of my time as ambassador. I made 211 visits outside Bonn, 50 official visits to German cities, 36 to universities, and 125 for speaking appearances. Of my speaking engagements, 57 could be considered major speeches that averaged perhaps five thousand words. These usually received wide German and often American media coverage. Nineteen were published in the *State Department Bulletin.* Since internal commercial air transport is not well developed in Germany, I traveled primarily by car. Only occasionally was the state railway used; on a number of occasions I used private trains loaned me by the military. I had access to, and often used, one of the planes assigned to our air attaché, and occasionally I borrowed a jet plane from our NATO air command in Wiesbaden for long trips.

Too much of an ambassador's time is consumed by business-social activities, but few of these are strictly social or personal. My wife and I gave 526 such affairs, hosting 14,875 people. These included 220 luncheons, 95 receptions and cocktail parties, 205 dinners, 7 breakfasts, 2 teas, 2 concerts, and 3 large dances. The embassy staff, including our excellent cook, who was with us the entire time, and our maitre d', were highly professional and tireless. After preparing for a luncheon for twenty they would not bat an eye if a dinner for thirty was added for the same evening.

The purpose of embassy entertaining is largely to enable important visiting U.S. officials to meet high German officials, other German dignitaries, and our embassy staff. Although it is the national capital, Bonn is a relatively small, provincial city with little social life like that of London, Paris, or Rome. For us this was a godsend. Other entertaining centered around anniversary and ceremonial occasions. Dinners tendered my wife and myself by diplomatic colleagues and local dignitaries were reciprocated. Occasionally a dinner or a dance was given just for the pleasure of the occasion. Germans do not entertain or want to be entertained on weekends. Few entertain in country homes. Dress for dinner was usually black tie. My wife made an effort to feature indigenous American dishes; those suitable for formal occasions, however, were limited. We often served American wines but more often Moselle or Rhine wines.

The embassy's annual Fourth of July reception is such a burden on the ambassador's budget that efforts have been made, unsuccessfully, to eliminate it. We gave four such receptions, dividing each into two parties, one for high German officials and diplomats, and one for all others. Each year we invited 2,000 people from all over Germany, expecting about 1,200. Resident Americans, who are not numerous in Germany, have come to expect such parties and would be offended if they were eliminated. The possibility of rain is always a threat, since the residence could not accommodate that many people. Tents, apart from being quite expensive, were really not feasible, for lack of space.

When it did rain, we successfully employed a system which I believe was our own invention. Guests were divided into three groups, invited, respectively, for 4–5 P.M., 5–6 P.M., and 6–7 P.M., but only in the event of rain. Germans are so punctilious in such matters that the one time it rained they came and went precisely in accordance with their assigned times.

During our five years my wife and I received a total of 3,196 invitations of all sorts, of which we could accept only 671, or about one-fifth. Refusals represented conflicts, came during absences from the city, or were to events of lesser importance. We regretted that we seldom received invitations for small, informal dinners or from young people of lesser rank. Germans are very rank conscious as concerns both invitations and acceptances. I received in my office 1,228 outside visitors during five years. This, of course, is few in comparison with larger capitals.

Many of our visits within Germany were for special occasions, some of which were particularly pleasurable. Each year we attended the *Kieler Woche* in the pleasant old Hanseatic town of Kiel. Each year we stayed at the local yacht club, went sailing with the minister president of Schleswig-Holstein, and enjoyed the entertainment provided the Bonn diplomatic corps and other visitors. We also attended faithfully the famous annual Horse Show at Aachen, at which the Germans demonstrated their great skill in dressage.

In West Berlin we visited the annual *Grüne Woche* of agricultural exhibits and entertainment, originated long ago as a kind of state fair for the Prussian landed gentry living around Berlin. It used to provide an opportunity for young members of the Junker class to meet one another at tea dances and arrange marriages. We usually visited the annual International Berlin Film Festival, which included American entries. One year we attended the Wagner festival in Bayreuth, featuring performances from "The Ring." We were given the box belonging to the composer's daughter-in-law and were shown Wagner's house.

We tried each year to attend social events involving American participation in various parts of Germany. One was the Atlantic Ball in Frankfurt, where there was a large American community; another was the annual Magnolia Ball in Munich, one of the several thousand activities of the Fasching season. On one occasion I had the honor of opening the ball by waltzing with the queen of Fasching, the king having broken his leg. Masked carnivals are celebrated just before Lent, especially at Cologne and Mainz in the Rhineland—gay affairs with colorful and imaginative costumes. The season includes outdoor parades and indoor balls with masked dancing. On two occasions we attended the beer-drinking Munich harvest *Oktoberfest*, which occurs in September. Beer is consumed with fifteen thousand others under one great tent. For a small fee one can direct the band.

Germans are a serious-minded, hard-working people, but they have their lighter side. They are hospitable and attach great value to home and family entertaining. With an introduction, a foreigner is received most hospitably. Although Germans are cautious in extending close friendship and men use first names only after long acquaintance, once a friendship is made a German is a thoughtful and loyal friend for life. We were in Germany long enough to make firm friendships. Our personal social life in Germany was very rewarding and has over the years brought back many pleasant memories.

John F. Kennedy's "Ich bin ein Berliner" Speech June 26, 1963

Two thousand years ago the proudest boast was "Civitas Romanus sum." Today, in the world of freedom, the proudest boast is "Ich bin ein Berliner."

There are many people in the world who really don't understand, or say they don't, what is the great issue between the free world and the Communist world. Let them come to Berlin. There are some who say that Communism is the wave of the future. Let them come to Berlin. And there are some who say in Europe and elsewhere we can work with the Communists. Let them come to Berlin. And there are even a few who say that it is true that Communism is an evil system, but it permits us to make economic progress. "Lasst sie nach Berlin kommen."

Freedom has many difficulties and democracy is not perfect, but we have never had to put a wall up to keep our people in, to prevent them from leaving us. I want to say, on behalf of my countrymen, who live many miles away on the other side of the Atlantic, who are far distant from you, that they take the greatest pride that they have been able to share with you, even from a distance, the story of the last eighteen years. I know of no town, no city, that has been besieged for eighteen years that still lives with the vitality and the force, and the hope and the determination of the city of West Berlin. While the wall is the most obvious and vivid demonstration of the failures of the Communist system, for all the world to see, we take no satisfaction in it, for it is an offense not only against history but an offense against humanity, separating families, dividing husbands and wives and brothers and sisters, and dividing a people who wish to be joined together.

What is true of this city is true of Germany—real, lasting peace in

Europe can never be assured as long as one German out of four is denied the elementary right of free men, and that is to make a free choice. In eighteen years of peace and good faith, this generation of Germans has earned the right to be free, including the right to unite their families and their nation in lasting peace with good will to all people. You live in a defended island of freedom, but your life is part of the main. So let me ask you, as I close, to lift your eyes beyond the dangers of today to the hopes of tomorrow, beyond the freedom merely of this city of Berlin, or your country of Germany, to the advance of freedom everywhere, beyond the wall to the day of peace with justice, beyond yourselves and ourselves to all mankind. Freedom is indivisible, and when one man is enslaved, all are not free. When all are free, then we can look forward to that day when this city will be joined as one—and this country, and this great continent of Europe—in a peaceful and hopeful glow. When that day finally comes, as it will, the people of West Berlin can take sober satisfaction in the fact that they were in the front lines for almost two decades.

All free men, wherever they may live, are citizens of Berlin, and therefore, as a free man, I take pride in the words "Ich bin ein Berliner."

Bibliography

Acheson, Dean. "The Practice of Partnership." *Foreign Affairs* 41 (January 1963).

Adenauer, Konrad. *Memoirs, 1945–1953.* Trans. Beate Ruhm von Oppen. London: Weidenfeld and Nicholson, 1966.

Almond, Gabriel A., ed. *The Struggle for Democracy in Germany.* New York: Russell and Russell, 1965.

American University Foreign Area Studies. *Area Handbook for the Federal Republic of Germany.* Washington, D.C.: GPO, 1975.

Bahr, Egon. "Renunciation of Force and the Alliance." *Aussenpolitik* (English ed.) 24, no. 3 (1973).

Balfour, Michael. *West Germany: A Contemporary History.* London: Croom Helm, 1982.

Ball, George. *Diplomacy for a Crowded World: An American Foreign Policy.* Boston and Toronto: Little, Brown, 1976.

Barnet, Richard J. *The Alliance.* New York: Simon and Schuster, 1983.

Batty, Peter. *The House of Krupp.* New York: Stein and Day, 1967.

Binder, David. *The Other German: Willy Brandt's Life and Times.* Washington, D.C.: New Republic, 1975.

Birrenbach, Kurt. "The West and German Ostpolitik: The German Opposition View." *Atlantic Community Quarterly* 9 (Summer 1971).

Bohlen, Charles E. *Witness to History, 1929–1969.* New York: W. W. Norton, 1973.

Bowie, Robert. "Tensions within the Alliance." *Foreign Affairs* 42 (October 1963).

Brandt, Willy. "Germany's 'Westpolitik.'" *Foreign Affairs* 50 (April 1972).

———. *Peace: Writings and Speeches of the Nobel Prize Winner, 1971.* Bonn: Verlag Neue Gesellschaft, 1971.

———. *People and Politics: The Years 1960–1973.* Boston: Little, Brown, 1976.

Braunthal, Gerhard. *The West German Social Democrats, 1969–1982: Profile of a Party in Power.* Boulder: Westview, 1983.

Buchan, Alistair. "Partner and Allies." *Foreign Affairs* 41 (July 1963).

Catudel, Honor O'M. *Kennedy and the Wall Crisis: A Case Study in U.S. Decision Making.* Berlin: Berlin-Verlag, 1979.

Chalmers, Douglas A. *The Social Democratic Party of Germany: From Working-Class Movement to Modern Political Party.* New Haven: Yale University Press, 1964.

Childs, David. *From Schumacher to Brandt: The Story of German Socialism, 1945–1965.* Oxford and New York: Pergamon, 1966.

Clay, Lucius D. *Decision in Germany.* Garden City, N.Y.: Doubleday, 1950.

Craig, Gordon A. *The Germans.* New York: G. P. Putnam's Sons, 1982.

Crawley, Aidan. *The Rise of Western Germany, 1945–1972.* London: Collins, 1973.

Dahrendorf, Ralf. *Society and Democracy in Germany.* New York and London: W. W. Norton, 1967.

De Rose, François. "Atlantic Relationships and Nuclear Problems." *Foreign Affairs* 41 (April 1963).

Dönhoff, Marion. *Foe into Friend: The Makers of the New Germany from Konrad Adenauer to Helmut Schmidt.* London: Weidenfeld and Nicholson, 1982.

Donovan, Hedley. *Roosevelt to Reagan.* New York: Harper and Row, 1985.

Dornberg, John. *The New Germans: Thirty Years After.* New York: Macmillan, 1976.

Droge, Heinz, Fritz Muench, and Ellinor von Pottkamer. *The Federal Republic of Germany and the United Nations.* New York: Carnegie Endowment for International Peace, 1967.

Dulles, Elanor Lansing. *One Germany or Two: The Struggle at the Heart of Europe.* Stanford: Almquist and Wiksell, 1965.

Edinger, Lewis J. *Kurt Schumacher: A Study in Personality and Political Behavior.* Stanford: Stanford University Press, 1965.

———. *Politics in Germany: Attitudes and Processes.* Boston: Little, Brown, 1968.

Erhard, Ludwig. *Germany's Comeback in the World Market.* Trans. W. H. Johnston. New York: Macmillan, 1954.

Erler, Fritz. "The Basis of Partnership." *Foreign Affairs* 42 (October 1963).

Gatzke, Hans W. *Germany and the United States.* Cambridge and London: Harvard University Press, 1980.

Goergey, Laszlo. *Bonn's Eastern Policy, 1964–1971: Evolution and Limitations.* Hamden, Conn.: Archon Books, 1972.

Goldman, Guido G. *The German Political System.* New York: Random House, 1974.

Goldsborough, James O. "The Franco-German Entente." *Foreign Affairs* 54 (April 1976).

Griffith, William E. *The Ostpolitik of the Federal Republic of Germany.* Cambridge: MIT Press, 1978.

Grosser, Alfred. *Germany in Our Time.* New York: Praeger, 1971.

———. *The Western Alliance.* Trans. Michael Shaw. New York: Vintage, 1980.

Haffner, Sebastian. *The Rise and Fall of Prussia.* London: Weidenfeld and Nicholson, 1980.

Haftendorn, Helga. *Security and Détente: Conflicting Priorities in German Foreign Policy*. New York: Praeger, 1985.

Hahn, Walter F. "West Germany's Ostpolitik: The Grand Design of Egon Bahr." *Orbis* 16 (Winter 1973).

Hanrieder, Wolfram. *The Stable Crisis: The Two Decades of German Foreign Policy*. New York: Harper and Row, 1970.

Heathcote, Nina. "Brandt's 'Ostpolitik' and Western Institutions." *World Today* 26 (August 1970).

Hillenbrand, Martin J. *The Future of Berlin*. Montclair, N.J.: Allenheld, Osmon, 1980.

———. *Germany in an Era of Transition*. Paris: Atlantic Institute for International Affairs, 1983.

Hiscocks, Richard. *The Adenauer Era*. Philadelphia: Lippincott, 1966.

Johnson, Lady Bird. *A White House Diary*. London: Weidenfeld and Nicholson, 1970.

Johnson, Lyndon B. *The Vantage Point*. New York: Holt, Rinehart, and Winston, 1971.

Jonas, Manfred. *The United States and Germany: A Diplomatic History*. Ithaca: Cornell University Press, 1984.

Kaiser, Karl. *German Foreign Policy in Transition: Bonn between East and West*. London and New York: Oxford University Press, 1968.

Kennan, George. "Polycentrism and Western Policy." *Foreign Affairs* 42 (January 1964).

Kennedy, John F. *The Burden and the Glory*. New York: Harper and Row, 1964.

Kiep, Walter Leisler. *A New Challenge for Western Europe: A View from Bonn*. New York: Mason and Lipscomb, 1974.

Kissinger, Henry. *White House Years*. Boston and Toronto: Little, Brown, 1979.

Landauer, Carl. *Germany: Illusions and Dilemmas*. New York: Harcourt, Brace, 1969.

Laqueur, Walter. *Germany Today: A Personal Report*. Boston and Toronto: Little, Brown, 1985.

Livingston, Robert Gerald. *The Federal Republic of Germany in the 1980's: Foreign Policies and Domestic Changes*. New York: German Information Center, 1983.

———. "Germany Steps Up." *Foreign Policy* 22 (Spring 1976).

Loewenberg, Gerhard. *Parliament in the German Political System*. Ithaca: Cornell University Press, 1966.

———. "The Remaking of the German Party System: Political and Socio-Economic Factors." *Polity* 1 (Fall 1968).

Majonica, Ernst. *East-West Relations: A German View*. New York: Praeger, 1965.

Manchester, William. *The Arms of Krupp*. New York: Bantam, 1970.

Merkl, Peter H. *Western German Foreign Policy: Dilemmas and Directions*. Chicago: Chicago Council on Foreign Relations, 1982.

Merritt, Richard L., and Anna J. Merritt. *West Germany Enters the Seventies*. New York: Foreign Policy Association, 1970.

Morgan, Roger P. "The Federal Republic of Germany." In Stanley Hening, ed., *European Political Parties*. New York: Praeger, 1969.

————. *The United States and West Germany, 1945–1973: A Study in Alliance Politics.* London: Oxford University Press, 1974.

Myers, Kenneth A. *Ostpolitik and American Security Interests in Europe.* Washington: Center for Strategic and International Studies, Georgetown University, 1972.

Nagle, John D. *The National Democratic Party: Right Radicalism in the Federal Republic of Germany.* Berkeley: University of California Press, 1970.

Noelle-Neumann, Elizabeth. *The Germans: Public Opinion Polls, 1967–1980.* Westport, Conn., and London: Greenwood Press, 1981.

Noelle-Neumann, Elizabeth, and Erich P. Neumann. *The Germans: Public Opinion Polls, 1947–1966.* Allensbach: Verlag für Demoskopie, 1967.

Prittie, Terence C. F. *Konrad Adenauer, 1876–1967.* Chicago: Cowles, 1972.

————. *The Velvet Chancellors: A History of Post-War Germany.* London: Frederick Muller, 1979.

Roberts, Frank. "The German-Soviet Treaty and Its Effects on European and Atlantic Politics: A British View." *Atlantic Community Quarterly* 9 (Summer 1971).

Roberts, Geoffrey K. *West German Politics.* New York: Taplanger Publishing Company, 1972.

Ryder, A. J. *Twentieth-Century Germany: From Bismarck to Brandt.* New York: Columbia University Press, 1973.

Schlesinger, Arthur. *A Thousand Days: John F. Kennedy in the White House.* New York: Greenwich House, 1965.

Schmidt, Helmut. *Perspectives on Politics.* Boulder: Westview Press, 1982.

Schoenbaum, David. *The Spiegel Affair.* Garden City, N.Y.: Doubleday, 1968.

Schweigler, Gebhard. *West German Foreign Policy: The Domestic Setting.* New York: Praeger, 1984.

Slesser, Sir John. "Control of Nuclear Strategy." *Foreign Affairs* 42 (October 1963).

Sorensen, Theodore S. *Kennedy.* New York: Harper and Row, 1965.

Spaak, Paul-Henri. "Hold Fast." *Foreign Affairs* 41 (July 1963).

Stehlin, General Paul. "The Evolution of Western Defense." *Foreign Affairs* 42 (October 1963).

Thomas, W. Hugh. *The Murder of Rudolph Hess.* New York: Harper and Row, 1979.

Vali, Ferenc A. *The Quest for a United Germany.* Baltimore: Johns Hopkins University Press, 1967.

Weymar, Paul. *Adenauer: His Authorized Biography.* Trans. Peter de Mendelssohn. New York: Dutton, 1957.

Wighton, Charles. *Adenauer: Democratic Dictator.* London: Frederick Muller, 1963.

Woodrow Wilson International Center for Scholars. *The Federal Republic of Germany and the United States.* Boulder: Westview Press, 1984.

Index

Abrasimov, Peter Andreyevich: McGhee and, 49, 95–97, 120; background of, 94; East Berlin and, 96; Test Ban Treaty discussion, 96; Autobahn incident, 120

Abs, Herman, 69

Acheson, Dean, 6, 81, 227

Action Committee for a United States of Europe, 79, 232, 233

Adenauer, Konrad: relationship with de Gaulle, 1, 21, 23–24, 31, 34–35, 110, 149–50, 158, 220, 221; rivalry with Erhard, 1, 31, 35, 37, 38, 81, 104, 105, 133, 147, 149, 150, 199, 200; McGhee and, 5, 26–31, 32–35, 41, 109–10, 134, 150, 159, 268; U.S. and, 6, 22, 30, 136, 161–62; Lübke and, 16; Cold War and, 20; France and, 20, 21; supported by Eisenhower, 21; supports Schuman Plan, 21; European Unity and, 21, 31; reunification and, 21, 93; Cuba and, 22; Spiegel affair, 22; relationship with Kennedy, 22, 29, 31, 35, 59, 61, 91, 220; Johnson and, 22, 128, 159, 217, 221; on British EEC entry, 22, 135; on Franco-German treaty, 29–31, 36, 110; rivalry with Brandt, 31, 51, 62; favors MLF, 31, 86–87, 158; and Hitler, 32, 34; SPD and, 33; on Harriman-Hailsham test ban, 34; on Limited Test Ban Treaty, 34, 35, 89; Gerstenmaier and, 35; McNamara and, 89–91; McCloy and, 102; Rusk and, 108–9; on East-West trade, 108–9, 125; East-West relations, 109, 124; reactions to the Wall, 121, 125; Ostpolitick and, 125; death of, 132, 220; on French-German relations, 134, 163; NATO and, 135; on USSR, 135;

Schröder and, 151, 158; Kissinger and, 158; *New York Times* interview, 159; Grand Coalition and, 189; supports Kennedy Round, 226

Ahlers, Conrad, 22

Albertz, Mayor, 152

Algeria, 31, 34

Ambassadorial Group, 145

American University, 26

Annual Congress of the Socialist Unity party, 213

Armed Forces Europe (USAREUR), 63

Atlantic partnership, 133, 173: nuclear weapons and, 11; Kennedy speech, 59; McGhee and, 82, 134; Brandt and, 119; Erhard and, 119, 130; France and, 247; Kiesinger and, 247

Augstein, Rudolph, 161

Bahr, Egon, 51, 126, 176, 242

Ball, George, 56, 80–82, 107–8, 117, 183, 185, 242

Barzel, Rainer, 200, 253–54

Beitz, Berthold, 77–79, 111

Belgium, 31, 137

Berlin, 28, 44–45, 98, 152–54, 170, 173, 272–73: role in East-West relations, 7, 45, 78; FRG responsibility for, 8, 49; U.S. commitment to, 8, 96–97, 159; Adenauer and, 22, 28; Kennedy and, 28, 58–59, 90, 272–73; Brandt and, 28–29, 50–52; Erhard and, 38, 119, 129; USSR and, 44–45, 120, 238, 243, 248; Philharmonic, 45; McGhee and, 45, 47, 101, 152; Bonn Group and, 47; Senate, 48, 119, 129; City Parliament, 50; blockade of, 51; Brigade, 55, 63; Docu-